£40

State policies and techno-industrial innovation

The last ten years have seen the rapid growth of science-based industries in Western countries, with governments encouraging the production of high-tech goods. The role of the state in techno-industrial innovation is the focus of this study, which draws on an international research network to give a comprehensive and detailed survey of national strategies in this area.

The success of techno-industrial innovation varies from country to country, according to scientific capability and the availability of export and domestic markets. The contributors to this book provide a comparative perspective, using case studies of five different sorts of technological innovation in Europe, Japan and the USA. They explore the various dimensions of the problem and examine whether active state policies are appropriate for science-based developments. They also discuss the changing patterns of state policy, and give a critical analysis of the ideologies underlying the concept of innovation, drawing attention to the risks attached to successful national participation in world markets.

State Policies and Techno-Industrial Innovation will be of interest to specialists in political science and economics, as well as to students and teachers of business studies, geography, regional studies and sociology.

Ulrich Hilpert teaches at the Free University of Berlin, where he is Chairman of the European Consortium for Political Research (ECPR) Group on Politics and Technology and Director of the ECPR Research Group on Technology, the State and Unintended Consequences.

State policies and techno-industrial innovation

Edited by
Ulrich Hilpert

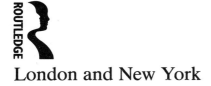

London and New York

First published 1991
by Routledge
11 New Fetter Lane, London EC4P 4EE

Simultaneously published in the USA and Canada
by Routledge
a division of Routledge, Chapman and Hall, Inc.
29 West 35th Street, New York, NY 10001

© 1991 Ulrich Hilpert

Printed in Great Britain by
Billing & Sons Ltd, Worcester

T
173
.8
STA

British Library Cataloguing in Publication Data

State policies and techno-industrial innovation
    1. Industries. Technological innovation. Policies of
    governments
    I. Hilpert, Ulrich, *1951*
    338.064
    ISBN 0-415-04268-2

Library of Congress Cataloging in Publication Data

State policies and techno-industrial innovation / Ulrich Hilpert,
    editor.
    p. cm.
    Includes bibliographical references and index.
    ISBN 0-415-04268-2
    1. Technological innovations. 2. Technology and state.
    I. Hilpert, Ulrich, 1951–
    T173.8.S72   1991
    338.9'27–dc20   90-8779
                                                     CIP

Contents

Contents

Contents

vii

Preface

Changes in the international division of labour have fostered a strong tendency in the leading Western industrialized countries towards the creation of science-based industries, and an orientation towards high tech goods and the production of high value-added products. It is interesting in this situation that government ideologies are characterized by the dominance of neo-conservative and neo-liberal concepts. At the same time there is a discussion both on *rolling the state back* and on the *appropriate state policy for techno-industrial innovation*. Many questions have been raised concerning the success of countries participating in these new high tech world markets and in the global race for innovation. Experiences and results of such political attempts to introduce development vary widely between countries and technologies, within countries and industries, according to the scientific capabilities and the availability of export and domestic markets. Many of these questions can be analysed in an appropriate way only if the research is done on a comparative basis. This provides the opportunity to become aware of national or technological specialities and of the underlying conditions that form convergent situations and results in different countries and technologies.

This book aims at a discussion of these various dimensions of the problem and at making a contribution on the question of whether science-based developments do require active state policies. In particular it is concerned with the design of state policy and its correspondence with initial conditions (such as the position in a changing international division of labour, the available markets, and appropriate industrial and research structures). Dealing with policies on techno-industrial innovation brings us to a discussion of the *role of the state in highly developed capitalist* vc *societies*. A first step in this direction was taken when I had the

ix

opportunity to organize and chair the workshop on *Politics and Technology* that was held in Amsterdam, April 5-10, 1987, with the annual *Joint Sessions of Workshops* of the *European Consortium for Political Research (ECPR)*. One of the fields we worked on was the role of the state in techno-industrial innovation and what conditions are required to generate innovation in particular national settings. Some of the papers included in this volume have been developed from this workshop, others have been added afterwards from the *Standing Group on Politics and Technology, affiliated to the ECPR*, that was founded in Amsterdam.

This international research network provided the basis for this book. The idea was to have a book that gives some general ideas about the role of the state regarding techno-industrial innovation, about the changing patterns of policy, and about new problems of policy designing (Part I). Thereafter techno-industrial innovation in the larger European countries is explored. They are diverging with regard to their competitiveness in international markets as well their initial conditions (Part II). Here, simultaneously, attention is given to the differences between infrastructure technologies (such as telecommunications systems and energy technologies) that require sizeable markets, and innovations leading to new products that create a market by emerging and offering new opportunities in various fields of application (such as biotechnology and microelectronics). Having explained the importance of appropriate markets, the opportunities of countries with large internal markets (such as in the United States, Japan and the European Communities) to realize the beneficial economic effects of techno-industrial innovation and the continuing importance of scientific capability are discussed (Part III). Paying close attention to initial conditions (such as strong and innovative industrial structures, capable and appropriate research structures, and available markets), there remains the question, whether and in what ways the small industrialized countries will participate in the innovating world economy (Part IV). Important differences between countries with regard to their settings and the forms of growth that are realized, as well as the particular role of state policies and the concrete initial conditions, are discussed here. Finally, the conclusions relate state policies and techno-industrial innovation to changes in international markets. But, in addition, they draw attention to the special situation of the currently innovative countries and to the risks attached to successful national participation in the world markets. State policies may lead to the internationalization trap and unintended consequences.

It was the editor's particular concern to develop this book on a strongly comparative basis, because the reader will benefit from discovering convergencies and divergencies. So, in general, there are at least two contributions in this book that deal with each country. This provides an opportunity to read it in six ways:

- With regard to the problem of state policy on techno-industrial innovation as explained above;

- With a particular interest in country studies by selecting particular chapters and information;

- By asking what the special conditions are for success in particular technologies and why patterns of development vary;

- With a particular interest in the question, whether the emergence of new technologies can change the international division of labour and provide an opportunity for state-led participation in new world markets;

- With regard to the growing importance of the generation of techno-scientific progress and the importance of state policy in the field of scientific research;

- As a critique of the ideologies that are embodied in the concept of innovation and an evaluation of their concrete effects.

In dealing with the national policies on techno-industrial innovation this book is not designed to discuss the context of this process in general. There is a further volume, *Regional Innovation and Decentralization,* edited by Ulrich Hilpert, simultaneously forthcoming from Routledge in 1991, that gives additional information on the conditions for successful state policies at different levels of government. Both books together show the trends that are introduced by innovation and innovation policies. This book may contribute to the discussion of *how to be innovative*, but it also may enable one to assess *whether countries can be innovative* in particular cases - the internationalization trap and unintended consequences are right to the fore in many countries.

Ulrich Hilpert
Berlin

Part I

Introduction and General Perspectives: The Changing Role of the State in Techno-Industrial Innovation

1

The State, Science and Techno-Industrial Innovation

A New Model of State Policy and a Changing Role of the State

Ulrich Hilpert

It is surprising: industrial decline and economic growth based upon technological innovation both call, simultaneously, for attention. In addition, policy-making based on bargaining with interest groups, regulating the decline of sectors, is experienced. There are calls for state policies that are appropriate to foster future techno-industrial innovation. On the one hand established ways of policy-making continue and can be studied. On the other hand it is often argued that the participation of the interest groups is counter-productive and that state policies in this field have to be developed on a purely rational basis of scientific findings and economic opportunities. The state is expected to play an outstanding role in introducing techno-industrial innovation: (i) organizing academic research so that its structure and its techno-scientific progress serves the needs of innovation, (ii) organizing markets for new science-based products that are appropriate in size to encourage the creation of new and innovative industries, and (iii) to create circumstances that are appropriate for general innovative potential of the nation's industries and to provide the incentives for them to engage in fields that are regarded as being likely to be highly profitable.

This requires a state very different from any that we have previously experienced and it requires the surrender of the established model of policy-making. The *state comes back in* (Skocpol) at a time when it was said that *private government* (Schmitter and Streeck) is the dominant model. But the state when dealing with techno-industrial innovation is completely different from that which designs Keynesian programmes in economic and labour policy. Here it is not the size of the programmes that is important, and whether interest groups are involved in industrial, employment or ecological issues: simply because they do not exist forecasting of the consequences of techno-industrial innovation is highly difficult and uncertain. The policies that this state designs when fostering techno-industrial innovation are concerned with potential markets, capable national industrial structures, innovative academic research and the problem of realizing technology transfer between science and industry. Here the state does not react to strong social interests or to an economic crisis: the state is active, it takes a leading role.

Given the new role of the state in techno-industrial innovation and the erosion of corporatist policy-making, the design of state policy looks to the initial conditions of the innovation process itself rather than to interest groups. The differences between countries with regard to national state policies in techno-industrial innovation would have to be explained on the basis of a new model. This new role of the state requires a redefinition of the role of interest groups and of the relation between politics and socio-economic development. This must explain the extent to which techno-industrial innovation is related to appropriate state policies. The *new* role of the state can be understood only when the process of techno-industrial innovation is understood, in particular its relationship to the changing international division of labour and the initial conditions for successful innovation (such as appropriate industrial structures, capable research structures and sizeable market).

1. The Changing International Division of Labour.
Western Economies between Crisis and Boom

In the Western industrialized countries, the 1970s and the 1980s, have been characterized by the effects of economic crisis and industrial decline in many industrial sectors. The "oil-crisis" in 1973 and the major price rises of 1979 and 1982 were for some time regarded as the reason for the intensifying economic crisis. These sudden price movements have drawn away a lot of purchasing power, but have masked the underlying change of the international division of labour that was more important and that introduced structural problems for Western economies. Before, the international division of labour was characterized predominantly by the Western industrialized countries being the producers of industrial products and by the countries of the Third World supplying raw materials or agricultural products. Today more and more industrial products are manufactured in former Third World countries. These countries' experience, in becoming Newly Industrialized Countries (NICs), indicates the fundamental change in the international division of labour. Mass production based on low production costs, cheap labour and very low requirements for the qualification of labour were the ways in which these countries first emerged in world industrial markets. Step by step some of these countries engaged in more sophisticated products, such as microelectronics, software and chemical products from Brazil, India, Korea, Singapore or Taiwan (Adler 1986; Wiemann 1985; Chung 1983; Clarke and Cable 1982; Chaponière 1987; Meyer-Stamer 1987).

So, the Western industrialized countries - and the Western European ones in particular - were confronted with two problems at the same time: (i) the emergence of new and strong competitors in international markets and (ii) the enormous increase in prices for raw materials that drew away the capital needed to introduce the structural changes required. The interrelatedness of international markets emphasized the importance of national labour costs and the advantages given to low wage countries. This challenge to the established international division of labour provided the opportunity for the NICs to become an important part of the world economy, even though they were badly affected by budgetary crisis, and drove the widespread

Fordist mode of capital accumulation into the crisis that has been discussed intensively since the early 1980s. The social and industrial development that took place in these NICs, the attempts of the petroleum exporting countries to introduce rapid modernization, and the need for modernization in industrialized countries, together introduced an enormous and rapidly increasing demand for highly sophisticated products (Hilpert 1985).

This change in the international division of labour introduced two controversial tendencies in industrialized countries: firstly, the decline of old, labour intensive industries engaged in mass production and, secondly, a boom in plant construction, in highly specialized industrial sectors, and in high tech industries. The most impressive and characteristic examples of these tendencies include the decline of mining, steel and shipbuilding industries and the booming microelectronics, machine-tool making and chemical industries. This development clearly highlights the structural conditions that influence the extent of the national affectedness by industrial decline or participation in economic boom. The importance of high tech was shown impressively by the case of microelectronics. There the ability to generate techno-scientific progress and the availability of markets was shown to form the initial conditions necessary to participate in the economic benefits of these new technologies. The United States and Japan became the leaders in these associated international markets. The more these products promised innovative effects in mature industries and advantages to their users within their immediate competitive situations (Piore and Sabel 1984), the more demand increased. The salvation of existing industries, facing problems of market situation, and/or competitors from low wage countries, lay where the appropriate high tech solution was available.

A clear relationship between techno-scientific progress and socio-economic development was indicated by this case. It was this example, represented first of all by the success of Silicon Valley and along Route 128 (Dorfman 1983; Saxenian 1981), that was used to argue against the engagement of the state in steering economic development, to argue for the vitality of capitalist economy and to regard the "spirit of enterprise" as the most important and fruitful concept for mastering the changing inter-national division of labour. National problems in participating in these booming developments have been blamed on ideological blindness and a lack of awareness of the social benefits of entrepreneuriship. Because of the inappropriateness of large Keynesian programmes for job generation the state was blamed for hindering the process of techno-industrial innovation and inhibiting the economy's vitality. In politics, these changes in the international division of labour during the 1980s, have converged with the dominance of neo-conservative or neo-liberal ideologies in Western industrialized countries.

This view left aside the unique situation of microelectronics and paid no attention to the situation that did exist where such developments took place. Here, it was the availability of techno-scientific advances that formed the basis for innovative products. The demands of NASA and the Pentagon formed the market for these high tech products but, because of the size this market was too small for big firms, large enterprises did not develop in this field. So, small firms played the role of basic innovators. They formed the core of the new microelectronics industry in the United States. The large American market offered a great advantage for the economic exploitation of innovatory products, and there was no explicit state innovation policy that led to these processes of techno-industrial innovation (Bruun 1980). In contrast to the situation in declining industries, this promised a future of economic growth and boom insofar as freedom of engagement is given to the "spirit of enterprise" and the prevalent pattern of state regulation and programmes would be superseded. The high tech industries that form the model for economic growth require specific and highly qualified labour. High wages for scarce labour highlighted the supposed obsolence of labour organizations and these highly paid employees show little interest in them.

But the presentation of this model for adjustment to changes in the international division of labour showed a lack of awareness of the role of the state when funding the research that is basic to the new technologies, and when providing the market for the new products. It also pays no attention to the unique situation within microelectronics that innovation could take place without an established industry prepared to utilize it. The partial crisis in Western economies introduced by the emergence of producers from NICs in international markets drove Western countries into a strong orientation towards innovation. The innovation process must be built upon available techno-scientific advances, upon industries equipped to make use of it and upon markets that are of a sufficient size. Techno-industrial innovation, though a common aim of Western states seeking to solve their socio-economic problems, requires specific initial conditions and these normally include the requirement for an active state.

2. Science, Industries and Markets - Initial Conditions for State Induced Techno-Industrial Innovation

2.1 Techno-Scientific Progress and Changing Competitive Relations

When the changing international division of labour drives the industrialized countries to concentrate upon techno-industrial innovation and modernization, while regulating the decline of industries that cannot stand the competition of the NICs, a much increased importance is given to the generation and availability of techno-scientific progress. The developments in microelectronics highlight this tendency. For defence reasons the Pentagon funded the development of new and more efficient calculators. In 1948 the Bell Laboratories developed transistors and provided access to a new era of data processing. The research at M.I.T., also funded by the American defence ministry, became fundamental for the development of this American industry and its dominant position in industrial markets. The use of semi-conductors and the development of micro-chips have marked a further step in the improvementHof micro-computers and their increasing efficiency.

Techno-scientific progress was the basis of this development. The catching up by the Japanese industry indicates that a strong position in international markets can be realized on the basis of licences as well as by the generation of such progress itself. This revitalization of the importance of scientific findings the introduction of vital economic developments and for achieving dominant in particular world markets takes place in the case of reverse engineering.[1] Here, the products are bought and engineers reconstruct the way they function and the way they are built. In microelectronics and computers in particular, this formed the basis of many products coming from South-East Asia and South America. From the standpoint of engineering, micro-computers are rather uncomplicated products, so the costs of wages make up an important part of production costs so that producers from NICs have advantages in international markets (Adler 1986; Meyer-Stamer 1987; Wiemann 1985).

However it is interesting to note that this devaluation of techno-scientific progress is limited very much to particular situations like the one above. Brazil's successful microelectronics industry is limited to micro-computers: large computers still have to be imported. So any tendency for the devaluation of techno-scientific progress in the scientifically most advanced countries affects relatively uncomplicated products and is related to the saturation of NICs' domestic markets for these products. Close attention to other fields of techno-industrial innovation reveals a very different situation. The introduction of microelectronics and high quality software into machine-tool making equipment has lead to the dominance of Swiss and German firms in the World Market. CAD/CAM equipment, in general, shows the continuing dominance in the traditional division of labour. The increasing use of robots in manufacturing (in particular in automobile industries) reveals the opportunity for innovation in mature industries and their ability to maintain their competitive position (Kern and Schumann 1986; Sabel, Herrigel, Kazis and Deeg 1991). It also reveals the urgent need for techno-scientific progress and the limits of reverse engineering. The generation of techno-scientific progress is becoming more and more important to economic success or failure (Hilpert 1987 and 1989).

The microelectronics revolution highlights two general tendencies: (i) techno-scientific progress as such does not create long-lasting advantages unless its application is very complex and requires high quality research facilities, or unless its application cannot be reconstructed from the final product; (ii) techno-

---

[1] See *Business Week*, July 28, 1986, and *Far Eastern Economic Review*, November 13, 1986.

scientific progress can contribute to a favourable competitive position when enabling innovation in mature industries or when leading to large-scale technologies with high start-up costs and which require significant engineering knowledge about large plants. In both cases, effective research structures and the generation of techno-scientific progress are very important. Besides microelectronics, the new telecommunication systems, biotechnology, aircraft and energy technologies (the non-nuclear ones in particular) are current examples of the role of techno-scientific progress influencing the way in which the international division of labour develops.[2]

The importance of these new technologies for future socio-economic development is their redefining the essential conditions for national economic competitiveness. They are of outstanding importance for particular industries and national economies in general. So competition by price in these markets is replaced more and more by competition in quality in science-based products. It is the innovativeness of these science-based products that gives advantages to their users and creates a market for them as soon as they are available. The generation and application of techno-scientific progress, therefore, provides high profits both for those who are the first to sell them and those who are the first to utilize them. This forces the leading industrialized countries to enter this innovation race, or risk being cut off and forced to enter into direct competition with NICs.

The generation of techno-scientific progress, that forms the basis of these processes of techno-industrial innovation, shows variations both in technological concept and between countries. With regard to microelectronics, in all Western industrialized countries the electro-technical or electronics industries are regarded as among the most innovative ones. After the general concepts of transistors and micro-chips had been developed the progress was very much characterized by the generation of additional progress. That can be done best by the firms themselves making use of the academic research in this field. Similar situa-

---

[2] Very interesting examples of science-based developments are new materials, artificial intelligence, outer-space technologies, rapid train systems etc. that have been introduced very recently.

tions can be identified in the aircraft and telecommunications industries. Here, the techno-scientific progress is based upon existing proven scientific concepts being incorporated into new high tech products.[3] But biotechnology and energy technologies are characterised by the vital role of first-rate academic research.[4] They highlight the importance of breakthroughs in scientific research for the achievement of techno-scientific progress.

It is this situation that must be comprehended as a fundamental imperative of the innovation process and also in understanding the strategic role that techno-scientific progress plays in determining the national competitive position. The less industries are able to introduce the innovation from within their own capacities, the less able they are to reach an advantageous competitive position in international markets. The more academic research is required to generate the techno-scientific progress necessary to design new technologies, or to provide basic findings, the more the national competitive position in international markets is related to a country's academic research structure.[5] Industrial research hardly forms a basis for such developments and the public funds that have to be spent for these purposes are of vital significance. So, a close correspondence between existing efficient academic research structures and increased injection of appropriately directed public funds is required for the generation of economically essential techno-scientific progress.

In addition to the research facilities the state policies are fundamentally important in other respects. A typical example is

---

[3] See the contributions of Desmond Hickie, Jill Hills and Peter Humphreys to this book indicating the importance of effective industrial research in these cases.

[4] See the contributions of Ulrich Hilpert and Takayuki Matsuo in this book. There the importance of countries' highly efficient academic research is indicated.

[5] See the contributions of Ulrich Hilpert, Wendy Faulkner and Luigi Orsenigo, Takayuki Matsuo, Andrew Jamison and Rob van Tulder in this book. There the role of efficient research structures for national competitive positions in the global techno-industrial innovation is discussed.

the development of non-nuclear energy technologies in West Germany (Hilpert 1989). There, the development of highly innovative technological concepts relies heavily upon academic research. The different types of solar technology (the use of wind energy and the development of biogas plants) early illustrate this tendency while in the use of coal or in the optimization of traditional power plants the role of academic research is much less significant for the design of the technology. This pattern shows up in other technologies and other countries as well. In West Germany the generation of techno-scientific progress in the field of biotechnology is based intensively upon academic research. Academic participation in this programme is even higher than in energy technologies. The funds spent on these fields of research are fundamentally important for the generation of the techno-scientific progress that is required to underpin innovation.[6] So, the United States has not only the largest biotechnology programme in the world but also the leading position in the relevant basic research (Sharp 1985). In France, the cases of solar technology and biotechnology indicate the great importance of government funding and of the generation of techno-scientific progress.

The importance that is given to the generation of techno-scientific progress and to the role of academic research is probably most impressively demonstrated by Japan. The Technopolis programme aims at the preparation of the country for participation in a world economy that is dominated more and more by high quality, science-based products (Tatsuno 1991). Japan's R&D has recently been moving from its previous dependence on foreign technology to a position of independent and autonomous development. Although the Japanese technological levels still lag somewhat behind those of the U.S. and Europe there are strong efforts being made in basic creative technology. The Japanese success in biotechnology is an impressive example. Besides funding research, the state is most important for reorganizing and changing the R&D system. A collaboration between government, industry and universities has been introduced. The uni-

---

[6] See the contributions of Wendy Faulkner and Luigi Orsenigo, and Ulrich Hilpert to this book.

versities have become much more important for developing original and creative technology than ever before.[7]

It is interesting and characteristic that the industrial adjustment to changing competitive positions, because of the strong yen, lead to a concentration on the generation of techno-scientific progress and an increasing role of state policies. Less efficient research structures and insufficient activity by the state in fostering the conditions that may lead to the generation of techno-scientific progress have contributed to problems that Italy and Great Britain have to face in this regard (Adams and Orsenigo 1988).[8] The lack of an effective research structure leads to a situation where countries cannot participate in highly profitable new world markets unless they depend upon licensing.

The lack of the necessary initial conditions for techno-industrial innovation causes problems for small industrialized countries as well. Limited resources and less international political and economic clout hinder the small countries' engagement in industrial sectors in which every actor invests in the same technology. Instead, the combination of high and medium tech seems to be more appropriate and leads to a dynamic and flexible economic structure that is able to adjust to economic change.[9] The generation of the necessary techno-scientific progress and its availability play an important role in maintaining an advantageous position in the international division of labour. So, these small industrialized countries pay particular attention to the spreading of R&D to small firms and research institutes. But, as in larger European countries, here the problem of utilizing different research structures arises. In small countries in general large enterprises are highly important. The Swedish example shows that military procurement plays an important role in microelectronics whilst the Danish story indicates the small role

---

[7] See the contribution of Takayuki Matsuo to this book.

[8] See the contribution of Wendy Faulkner and Luigi Orsenigo in this book.

[9] See the contribution of Rob van Tulder in this book. There the difficulties of small countries participating in an innovating world economy and the way of dealing with the dominance of science-based development is explained.

of academic research in technical or technological application.[10] So, small industrialized countries have to do more than just avoid competition with larger countries in particular fields of research, and even the use of small firms in general is no guarantee for success. They still depend greatly on their existing research and industrial structures, their capacity to innovate and to generate techno-scientific progress and on the correspondence of their national ability to innovate with the opportunities provided by the international division of labour.

Thus competitive relations are changing: the quantitative problem of reducing the production costs in the area of core technologies is replaced by the qualitative problem of generating the most advanced and most appropriate techno-scientific progress. The more this form of progress turns out to be essential for future development, the more the national research structures' efficiency and capability becomes vital with regard to socio-economic development. Here, it is the increasing importance of academic research (rather than the support of industrial research) that introduces a new approach into the growing field of state research and technology policy. The more the generation of techno-scientific progress becomes an initial condition for adjusting to changing competitive relations, the more it is state policy that provides the basis and the direction of innovation. Different research structures and different volumes of resources are generating a variety of policies for techno-industrial innovation, but providing the conditions for productive techno-scientific progress leads to innovation itself only insofar as it is congruent with the existing industrial structure and its innovative capacity.

2.2 Industrial Structures and the Participation in Science-Based Development

The Western industrialized countries' increasing orientation in high value added products has made the process of techno-

---

[10] See the contributions of Rob van Tulder and Andrew Jamison in this book. In addition to Rob van Tulder's argument on introducing techno-scientific progress for making the industrial structure more flexible, Andrew Jamison gives particular reference to the history of science structures in small countries and their role in the current innovation process.

industrial innovation the core problem of future economic development. But the fields of techno-scientific progress do not cover all industrial sectors in advanced industrialized countries and, in addition, not every single event in this progress contributes to the management of the economic crisis in these countries. Even though techno-industrial innovation depends greatly on appropriate scientific progress, new products may be mass-production goods with relatively less rates of value added and make relatively few demands upon the labour engaged in their manufacture.

The example of semi-conductors highlights this development. Although this is an essential part of the high tech microelectronics industry and although its development requires intensive research, the manufacturing is done predominantly by cheap unskilled or semi-skilled labour.[11] Consequently, more and more manufacturing is transferred to the NICs that offer major advantages because of low wages.[12] The advanced industrialized countries are concentrating on the latest advances (such as the super-chip) that cannot be produced by the NICs at least for the present. On the other hand, it was the use of microelectronics that provided the opportunity for innovation within old and mature industries and counterbalanced the NICs advantage of cheap labour. The development of CAD/CAM machines and the use of microelectronics introduced a recovery in the textile and watch-making industries (Scharpf and Schnabel 1980). The success of Swiss and West German machine-tool-making industries is probably the best known example of the importance of qualified labour and the use of new technologies (Sabel, Herrigel, Kazis and Deeg 1991). But techno-scientific progress, or the use of very advanced technologies, cannot stop the decline in the coal mining, steel and shipbuilding industries.[13]

---

[11] Dorfman (1983) reports on Silicon Valley that 50% of the labour employed in chip production are migrant workers from Mexico or the Philippines and among these 70% are women.

[12] The microelectronics industries in Brazil and South Korea indicate this quite clearly (Meyer-Stamer 1987; Adler 1986).

[13] On the other hand, the concentration on science-based industries can draw attention away from the innovative opportunities in the manufacturing industries. For the importance and problems of this economic sector see the contribution of Stephen S. Cohen and John Zysman in this book.

Participation in science-based development is linked to the appropriateness and the capacity of each national industrial structure. The history of the microelectronics industry gave the impression that science-based industries must have strong links to research but need little or no roots in the established industrial structure. Were this true, it would mean that techno-industrial innovation is adaptable independently of national industrial history. But microelectronics emerged in a situation where none of the large firms wished to engage in it, in particular because they lacked both the structure and orientation to do so. Thus new firms could engage in an open market and develop according to their innovativeness. In contrast, the non-nuclear energy technologies, biotechnology, telecommunications systems or new aircraft must be based upon particular industries that already exist and that are aware of the innovative potential of new relevant technologies.[14] Therefore participation in science-based development can only take place outside existing industrial structures and be based exclusively on techno-scientific progress only in rather unusual circumstances, and then only to a limited extent.

This differentiation according to the industrial structures is a very important differentiation, because: (i) it restricts the opportunity to participate in concrete innovation processes to those countries that have capable industries in the field in question; (ii) it influences the extent of the future benefits to be accrued according to the current position of the national industries in international markets; and (iii) it favours those countries that possess these industries rather than those faced by the problems of industrial decline. This means that, whilst the qualitative basis of techno-industrial innovation relies upon an effective research structure, the results of this research have few opportunities to be incorporated into innovations if they are not associated with the quantitative element of a strong position in present world markets. This, of course, gives a particular advantage to the United States. It is probably the only country that, in

---

14 See the contributions of Ulrich Hilpert; Peter Humphreys; Wendy Faulkner and Luigi Orsenigo; Jill Hills; James Miller, Volker Schneider and Thierry Vedel; and Desmond Hickie who indicate the importance of already existing industries.

addition to its strong research structure, is prepared to make use of nearly any new technology because in almost any industrial sector it has enterprises that are well placed in international markets.

The industrial structure's general adaptability to techno-scientific progress and the strength of its leading enterprises makes innovation a much easier process than in situations where such preparedness does not exist. Size, even in innovation that is characterized by qualitative issues, remains an initial condition for success. Similarly the Japanese situation has strong advantages for successful participation in techno-industrial innovation although for Japan exports to Third World countries are still much more important than is the case in other Western industrialized countries.[15] So, it is not surprising that the United States and Japan lead in all next generation concepts in the fields of microelectronics and telecommunications systems. These expensive technologies require enormous research expenditure and successful innovation depends upon the national industrial structure's particular market opportunities (Morgan and Webber 1986), an initial condition that exists in these countries, but that does not exist in a similar way in the West European countries.

As long as the dominant countries can manage to participate in innovation, the situation that existed in the early stages of microelectronics cannot be reproduced and keeps competing firms to a large extent out of the markets. The problems of Airbus Industrie indicate this difficulty even though the product may be technologically more advanced and its use may be economically rational. A successful break into the world market and participation in the global process of techno-industrial innovation, therefore, requires the availability of an event in techno-scientific progress that provides the opportunity to potential users which the established and dominant enterprises cannot offer. This exceptional situation is unusual because the countries that meet the initial conditions engage in fields of relevant research whilst potential competitors can spend limited funds on it. Thus the strong West German position in international markets for chemical and pharmaceutical products creates a valuable opportu-

---

[15] See the contributions of Jill Hills and Takayuki Matsuo in this book.

nity to participate in biotechnological innovation, while less strong enterprises in other West European countries can do little more than attempt to work within their established market position and are thus weakened in the international race of innovation (Sharp 1985).[16]

This situation already causes severe problems for larger European countries (such as Italy, Britain and to some extent for France) and is even more serious for small countries. Their industrial structures possess neither the range of sectors nor the variety of markets of the larger economies. But, in addition, there are two conditions that influence their participation in science-based development: (i) in small countries development is linked to another larger country in Europe, and (ii) the direction of industrial R&D in the smaller countries is dominated by the larger companies. It is these particular linkages, with regard to supply and innovative orientation, that make innovative processes in a small country to a large extent a residual outcome of events in the larger country to which it is linked.[17] Established links that have led to very specific industrial structures, at least in some sectors of industry, provide access to innovation. On the other hand, the importance of large enterprises to small countries creates a strong and close dependency regarding their participation in science-based development.

Small countries, therefore, to some extent develop or decline rather like regions in larger countries. Here, findings in research on regional innovation help one to understand the role of industrial structures. Thus it can be shown that the increase of flexible production systems, the increases in services and growing participation of small and medium-sized firms do not introduce innovation and growth except alongside parallel developments in dominant industrial sectors in the same direction (Neumann 1991; Sabel, Heerigel, Kazis and Deeg 1991). Similar organizational structures can be found in declining regions, as well as in booming ones. To small countries this creates the problem that their industrial structures need links that transcend the

---

[16] See the contributions of Wendy Faulkner and Luigi Orsenigo, and Ulrich Hilpert in this book.

[17] See the contributions of Rob van Tulder and Andrew Jamison who indicate the need for specific concepts in the small countries.

national level and so reduce national opportunities to orientate towards innovative development. The national dependency on the larger companies also reduces their capability to make basic changes.[18] The importance of these firms to the national economic and employment situation calls for a support or an engagement that hinders critical economic developments but might not necessarily bring innovation with it.

Thus developments similar to those that make regions part of the innovation process or condemn them to industrial decline, because of their industrial structures, also mean that some small countries are on the winning side (e.g. Sweden) and others are among the losers (e.g. Belgium). But in contrast to regions and regional governments, the capability of a national government can help to introduce structural changes more rapidly and more effectively. Although in particular regions such as Terza Italia, Baden-Württemberg or Rhône-Alpes small innovative firms are an important element of the organizational structure of regional industries and their economic development, they have little importance on the national level. But in smaller countries such firms are an important instrument for the small countries' participation in science-based industries.[19] Here these firms help to find a way out of the structural dilemma where the small countries and their states lack the funds to engage successfully in the international race of techno-industrial innovation and where they require a linkage to developments in industrial structures outside the country.

The innovation process in small countries needs relative little reference to high tech development, but it requires a combination of high and medium tech as well as specialization on the needs of particular market niches. That introduces an industrial structure that is dynamic and flexible enough for adjustment to technological changes. This again shows the close similarities to developments that can be seen on the regional level. But what makes the example of the small countries so interesting is the way they indicate the importance of national industrial structures. Even though some of them may show an ability to find a

---

[18]   See Andrew Jamison's and Rob van Tulder's contributions.

[19]   See Andrew Jamison's and Rob van Tulder's contributions.

place in global processes of innovation, they also highlight the determinant role of existing industrial structures and the important role of the state in managing the situation. The extent to which national industrial structures are related to science-based developments, rather than to the competition among Fordist industries, determines their participation in the benefits of high tech. State support plays an important role here. The more resources that have to be spent on regulating decline or modernizing older industries, the fewer are the opportunities to introduce participation in the new developments.[20] High tech industries do not break with industrial history. They increase the pressure on state policy-makers to design an appropriate solution. The smaller the countries and the lower the share of their industries in the international division of labour then the more states are required to assure their continuing socio-economic development.

2.3 Markets and the Realization of Innovation

Innovation until the early 1970s was identified almost totally with processes of rationalization in production. Existing competitive relationships had been based upon production costs. More efficient machinery and the replacement of expensive labour in mass production was required. Innovation, therefore, was a process that had to take place and had to be financed, but it required relatively little wide-ranging preparation and organization beyond some discussion agreement regarding social questions and industrial relations issues. The question of new markets did not arise, because a clearly defined demand was supplied and in a known market. The emergence of microelectronics indicated, for the first time, that innovation and markets for new technologies do not apply exclusively to the need for rationalization but point to the creation of new markets simply because of the variety of opportunities for application that present themselves. Here, the market was formed out of the

---

[20] Pamela Adams and Luigi Orsenigo (1988) raised the question with regard to Italy's problem of its southern parts. The money spent there gives little opportunities to spend the funds required to engage in the international race of techno-industrial innovation to the extent that is necessary.

potential use in different industrial sectors and, therefore, was dependent upon the access of potential users and their anticipated benefits. Another characteristic example is provided by energy technologies. Until the early 1980s increasing prices have provided the opportunity to make use of other sources of energy than fossil fuels. The market used fossil fuels that could be substituted and all industrialized and newly industrializing countries attempted to reduce their dependency on oil imports.

Appropriate market structures are a necessary initial condition for the realization of techno-industrial innovation. But the structure of science-based industries has shown the need for strong government funding, whose amortization requires larger markets. The access to potential markets is, therefore, a major advantage in this process. Countries that have large internal markets are in a much better position than medium or small ones. The availability of new techno-scientific findings and the existence of industrial structure that is prepared to make use of them greatly reduce the significance of the market question. No arrangements with other countries have to be made to form the market. National policies are quite sufficient. The national industries' positions in international markets also contribute to these initiatives and avoid problems of amortization in expensive technologies. The United States internal market in solar technology makes up about 25% of the world market. In telecommunications systems this increases to about 40%. This situation reduces the commercial risks of the new technologies. Strong innovation processes can be introduced and the advantageous position in international competition brings additional economic benefits. The Japanese success in the telecommunications sector also highlights the importance of a large internal market (that makes up about 15% of the world market).

Because large markets benefit competitors, the size of markets needed to amortize investments creates a major problem for countries with smaller internal markets. Techno-industrial innovation related to the development and manufacturing of solar technologies indicates the importance of potential markets quite clearly.[21] Besides the United States there is no industrialized country that has any internal market for this technology of any consequence. Without such markets even appropriate industrial structures cannot make use of the techno-scientific progress that is available. Thus France makes use of the French-dominated Franc Zone to find the market that is needed for industrial production, and West Germany gets access to valuable markets by agreements with NICs. This model of innovation is also used by both countries to some extent regarding new telecommunications systems.

But while in solar technology it was the lack of internal markets, in telecommunications the problem is one of insufficient size of internal markets (Morgan and Webber 1986). These deficits in size are regarded as handicaps to efficient growth and competitiveness. So forming effective firms and getting access to external markets has become an aim of state policy in telecommunications. While in the case of teletex systems in a large country like the United States private firms (because of their size and expertise in different fields) can realize the innovation and introduction, in European countries (with their smaller markets) state intervention is required. Here, it is only the state that can guarantee coordination of economic development, technical standards and creation of new markets. Simultaneously, it assists with export opportunities.[22] Although the French telecommunications industry did quite well because of the complete modernization of the French telephone system, it could not develop a strong position in international markets. Growth rates slowed down remarkably and there has been no increase of jobs in the industry. Probably more importantly it is the case that the older strong development does not lead readily into the development of next generation telecommunications systems.

---

[21] See the contribution of Ulrich Hilpert in this book.

[22] See in particular the contributions of Peter Humphreys on telecommunications and that of James Miller, Volker Schneider and Thierry Vedel on Videotex systems in this book. They give special attention to the creation of markets, to state policies and to the importance of the state and exports in the case of European industrialized countries and Canada.

British state policies in telecommunications aimed at deregulation and the introduction of services that would generally support British competitiveness by creating markets for advanced high tech telecommunication services.[23] But these new markets neither are large enough for amortization of the investments, nor do they contribute to employment growth in this industrial sector in Britain. There was a loss of 17,000 jobs between 1982 and 1985 (Morgan and Webber 1986). The market orientation of this policy neglected the country's industrial capability to innovate and to supply these new demands. West German strategies will avoid these problems by continuing the PTT's monopoly in the central services while introducing a liberalization in the use of consumers' equipment. This provides the opportunity to contribute and to strengthen the country's firms engaged in this field.

The problem of an insufficient market for the amortization of the new system remains, but the example of the European Airbus Industrie indicates that agreements and *concertations* of European countries with regard to technology development, manufacturing, and creation of a large market do not at least immediately bring success in the marketplace.[24] Although 18% of the world's air traffic take place within the EEC and although this is expanding rapidly, the technologically advanced Airbus needs strong state support to find its place in world markets. American manufacturers continue to have total dominance making up 94% of this sector in 1970 and 96% today. The circumstances of this European industry ask for more than simple access to a large market. It has to develop a complete range of goods and services that meet the air carriers' needs and it takes time until air carriers need to replace their aircraft. But the situation that is most different from the one in telecommunications is the critical development for national aircraft industries when the Airbus Consortium was established. The telecommunications industries in the larger European countries are capable of developing new systems and, in general, do well economically

---

[23]   See the contribution of Peter Humphreys to this book.

[24]   See the contribution of Desmond Hickie in this book. He indicates that there are market peculiarities that have to be taken into regard as well.

these key industries.[28] These manufacturing industries are more than the simple recipients of these products: they are the clients to whom scientific research must unfold its full benefits. The state in a larger country is in a very difficult situation. It has to design policies that take account of the capabilities of its research system, its established industries and the available markets, as well as the potential opportunities of the consuming industries. Federally organized countries, such as the United States or West Germany, have shown some capacity to optimize initial conditions and to achieve the participation in an innovating world economy politically, even where sizeable markets are not available. The type of technology and the form of its contribution to innovation plays an important role both in economic development and the design of state policy.

A different situation can be identified in those technologies that are based on highly intensive and expensive research and that therefore aim at large markets. Biotechnology, new materials and the next generation of chips are impressive examples. Their research and development requires large funds, so that only a small number of countries are prepared to participate in this innovation. But the products based on this techno-scientific progress, in general, are placed in traditional markets. Biotechnological progress leads to the manufacturing of products that have been produced in traditional ways before. New micro-chip systems are placed in markets that have been created and supplied by the older chips. New materials will find a ready market as well (e.g. new ceramic engine blocks will replace those still made out of metal). So the markets are already formed and the producers that engage here have to make use of new technologies to remain in these markets. Here, it is the need for access to new markets that is crucial. An insufficient participation in international markets can then make the full engagement in particular technologies irrational.

But in addition to this orientation towards established industrial structures and to market access, this techno-scientific pro-

---

[28] See the contribution of Stephen S. Cohen and John Zysman in this book. After all the orientation in science-based industries they call attention to the risk of losing the manufacturing basis that forms an important part of a nation's industry.

gress provides opportunities to supply needs that did not exist before these new technologies offered a variety of new applications. Biotechnology can lead to the development of new chemical products that may be less harmful, or to new pharmaceuticals that fight new diseases. New micro-chips can lead to systems that can deal with complicated processes or to the development of more advanced systems in artificial intelligence. And new materials may offer solutions to problems that have been insoluble. So heavily science-based technologies are in a position to create markets by themselves as long as their application promises a benefit or an advantage to the potential user. Here no organization of markets is required and, because of the emergence of new markets, the market access of the existing industrial structure is of limited importance.

Given such breakthroughs at the frontier of scientific research, even small industrialized countries, or those that have not been among the advanced ones in this particular market segment, can benefit from the economic effects. This does not reduce the importance of markets for the realization of techno-industrial innovation. It makes the situation even more complicated. In countries where the industrial structure and the access to the markets necessary for engagement in particular science-based development is present, there will be the opportunity for participation in the new world markets that will be created on the basis of new applications of techno-scientific progress. But in those countries where these initial conditions cannot be created the position will be precarious. Disengagement from this extraordinarily expensive research will cut these countries off from new world markets that may emerge. Engagement requires enormous funds but offers an uncertain pay-off.

The less appropriate the industrial structure is, with regard to participation in current science-based developments, the less will enterprises engage in investing for uncertain future opportunities. State policies are required to avoid a rapidly growing technology gap, even though the initial conditions for state-induced techno-industrial innovation do not exist. In countries where the initial conditions for techno-industrial innovation can be arranged, the state plays an important role in supporting scientific research that generates progress that fits with the established industrial structure and assists the access to markets that

27

finally allows the innovation to materialize. Research, industry and markets form the initial conditions for innovation. The long lead times of the new technologies, from the first engagement in scientific research to the presentation of the product in the market, create remarkable risks for firms and give a major role to the state which supports academic research and designs policies for techno-industrial innovation.

3. Changing Policy-Making in Techno-Industrial Innovation and the New Role of the State. The Political Generation of Innovation

3.1 New Requirements of State Policies and the Erosion of Interest Groups' Impact on Policy-Making

The process of techno-industrial innovation today differs fundamentally from any previous innovation. Though the innovation that has taken place in earlier stages of industrial history has relied on the application of findings in academic research and whilst there has existed a wide range of contacts between science and industry; the current process of techno-industrial innovation is characterized by the creation of industries that are science-based industries so that the generation of techno-scientific progress is encouraged and perceived more instrumentally. National science structures form more than a general source of education and qualified labour, and they are more than a pool of potential scientific findings that may be utilized for innovation processes. To the extent that techno-scientific progress became the germ cell of techno-industrial innovation, the national structures of scientific research that are generating this initiative and central element of the innovation process can determine the destiny of the socio-economic system's future economic development. Industrial structures and markets are important for the realization of this techno-industrial innovation, but techno-scientific progress has to be taken as the event that catalyses change.

Because of the enormous funds that have to be spent on research for generating techno-scientific progress relative to the limited resources available, decisions have to be made concerning the field and the aims of research. Equally, because of the importance of producing techno-scientific findings quickly to avoid economically disadvantageous time lags when bringing products to market, decisions have to be made concerning the extent of national engagement in particular technologies. This, again, indicates the fundamental difference with previous processes of innovation. While earlier innovations enabled the same products to be produced more effectively, and on the basis of the replacement of expensive labour, current innovation aims at the technology itself introducing a qualitative change, hence making the resultant product a science-based product in its purest sense. Without any doubt the orientation of Western science is towards the needs of industry. Although applied and basic research are getting closer the general orientation towards applications remains dominant. So techno-scientific progress is highly important for inducing the process of innovation.

State policies that aim at the introduction of this process give particular importance to the support of academic research in fields that may turn out to be economically interesting (Hilpert 1989; Faulkner 1986). The lead times of technology development from the early engagement in support of research to the final design of the concept are still very long and can take about twenty or thirty years. In the early days decisions are made on the basis of different scientific opportunities (in scientific alternatives) and support is given to research that is expected to be of economic importance or which interests countries with competing industries. Besides a general expectation to innovate no particular form of innovation is expected, nor can any of the particular effects of innovative developments be foreseen. State policies are designed in the field of techno-industrial innovation, at least at this highly important initial stage, on the basis of general scientific opportunities and uncertain economic expectations. There is hardly any room left for an impact of interest groups on policy-making because the situation is vague and the possible economic effects are very unclear. So, it is surprising that in the industrialized countries, no matter whether they have large or small internal markets, or whether they have shown corporatist or non-corporatist structures, similar fields of political engagement and state support exist (Junne 1984; Sharp 1985). No bargaining process takes place in a deterministic way. State policies do not follow societal interests but, in contrast, they anticipate future developments of the socio-economic system.

The realization of techno-industrial innovation therefore takes place in a situation that is created by the state's orientation towards economic development and the state's support of scientific research. The innovatory outcome itself is, of course, much closer to particular societal interests than the general introduction. But this realization of techno-industrial innovation takes place in a situation prepared by the state policies that were introduced many years before. The economically interesting innovation that is in question is one based on a techno-scientific progress which serves the country's industry structure and some industrial sectors in particular. The organization of markets (internal as well as external) is rather a question of economic rationality than one of the interest groups' impacts. So the engagement of the enterprises that finally leads to the innovation follows the lead of the state.

To the extent that the state meets the new requirements of its new policy successfully, interest groups become much more important with regard to the final outcome of this policy. Given the case of techno-industrial innovation that relies on the availability of markets it is interesting that interest groups are important for the implementation of the policies, but less important for their design. The deregulation debate in telecommunications services and new media illustrates international market pressures towards the location of investments in deregulated environments and regarding the economic importance of these new technologies (Lehmbruch 1988). No matter whether there is a strong corporatist tradition or not there is a convergence of policy responses to new media.[29] But the more state policies become important the more importance is given to the underlying ideology.

At the far end of the innovation process there is the highly concrete process of technology assessment that influences the basis of the form that innovation takes in a society. At that stage the process of techno-industrial innovation might be regarded as most open to the impacts of interest groups. But technology assessment relies on appropriate and available scientific knowledge. So, a twofold dilemma is introduced that militates an

[29] See the contribution of Kenneth Dyson to this book, who indicates the convergences between Great Britain, France and West Germany.

important role for interest groups: (i) the required scientific knowledge refers to particular technologies; but this knowledge is not ready to be produced as neither a state of development close to its final form has already been reached nor its field of application is known; here the problem of a just-in-time production of scientific knowledge emerges and, in general, cannot be solved until the moment of decision is very close at hand; (ii) the required scientific knowledge would have to be produced by a science that follows up the idea of innovation and is designed for this purpose in this context. Alternative knowledge can hardly be produced by a science that follows the intrinsic logic of the established socio-economic system.[30] So interest group participation in policy-making on techno-industrial innovation does not happen.

This erosion of interest groups' impact on policy-making in techno-industrial innovation creates a situation that is different from other policy fields. In fields such as labour, health, fiscal or economic policy, interest groups still play an important role in policy-making although differences in governmental ideologies introduce different levels of impact. While in these fields state policies aim at the continuation of the socio-economic system (with aims such as economic growth, low levels of unemployment, low social costs to the population's health) in techno-industrial innovation the aim is not continuing but radically changing. This difference requires explanation. It is a new role of the state that has to be investigated in conjunction with the generation of techno-scientific progress.

3.2 Organizing Techno-Scientific Progress and the New Role of the State

The erosion of interest groups' impact on policy-making and the particular attention that is given to international market pressures and opportunities introduces a setting that can be understood only when the link between the process of techno-industrial innovation and the role of the state are clarified. Here, two points have to be kept in mind: (i) the policies do not spring

---

[30] See the contribution of Frieder Naschold in this book, who deals with this problem of technology assessment.

from nowhere - they are designed within institutional structures and state bureaucracies that have developed established competences over the years; (ii) the existence of generally converging patterns of different technologies and countries indicates that particular reference should be given to the intrinsic logic of the innovation process, while the differences highlight the importance of ideologies for the state's response to changes in the international division of labour.

Ideologies and institutional structures will be examined first. With regard to the importance of the underlying ideologies for the design of the policy there is little to say since the emergence of conservative ideologies "Thatcherism" or "Reaganomics". It is certainly the path of innovation or industrial modernization that has primacy. But Britain and the United States are the only examples where such an approach is attempted in this pure way. Paying attention to other countries it seems that even the extraordinary weakening of corporatist structures has not given the opportunity to design policy according to the conservative model. Bureaucrats working on these policies do not change their way of doing their job after every election and changing governments are in need of their expertise no matter whether ideologies change or not. Governments are also in need of expertise from outside their own bureaucracies.

So, although there is an important change in policy-making style that is indicated by the erosion of the impact of interest groups there is also some continuity that is characterized by national traditions and mechanisms for accumulating change. This forms a context that includes more than the involvement of corporatist organizations. It is the national style in technology policy that is expressed here.[31] These national styles have roots in national history. The traditional national attitude towards science and technology plays as important a role as the national history of science and its relation to industrial applications. The roles of the state, of corporatist organizations and of large enterprises contribute to this particular setting as well as the size of the markets and traditions in adjusting to changing international markets. Policy-making in the field of techno-industrial innova-

---

[31] See also the contribution of Andrew Jamison in this book, who gives particular reference to the formation of national styles.

tion, therefore, finds a new setting because of the erosion of the outstanding role of interest groups, but it also incorporates a society's inherited attitude towards this process and its inherited institutional structures.[32]

This mix of philosophical approaches, social orientations and developments in industrial history combined with governmental ideologies is confronted by the sectoral characteristics of the industries concerned. The pressures of international markets and the changes in international divisions of labour are always the problems that specific national policies focus upon.[33] So, what the countries aim at is to organize techno-scientific progress as it represents the germ cell of national concepts for techno-industrial innovation. This means it is not only the initial conditions formed by the research system, the industrial structure and the availability of markets that differ cross-nationally but also the countries' national policy-making styles and the needs of the particular technologies in question. According to the countries' national styles and to the particular sectoral conditions they aim at organizing a situation that leads to the generation of techno-scientific progress that fits with the national industrial structure and the size of the markets to be supplied.

Paying attention to the generation of this necessary techno-scientific progress and to the research structures that form its basis makes the state's involvement clear. The importance of state action for techno-scientific progress has been identified clearly above. In addition one now has to recognize that, on the one hand, to new or modernized industries this progress forms the initial condition, while, on the other hand, state action is necessary to make the national research structures function. Even in the United States, which is usually at the very frontier of scientific research and where there is no need for a technological catching up, political support is needed to lead to the techno-scientific progress required. The large federal programme on

---

[32] See the contribution of Kenneth Dyson in this book, who indicates the importance of inherited institutional structures for policy-making on media.

[33] See the contributions of Kenneth Dyson, Jill Hills, Ulrich Hilpert, Peter Humphreys and Desmond Hickie who give particular attention to the reference of national policies to pressures of international markets.

biotechnology is a good example (Sharp 1985). The discussion as to whether military research creates benefits for non-military use indicates even more clearly the role of the state. Super-computers, super-chips and artificial intelligence are related to military research and contribute to the industrial sector of mili-tary goods that accounts for about 10% of the nation's gross national product. In this very specific industrial sector the state policy on techno-industrial innovation is concentrated to a large extent by the Pentagon, supporting the design of new and advanced weapons on the basis of appropriate techno-scientific progress. The application of this techno-scientific progress for other goods and other sectors of the industrial structure indi-cates to what extent the innovation process focuses upon techno-scientific progress.

Organizing the research structure with regard to the techno-scientific progress required in Japan has become a major state acitivity. So Japan's R&D type has recently been changing from conventional dependence on foreign technology to independent innovative technology.[34] This means a basic change in the coun-try's R&D system and the introduction of a new government-industry-university collaboration. Here again the function of the universities becomes much more important than before, in developing original and creative technologies. The Technopolis Strategy, besides its regional implications, serves this state-led orientation in science-based industries (Tatsuno 1986). Its full significance is indicated by the remarkable change with regard to the markets at which these industries aim. These new industries aim at markets that were formed predominantly by the advanced Western industrialized countries. Nevertheless it still experiences a great excess of imports from the U.S. and the EC countries whilst benefiting from a great surplus of exports to Asia and other developing countries.[35] Organizing the generation of techno-scientific progress is expected to foster the innovation process that will introduce a new and different industrial struc-ture.

---

[34] See the contribution of Takayuki Matsuo to this book.

[35] See the contributions of Jill Hills and Takayuki Matsuo in this book.

In West Germany this change in the industry's orientation in other markets is not required. There is already a strong focus on high value-added products. But the microelectronics revolution has shown the importance of effective research structures, and the development of energy technologies indicated the importance of state-induced techno-scientific progress for bringing about techno-industrial innovation (Hilpert 1989). The state's engagement in developing a competent national research structure in the field of biotechnology illustrates the importance of such progress and the strong and mostly dominant participation of academic research shows the way such innovation is introduced. While in West Germany this progress forms an incentive for enterprises to become involved and to realize the innovation, in France there is direct intervention in the process and a state-introduced linkage between science and industry that assures its application. In both countries the state's engagement in organizing an appropriate research system and in extending the instrumental function of science serves aims to preserve the established competitive position in highly attractive and fast growing markets for science- and technology-based products.[36]

The setting that is formed in countries plays an important role in the implementation of the state's policies. In contrast to the West German attempt to give incentives to private enterprises and the French interventionist concept, small countries cannot base themselves on a similarly broad research structure. Historical developments have given rise to particular conditions. National styles in technology policy not only introduce national variations but create concrete conditions on how to introduce techno-scientific progress.[37] The state's difficulties in utilizing the research structure, because of the strong academic but weak technological orientation in Denmark or the role of big firms and the military in Sweden, illustrate the attempts to create the condition leading to techno-scientific progress and at the same time illustrate how much the form of prevailing structures and relationships have to be taken into account. The examples of the Netherlands, Belgium and Switzerland, in addition, point to the

---

[36] See the contribution of Ulrich Hilpert to this book.

[37] See in particular Andrew Jamison's contribution in this book.

continuing domination of large companies for the organization of R&D in small countries and also to the attempts to spread R&D over smaller research institutes to generate the progress needed for the national paths in techno-industrial innovation.[38]

It is interesting to see that all Western industrialized countries aim at the generation of techno-scientific progress. The innovation process introduces an important change into state policies. While in other policy fields it is the bargaining with interest groups on government support or the allocation of particular funds or ongoing programmes, the focus of the policy in question here is that financial resources are not used for promoting ongoing processes but for preparing a situation that is expected to be of importance in the future. This means that decisions have to be made at a stage when particular processes have not already started and particular interests are not already in a position to generate political pressure. To be in a position to engage the developments of possible future markets and possible technological opportunities governments must anticipate conditions for uncertainty. Interest groups enter the situation when the final technology becomes more concrete; that is, when decisions have to be made on concrete paths of techno-industrial innovation and when technology assessment becomes possible. The decision on state policy comes before this. It is a decision on the field in which techno-scientific progress may be produced.

This process of policy-making takes place of course in the established organizational and institutional structure, but the role of the participants has changed due to politically introduced innovation. Under the surfaces of different national styles and settings there is the active organization of techno-scientific progress forming the basis of techno-industrial innovation that determines the future socio-economic development introduced by the state playing its new role.

4. A New Role of the State and a New Model for the Designing of State Policy

The appearance of the new role of the state with regard to the inducement of techno-industrial innovation highlights an impor-

---

[38]   See Rob van Tulder's contribution to this book.

tant change with regard to the medium that is used. Previously, governments gave incentives by spending money to support particular developments they had in mind. Now, because the process of techno-industrial innovation and participation in science-based industries determines participation in new and highly attractive world markets, less money is required to provide access to techno-scientific progress than to form the basis for enterprises' involvement. So, the new role of the state goes along with a new medium that is a further initial condition of the innovation process. There is an important change in the innovation process that has taken place with the emergence of new technologies and the attractive applications they offer. No quantitative incentive by offering money or reducing the costs of production can balance the strategic importance and advantage of the availability of appropriate techno-scientific progress.

To the extent that the new technologies create their new world markets by their appearance, the new role of the state concentrates on the generation of techno-scientific progress. So spending funds on promoting the enterprises' strategies would be inappropriate to assure their engagement in science-based developments and access to new world markets. In the way that effective research structures form the basis for techno-scientific progress a new role of the state is introduced. It also illustrates that state activity in this field provides the initial conditions for techno-industrial innovation and that the policy's design is to be understood in a way that makes reference to the intrinsic logic of the particular innovation processes. This brings us back to the initial conditions of state-induced techno-industrial innovation and to the way the state plays its role in this context. The difficulty in identifying convergences is caused by the varying situations in the cases of different technologies and by the different settings in different countries that create national styles. On the other hand, it is just this variation between technologies and countries that indicates the flexibility of state action. The analysis of state policies on techno-industrial innovation, therefore, shows how states play their new role in the varying situations of different technologies. It also shows that the erosion of interest groups' impacts in designing state policies is replaced by a new model that differs inasmuch as the initial conditions differ according to the concrete situation.

Techno-scientific progress, industrial structures and access to appropriate markets form these initial conditions. Although techno-scientific progress is highly important and may form the germ cell of the innovation process, it is the market that is basic to the realization of techno-industrial innovation. This means that state policies have to aim at a particular techno-scientific progress which, after its application by the industrial structure, leads to the supply of markets that are of the necessary size required for the investment's amortization. Thus there is a systematic interrelation between available markets and national orientations in the generation of techno-scientific progress. The size of available markets introduces variations, although the general model of concentrating on techno-scientific progress is common. Another variation, of course, is introduced by different established industrial structures that call for differently designed policy and hence variations in the techno-scientific progress that is produced.

This provides the opportunity to identify the convergences that lie below the surface of variations in the initial conditions. Similar designs in state policies on techno-industrial innovations correspond to some extent with the industrial structures of the Western industrialized countries. It also indicates structural advantages and disadvantages, in particular attempts to participate in new world markets and the changing division of labour. A comparison between countries and technologies then shows the opportunities and the importance of the state for continuing techno-industrial innovation and socio-economic development. Reconstructing the different initial conditions and policy designs on techno-industrial innovation illustrates the new role of the state and exemplifies its particular national settings. Given that the state plays this new role, the question has to be answered: do state policies on techno-industrial innovation vary with the size of the available markets?

Bibliography

ADAMS, Pamela and ORSENIGO, Luigi (1988), Tecnologie emergenti e politica industriale, in: HILPERT, Ulrich (ed.) (1988), 113-137.

ADLER, Emmanuel (1986), Ideological "Guerrillas" and the Quest for Technological Autonomy: Brazil's Domestic Computer Industry, in: *International Organization*, 40, Summer 1986, 673-705.

BRUDER, Wolfgang and ELLWEIN, Thomas (eds.) (1980), *Raumordnung und staatliche Steuerungsfähigkeit*. Opladen: Westdeutscher Verlag, 297p.

BRUUN, Michael O. (1980), Technology Transfer and Entrepreneurship, in: SAHAL, Devendra (ed.) (1980), 203- 214.

BUSINESS WEEK, July 28 (1986), The PC Wars: IBM vs the Clones.

CHAPONIERE, J.R. (1987), L'industrie électronique à Taiwan, in: *Industrie et Développement International*, Fevrier 1987, 61-70.

CHUNG, Jee-Man (1983), The Electronics Industry in Korea, in: *Monthly Review of the Korea Exchange Bank*, 17, 1983, 13-30.

CLARKE, Jeremy and CABLE, Vincent (1982), The Asian Electronics Industry Looks to the Future, in: *IDS-Bulletin*, 13, 1982, 24-34.

DORFMAN, Nancy (1983), Route 128: The Development of a Regional High Tech Economy, in: *Research Policy*, 12, 1983, 299-316.

DYSON, Kenneth and HUMPHREYS, Peter (eds.) (1986), *The Politics of the Communications Revolution in Western Europe*. London: Frank Cass.

FAR EASTERN ECONOMIC REVIEW, November 13 (1986), Crimping the Copiers.

FAULKNER, Wendy (1986), *Linkages between Industrial and Academic Research: The Case of Biotechnological Research in the Pharmaceutical Industry*. D Phil Thesis, Brighton: Science Policy Research Unit, University of Sussex.

HILPERT, Ulrich (1985), Economic Development in the Third World and Innovations in Industrial Structure in Industrialized Countries. The Example of West Germany and France, in: *Law and Politics in Africa, Asia and Latin America*, 18, 1, 1985, 49-64.

HILPERT, Ulrich (1987), Technology Transfer and the Role of Scientific-Technical Information, in: *Law and State*, 36, 1987, 121-135.

HILPERT, Ulrich (1988), *Politica e Tecnologia*. Monographie Issue of the Rivista Trimestrale di Scienze dell' Amministrazione. Milano: Franco Angelli, 1984p.

HILPERT, Ulrich (1989), *Staatliche Forschungs- und Technologiepolitik und offizielle Wissenschaft. Wissenschaftlich-technischer Fortschritt als Instrument politisch vermittelter technologisch-industrieller Innovation*. Opladen: Westdeutscher Verlag, 295p.

HILPERT, Ulrich (ed.) (1991), *Regional Innovation and Decentralization*. London: Routledge, Chapman & Hall Ltd, 330p.

JUNNE, Gerd (1984), Der strukturpolitische Wettlauf zwischen den kapitalistischen Industrieländern, in: *Politische Vierteljahresschrift*, 25, 2/1984, 134-155.

KERN, Horst and SCHUMANN, Michael (1986), *Das Ende der Arbeitsteilung? Rationalisierung in der industriellen Produktion*. München: C.H. Beck, 361p.

LEHMBRUCH, Gerhard (1988), *Neo-Conservative Policy Change in Comparative Perspective: Opportunities and Constraints in Strategic Choice*. Paper presented at the U.S.-German Symposium on "Technology, the State and Unintended Consequences", Washington, D.C., September 1-2, 1988.

MEYER-STAMER, Jörg (1987), *Politische Gesaltungsspielräume von Schwellenländern in der Mikroelektronik-Industrie - Die Beispiele Süd-Korea und Brasilien*. Lecture given at the University of Bochum, May 19, 1987, 27p.

MORGAN, Kevin and WEBBER, Douglas (1986), Divergent Paths: Political Strategies for Telecommunications in Britain, France and West Germany, in: DYSON, Kenneth and Humphreys, Peter (eds.) (1986).

NEUMANN, Wolfgang (1991), Politics of Decentralization and Industrial Modernisation. France and West Germany in Comparison, in: HILPERT, Ulrich (ed.) (1991), 209-226.

PIORE, Michael J. and SABEL, Charles F. (1984), *The Second Industrial Divide.* New York.

SABEL, Charles F., HERRIGEL, Gary, KAZIS, Richard and DEEG, Richard (1991), Regional Prosperities Compared: Massachusetts and Baden-Württemberg, in: HILPERT, Ulrich (ed.) (1991), 191-208.

SAHAL, Devendra (ed.) (1980), *Research, Development, and Technological Innovation. Recent Perspectives on Management.* Massachusetts & Toronto: Lexington Books, 274p.

SAXENIAN, AnnaLee (1981), *Silicon Chips and Spatial Structure: The Urban Development of the Santa Clara Valley.* University of California at Berkeley, Working Paper No. 345.

SCHARPF, Fritz W. and SCHNABEL, Fritz (1980), Steuerungsprobleme der Raumplanung, in: BRUDER, Wolfgang and ELLWEIN, Thomas (eds.) (1980), 12-57.

SHARP, Margaret (1985), *The New Biotechnology. European Governments in Search for a Strategy.* University of Sussex, SPRU, 149p.

TATSUNO, Sheridan (1986), *The Technopolis Strategy: Japan, High Technology, and the Control of the 21st Century.* New York City: Brady & Prentice Hall.

TATSUNO, Sheridan (1991), Building the Japanese Techno-State: The Regionalization of Japanese High Tech Industrial Policies, in: HILPERT, Ulrich (ed.) (1991), 227-242.

WIEMANN, Jürgen (1985), *Indien im Aufbruch. Industrialisierung, Industriepolitik und wirtschaftliche Zusammenarbeit.* Berlin: Deutsches Institut für Entwicklungshilfe, VIIIp. and 169p.

2

The Nature and Relevance of State Policy for Techno-Industrial Innovation

Kenneth Dyson

Behind the bold rhetoric of "intervention" or "deregulation" that has accompanied the attempts of West European governments to stimulate technological innovation in the last decade is secreted a rich story of failed ambitions, confusion, muddle and incoherence. Nevertheless, some lessons about state policy and techno-industrial innovation can be derived from this experience. Firstly, new technology policies provide a lesson about the pressures for, and the limitations on, state action. The result is a profound ambiguity in attitudes towards public policy. On the one hand, state action is wanted to create new markets (e.g. by public procurement or by agreeing international standards) and to share the burden of high and mounting research and development costs (e.g. by taxation or expenditure measures); on the other hand, the state is beset by external pressures and internal problems of coordination that make unified action difficult, if not impossible to achieve. For West European governments, of Left and of Right, new technology policies have been a learning process about the needs, complexities and limitations of state action. (Secondly,) the search for *the* role of the state in technological innovation distracts attention from the prevalence of change and uncertainty in public policy. On examination a shifting kaleidoscope of roles emerges, conditional on such factors as governmental ideology and sectoral characteristics and on newly emerging knowledge. In particular, the specific "micropolitics" of the firm and of the sector stand out as significant, for instance when a certain corporation or trade association emerges as a key beneficiary of government action. (Thirdly) over time public policy has a tendency to become bound up in the phenomenon of unintended consequences, whether of government's own past actions or of corporate or market behaviour. In other words, the "reactive" characteristics of public policy are ascendant. Public policy becomes driven by "threat avoidance". Governments learn to be more modest and "workmanlike" in style, thus reducing their exposure to difficulties and better safeguarding reputation. Public action comes to prefer less visible forms.

This chapter interprets the development of West European policies in the field of broadcasting and new media as a learning process about the limitations of state action and about the need for a more subtle and differentiated approach. The learning process involves a recognition of the "realities" of international market power and of the structure of domestic relationships within which governments act. Quite simply, West European governments cannot for long ignore the processes of internationalisation that affect "high-technology" markets and the market power of the major suppliers of "high-tech" products and services and their users. They learn about the consequences of being small states in world markets, of being open, vulnerable and dependent. Domestically, the fate of public policy is revealed to be bound up with the complex sectoral characteristics within government and industry. Caught up within this vortex of pressures, governments are disposed to identify their interests, including ideology, with certain corporate interests which are favoured and promoted by public policy. The consequence may be that ideology is reduced to an increasingly symbolic role, with a government "defending the bad against the worse" (e.g. the French Socialist new media policy after 1983); alternatively, as with the British Conservative government, certain corporate interests are gladly coopted as a means of more vigorously implementing ideology. In either case politics continues to matter, albeit in different ways. Beleaguered governments come to appreciate the quality and strength of their policy networks as assets in their own right, as their main hope of enhancing their capability for action.

1. New Markets, New Products: Techno-Industrial Innovation in New Media

Broadcasting provides an excellent case study of how West European states are responding to the challenge of new technologies. In this case a traditional sector, whose regulation has been governed by cultural values - the need to inform and educate as well as entertain the public - and whose operation has been public-service, is faced by new products, new markets and new "entrants". Public-service broadcasters have been seeking to protect and promote their interests in this altered context; whilst governments have had to revise regulatory arrangements in order to accommodate market and cultural values. In the process a new conception of broadcasting as an internationally tradable service or industry has emerged; "viewers" are being redefined as "consumers"; programmes are planned and presented as marketable "products"; and programme libraries are seen as assets to be exploited in international television and video markets. Technological changes have created an increasingly turbulent environment for state action, with the following major changes at work:

1. New video, satellite, cable and computing technologies and "high-definition" transmission standards are rapidly expanding the range, speed and quality of communications services and opening up huge new international markets for digital switching, transmission and reception equipment (Schiller 1982; Sterling 1984; Wenham 1982; Hollins 1984; Howkins 1982). The new equipment markets involve, for instance, communications satellites, direct broadcasting satellites (DBS), copper-coaxial cable, optic-fibre cable, digital switching exchanges, video-cassette recorders and digital television and radio sets; whilst examples of the new audio-visual (telematics) services are provided by extra radio and

television channels (terrestrial, cable and satellite), "one-way" or "interactive" data services like teletext and videotext and "value-added" services like electronic mail, facsimile, videoconferencing, "tele-banking" and "tele-shopping". As "broadband" cable communications (eventually leading to an "Integrated Services Digital Network") is seen as a core technology of the "third industrial revolution", so broadcasting - a traditionally closed and exclusive sector - "converges" with telecommunications and electronics (Dizard 1982; Toffler 1980). Governments are tempted to see broadcasting in a broader and more significant framework of techno-industrial innovation.

2. The growing international scale of broadcasting and new media markets (for equipment and services) has three consequences: (1) small, fragmented and closed European markets are seen as a major barrier to commercial success, with subsequent pressures to establish common European regulatory standards (e.g. on transmission, advertising, programme quotas) and for European collaboration in research and development to avoid enormous duplication and waste of expenditure; (2) governments seek to promote investment by regulatory conditions that either favour domestic equipment producers or service providers (building up "national champions") or favour corporate users of communications (notably the big multinational corporations); and (3) broadcasters and service providers seek to circumvent domestic regulation and undermine its effectiveness by "off-shore" operations (e.g. in Luxembourg), thus promoting an international process of competitive deregulation (Dyson 1986).

3. The entry of new actors into broadcasting from adjacent sectors, notably the press, film and financial giants, leads to increasing competition. New multi-media or communications conglomerates emerge, with the ability to mobilise capital on an enormous scale behind European and global ambitions (e.g. Rupert Murdoch, Robert Maxwell, Axel Springer, Leo Kirch, Robert Hersant and Silvio Berlusconi). New commercial satellite channels proliferate (like Murdoch's Sky Channel and the Springer/Kirch axis behind

SAT1), whilst Hersant and Berlusconi gained control of the new commercial fifth channel in France. This process of "market entry" is a direct threat to public-service broadcasters and to the traditional philosophy of regulation as trusteeship for the cultural heritage (Dyson and Humphreys 1986).

2. Governments under Pressure from Technological and Market Development

Government policies towards broadcasting and new media are located within the structures and dynamics of international markets and are subject to common problems of policy design and policy implementation. The consequence is powerful pressures for convergence in the role of West European states in this field. Indeed the impacts of turbulent international markets are part and parcel of the domestic problems of policy design and implementation. At one level, international market pressures seem to be promoting an interactivity of national policies, a process of "assimilative repetition" of experience elsewhere; at another level, problems of policy design and of administrative coordination and control are remarkably similar, producing a common shift from bold, "heroic" and "high-profile" policy to a more pragmatic and "low-key" brokerage politics. At varying speeds, and with often sharply contrasting attitudes of enthusiasm or reluctance, West European governments have learnt the same kinds of lessons. One main lesson has been a less "authoritative" and more self-restrained role for the state in regulating broadcasting and new media.

Three dimensions of convergence of regulatory policies need to be explored: international market pressures; problems of policy design and implementation; and an emerging reflexivity in legal arrangements. In particular, the international political economy of television programme production and distribution, of advertising and of communications technology equipment reflected already the emergence of large corporations, typically American or Japanese (Mattelart and Mattelart 1984; Schiller and Nordenstreng, 1981). These corporations had begun to think "global", to target world market share and to seek market entry into Western Europe through licencing deals and joint ventures.

45

Their international scale could be used as a strategic weapon against competitors and governments (Ohmae 1985). Aggressive and sophisticated corporate strategies were well developed by companies like Corning Glass (optic-fibre cable); Hughes Communications and RCA (satellites); Rupert Murdoch's News Corporation, Lorimar (the producer of *Dallas*), Harmony Gold and Viacom International (film and broadcasting); J. Walter Thompson, McCann Erickson and Young and Rubicam (advertising); and AP Down Jones and Citicorp (news and financial services). American and Japanese corporations were major agents of change in these international markets and, as we shall see, had various resources of power at their disposal to effect a relaxation of regulatory conditions in order to pursue their commercial interests.

Against this background two major changes were radically affecting the structure and dynamics of the international markets. Firstly, video and new cable and satellite channels were offering huge new markets in Western Europe for feature films, television series, cartoons etc. Accordingly, the prospects were for use of repeats on an even greater scale and a rise of imports to some fifty per cent (EC Commission 1983). Against the background of a long haul to profitability and a sharp rise in the production costs of television programmes, the new private satellite channels did not have significant funds for programming. Low-cost and easily available imports of television films, series and cartoons provided a solution for the new commercial operators, as they had done a decade earlier in the case of Italy. In the wake of deregulation of local "off-air" broadcasting Italy had become, by 1982, the world's largest importer of American television programmes and of Japanese cartoons. Television programme imports were closer to those of the smaller West European countries like Austria (43%), Denmark (46%) and Ireland (57%) (Varis 1984).

With the pending explosion of demand for low-cost programmes the other large West European countries looked like going the way not just of Italy but also these smaller countries. In other words, in a world of media giants all European states appeared to be "small states", open, vulnerable and dependent (Dyson and Humphreys 1986). The consequence was a threat of a media trade war between Western Europe and the United

States. Thus, in its draft directive of April 1986 on broadcasting the European Commission proposed European programme quotas to limit the import of film and television programmes from outside the EC. The implications were controversial, not just for editorial independence (as the BBC argued strongly) but also for the GATT process and the avoidance of new trade wars.

Secondly, with the development of new media the potential for the expansion of television advertising seemed enormous. Broadcasting would depend to a greater extent for its finance on the sale of airtime to advertisers: and, as an additional incentive for the "global players", Europe as a whole was a wealthy but as yet undeveloped advertising market compared to the United States and Japan. Growth potential was concentrated in the French and West German markets and in the possibilities with satellite broadcasting to develop new multinational advertising campaigns. The basic impediment to the development of the European advertising market seemed to be national legislative restrictions on amounts, styles and subjects of advertising. Advertising and commercial broadcasting interests were, accordingly, united in their desire to ease these restrictions.

Pressures from international markets seemed to be eroding the "substance" of regulatory sovereignty in four main ways. Firstly, particular domestic interests *used* changes in the international markets to legitimate deregulatory reforms at the national level: notably, certain sections of the equipment supply industry, private cable television firms, publishers and the advertising industry. Secondly, certain actors sought to flee domestic regulation by becoming multinationals or developing a role as "global players" seeking out "media havens": thus BT and Maxwell involved themselves in the Luxembourg Astra project for a medium-powered broadcasting satellite, Bertelsmann of West Germany teamed up with Luxembourg's CLT to launch the German-language satellite programme RTL plus; Berlusconi of Italy was active in France *(La Cinque)* and Spain; Murdoch developed links with Belgium's Groupe Bruxelles Lambert, the main shareholder in CLT of Luxembourg, to explore DBS proposals; whilst CLT itself was seen as "fleeing" Luxembourg as it established separate operating companies in Belgium (TVi) and West Germany (RTL plus) in conjunction with domestic publishers there. Thirdly, by threatening to locate their investments in more deregulated environments, multinationals encouraged a process of "international gamesmanship" as governments sought to use deregulation to attract jobs and earn tax revenue. In this way, "principled" opposition to deregulation gave way to a more pragmatic adaptation, for instance as SPD Hamburg sought to prevent Munich emerging as the more powerful media centre in West Germany. Fourthly, penetration of American capital was accompanied by penetration of American ideas, including a changed ideological climate in Western Europe. The "third industrial revolution" was accompanied by the model of American "deregulation" and "enterprise culture". "Americans in Europe" could be found in the British Conservative Party, the French centre-right RPR-UDF parties (e.g. Francois Leotard), the West German liberal FDP and the CDU/CSU, and the Dutch liberal VVD.

This combination of international market pressures seemed to suggest that Western Europe would follow American experience with a time lag, that ideological opposition from the West German SPD states or the French Socialists was doomed to failure - in short, that policies for new media would converge around a deregulatory model. On a liberal interpretation, government efforts to resist would only produce irrational outcomes that were unlikely to endure politically. On a neo-Marxist interpretation, such attempts to regulate could only "disguise" reality by fulfilling a function of legitimation for changes imposed by the underlying logic of the international political economy. Legitimation procedures were likely to be more elaborate, the higher the level of domestic public conflict generated by the implications of the new international political economy of broadcasting. And yet, however elaborate the committees of inquiry, the panoply of government-backed research and the systems of regulation, their role seemed essentially symbolic. From the perspective of international economy governments appeared to be cast in the common role of spectators.

The second main dimension of convergence of regulatory policies involves problems of policy design and policy implementation. At the level of policy design there is a complex problem of matching regulatory "tools" to regulatory problems (Hood 1984; Breyer 1982). The consequence is a degree of uncertainty and confusion about policy development that holds up the implementation process, a phenomenon that is graphically apparent in the protracted conflicts amongst the West German states about a common new media policy and in the new media "policy" of the French Socialists after 1981. For instance, on the one hand, threat to the domestic "cultural industries" and to "national culture" from cheap foreign imports suggests the importance of quotas for programming, to encourage domestic programme production and to restrain foreign programming; on the other hand, the problem of financial viability of new media indicates the need for a "liberal" attitude to programming and to advertising. Regulation also gravitated between the problem of "overmighty" subjects or "failed" national champions (the BBC and BT have in the past been seen in this way) and the problem of "the enemy from without" in the form of powerful and aggressive foreign companies (like Murdoch or Ted Turner). If the former suggests a solution of deregulation and foreign competition, the latter indicates a need to pick and privilege one or more national champions. Whilst different balances have been struck in different cases, the difficulty of matching regulatory tools to problems has generated a common phenomenon of uncertainty and incompleteness in policy development. Confusion has on occasion seemed to have been broken by *ad hoc* panic action, as by President Mitterrand in November 1985, only to be once again re-established (for details see Dyson and Humphreys 1988).

Across Western Europe there seems to have been a predictable policy cycle in new media policy: from heroic bold initiatives, through frustrated expectations and a "new realism", to recrimination as blame was allocated for failures of policy implementation. The same kind of problems of policy implementation has recurred across countries (Pressman and Wildavsky 1973). If the specific details have varied, similar problems of structural coordination and control have been apparent. Competing political and administrative interests have mutually frustrated each other, creating an impression of inertia. The "intelligence" function of policy makers and regulators has appeared extremely faulty, their activities being based on assumptions that are the product of the commercial and technological "hype" of particular interests and distorted by such structural sources as specialisation and interdepartmental rivalry

(Wilensky 1967). They have laboured in the face of information overload and sheer intellectual complexity. Technology competition, leading to new policy initiatives, has challenged the assumptions on which policy has been based and aggravated the implementation process. Thus cable television has been challenged by VCRs and by DBS; in turn both cable and DBS have been challenged by the new potential for "off-air" broadcasting in the wake of the Geneva frequency plan of 1984. As ever more technologies compete for viewers, so the financial prospects of each become more difficult to assess and the regulatory framework for each is placed in question. Also, the fact that these technologies are principally oriented to consumer markets subjects them to a high degree of complexity and rate of change (Zysman 1977). The pressures for flexibility of operation and pragmatic regulation mount as a consequence.

Not least, the regulatory policy process has been affected by the "shake-out" in industry as it was recognised that there would be a long haul to profitability. By 1987, as Sky Channel approached its fifth birthday, no satellite channel had made a profit. Sky Channel lost £5.9 million in 1986. "Lead times" for consumer penetration seemed to be long, perhaps seven to nine years. If potential demand was enormous, problems of programmes, delivery systems, marketing and finance were formidable. A major consequence of this "shake-out" was a strengthening of the position of new types of conglomerates and multinational alliances, both of which helped to mitigate risks (Dyson and Humphreys 1986). Particular beneficiaries were the big publishing groups which sought to stake out a key role in satellite and cable broadcasting. Thus the West German Springer group consolidated a dominant position in the SAT1 channel; Bertelsmann teamed up with CLT of Luxembourg to launch the RTL plus channel; Murdoch pursued a joint venture with Groupe Bruxelles Lambert of Belgium; whilst Maxwell acquired the major role in Britain as a cable television operator by buying Rediffusion, entered into a programming consortium with Silvio Berlusconi (Italy), Jerome Seydoux (France) and Leo Kirch (West Germany) for the French DBS satellite, and took part in a joint venture with BT and with MTV Networks (a subsidiary of Viacom International) to bring the American MTV, a 24-hours-a-day satellite pop music channel, to Western Europe.

The activities of multi-media conglomerates began to alter the balance of power in new media policy development; sectoral problems and characteristics affected policy design. In both Britain and West Germany the leading role of cable television operators and their needs was displaced by the interests of the new cable and satellite programmers. The latter's important regulatory gain was the liberalisation of the installation of satellite receiving dishes (SMATV); in some West German states satellite programmers were also given priority in the allocation of new terrestrial frequencies to give them more rapid audience penetration. Multi-media conglomerates introduced a dynamism of change into regulatory policies. Also, as they negotiated with successive governments, they benefited from a "learning curve" of experience, emerging as increasingly sophisticated political actors.

Finally, the combination of commercial risk and uncertainty with political "sunk costs" in new media policy produced the phenomenon of a complex intermingling of public and private power. This intermingling of powers found expression in two tendencies - towards "clientelism" as public agencies seemed to become spokesmen for specific commercial interests (agency capture) and towards "neo-corporatism" as governments sought to "orchestrate" private-sector solutions (Streeck and Schmitter 1985). In both instances the same trend was at work; regulators were increasingly pursuing promotional aims for the new media industry and, consequently, paid increasing attention to the interests of the regulated, who themselves had an incentive and capacity to dominate regulation (Stigler 1975; Petzman 1976). In practice the elements of "clientelism" and neo-corporatism were often difficult to disentangle. Once again, increasingly sharp international competition was causing governments to begin to see the fragmentation of the domestic industry as a problem and "concerted" action as a possible solution.

The third main dimension of convergence of policy responses to new media is very much a product of the first two: namely, a crisis of formal legal regulation, brought about by sheer complexity and the problems of managing escalating conflicts and a new speed of technological and economic change. At one level - the most obvious - confusion about regulation emerges as the forces in the new "broadcasting market" confront the require-

ments of the old "broadcasting constitution". At another level an
evolutionary change in regulatory policy seems to be underway:
from detailed and elaborate criteria for regulation and legalistic
"rule-oriented" reasoning towards legal self-restraint. Regulation
begins to adopt the characteristics of an adaptive and responsive
learning process (Teuber 1983; Nonet and Selznick 1978). A
greater caution about imposing clear substantive criteria for regulation is apparent cross-nationally: in technology specification
for cable and satellite systems, in the role of public-service
broadcasting in new media, in advertising, in quotas for foreign
and local programming, and in participation of the press in cable
systems. Little in the way of a new normative theory underlies
these regulatory developments, other than aims of industrial
promotion or "damage limitation". Policy makers sense the danger that the traditional type of regulation will either prove inef-
fective, with a subsequent loss of political credibility, or be too
effective, in which case major new industries will suffer in fiercely competitive international markets.

3. The Nature of State Policies for New Media

As government policies are located in domestic political contexts, diversity of contents and "style" are to be expected. Their
policies bear the clear imprint of political tradition (notably
inherited ideas about the nature and role of the state); of the
institutional structures of the state (e.g. whether and how it is
decentralised); of the nature and functioning of "pressure politics" (e.g. whether the most influential pressure comes from
within or outside the state apparatus); of the political ideology of
government; and of the inheritance of past policy making and
performance. The impact of each of these elements can be tra-
ced in the policies of the three major West European media
powers towards new technologies.

In the case of French policies towards broadcasting and new
media under the Socialists after 1981 one can note the traditions
of *etatiste* modernization (the idea of a single, integrated and
technologically ambitious cable system) and "national independence"; the impact of the government's commitment to a radical
decentralisation of the state (in the cooption of local authorities
as initiators, negotiators and co-financiers of the cable plan and

as co-managers of the local cable operating bodies); the influence of pressure groups internal to the state on the cable plan (in particular, the DGT, the posts and telecommunications administration); and, not least, there was the complex ideology of the government which fused together a faith in economic modernization and *etatisme* with the new theme of *autogestion* (self-management) (Cerny and Schain 1985). Indeed it was precisely the fusion of governmental ideology with political tradition that seemed to give such coherence, distinctiveness and power to the broadcasting and new media policies of the French Socialists.

Domestic political context seemed to account for the major differences of policies for broadcasting and new media in the West German case. Here the political tradition gave primacy to the procedural requirements of policy-making, lending a distinctive cultural style to regulation (Dyson 1982). Consensus building was a serious business, and in media policy involved elaborate committees of inquiry beginning with the *Kommission für den Ausbau des technischen Kommunikationssystems* (KtK, 1974-76) legitimation process for new policy initiatives. In West Germany the latter is the provision for judicial review that is associated with the overarching constitutional concept of the *Rechtsstaat* ("state based on law"). Judgements of the Federal Constitutional Court in 1981 and 1986 were to play a central part in the context of new media policy (Dyson and Humphreys 1988). The federal structure of the West German state was also to be of enormous significance in the development of (or rather difficulty of developing) new media policy. On the one hand, the federation had sole responsibility for telecommunications (i.e. laying and operating cable and managing satellites); on the other, the states *(Länder)* were exclusively responsible for cultural (and thus broadcasting) policy.

In the case of Britain the Thatcher government seemed to suggest a picture of coherence, distinctiveness and power in policy making that rivalled the French Socialists (though the aims were very different). Political tradition is again evident. In contrast to France, new media policy seemed to embody a suspicion and even distrust of government intervention that has been linked to the tradition of the "arm's length" state; according to the Cable and Broadcasting Act regulation was to be "light-touch" and reactive (Dyson 1980). In contrast to West Germany, there was an absence of self-conscious concern for procedural legitimation; bureaucratic negotiation and "majoritarianism" were seen as providing adequate legitimation. The institutional structures of the British state made Whitehall the centre of gravity in policy making (Richardson and Jordan 1979). In particular, the failure to involve local authorities (indeed their exclusion from any formal role in new media) points out the degree of centralisation, particularly in a comparison with France and West Germany. Not least, of course, there has been the impact of the pronounced neo-liberalism of the Thatcher government. Central to the government's ideology was the idea of "rolling back the frontiers of the state". In the Cable and Broadcasting Act emphasis was given to encouraging "new blood" into broadcasting by "light-touch" regulation, notably the inducement of new entertainment programming (the cable revolution was to be "entertainment-led") and by the ability to combine the functions of DBS operator and programmer and of cable provider, operator and programmer. If this ideology threatened the established system of public-service broadcasting, it had the virtue of consistency with the tradition of "arm's length government" in economic affairs. Market ideology gained a measure of coherence and power from this compatibility with political tradition.

    A broad analysis of regulatory policies for new media in Britain, France and West Germany reveals four major types of difference. Firstly there has been a significant difference in the character of political and policy debate. The regulatory debate began later in Britain (with the ITAP report Cable Systems of 1982) than in France (with the Nora/Minc report *The Computerisation of Society* of 1978) and West Germany (with the KtK report of 1976). In addition, the ITAP report lacked the professionalism of its French and West German counterparts. The KtK report was distinguished by its methodical analysis and assessment of the technological options; the Nora/Minc report by its scope and ambition. These reports made an important contribution to a vigorous substantive debate about *communication audiovisuelle* (the preferred French term) and *Neue Medien* (the preferred German term). Such terms seemed "foreign" and "theoretical" in British policy debate. In fact they reflected the

and the fifth and sixth channels were soon in the hands of entrepreneurs close to the government. In the British case vague regulatory criteria were accompanied by franchising and regulatory authorities (the Cable Authority and the IBA) whose powers were to be exercised secretively and unaccountably. Public hearings were not a feature of the work of the Hunt inquiry (1982) into cable expansion and broadcasting policy or of franchising by the Cable Authority and the IBA. Pragmatism and informality prevailed; there was no system of public law to discipline regulatory policy, no concept of some overarching state purpose to legitimate policy (Dyson 1980; Harden and Lewis 1986). Instead regulatory policy making lacked precision and coherence.

4. Conclusion: Does State Policy Matter?

The analysis of this chapter has underlined how complex and incomplete West European policies for broadcasting and new media remain. When the final shape of public policy is still difficult to discern, conclusions are bound to be somewhat tentative and provisional. The overall impression is of ambiguity in the role of the state. On the one hand, national and sectoral particularities seem to remain significant. On the other hand, international market pressures and processes of regulatory "gamesmanship" appear to combine with problems of policy design and implementation to "force" a pattern of convergence towards a "light-touch" mode of regulation. Policy is characterised by a predominance of promotional industrial aims and strongly collusive relationships between regulators and regulated. Over time one is more struck by the similarities than differences in legislation and practice, for instance between CDU and SPD states in West Germany.

West European governments seemed to be involved in a difficult but common learning process: learning about the implications for national power and prosperity of international interdependency, learning from domestic problems of policy design and implementation, and being "taught" by new media conglomerates which displayed great knowledge and political sophistication and were often emerging as well-coordinated "global" actors. Increasingly, regulation responded to, and increasingly sought to mobilise, powerful domestic interests in order to respond to the challenge of new large-scale broadcasting markets that were evading control. In the process, however, governments were faced with difficult problems of interdepartmental and intergovernmental coordination and control (compared to corporate actors) and often had very little notion what a "media policy" was, even what the media comprised. Their complex political problems of knowledge, capability, attention and will were reinforced by organisational problems and by ideological and cultural inhibitions deriving from liberal democracy ("the free flow of information" is difficult to block). Also, the behaviour of governments in broadcasting policy reveals the limitations of the metaphor of "gamesmanship". With the complex intermingling of public and private power regulators were unable to conform to the simple model of a neutral state acting as a referee. They were also "committed" players, though not always sure to what they were committed or how best to play.

This analysis would appear to suggest that new media entrepreneurs were about to "escape the state" to become an independent political force in Western Europe, a new "estate" serving its own interests. In this sense Berlusconi, Hersant, Murdoch and Maxwell seemed to represent a new type of "media mandarin" on a European scale, using their international scale, market sophistication and relative integration of strategic management to effect policies that suited them. Whilst these trends are very significant, such a thesis about broadcasting and new media does need qualification. In other words, the convergence thesis of the state simply legitimating market and corporate change can be overstated. Firstly, if national particularities are less evident as new media policies evolve, political debate continues to be nationally distinctive. Neither regulators nor the corporate actors can afford to ignore politically significant ideological reactions; the latter operate as an "environmental" constraint. Also, the special character of public authority - its "sovereignty" combined with democratic legitimacy - adds an asymmetry of hierarchy to relations of negotiation and pressure. The fact that in some contexts ideology and policy become increasingly separated only reinforces the problem and constraints of legitimation. As in the case of Hamburg, what particularities remain in new media legislation are of great political significance. Secondly, in sectoral policy and politics details are important, not just details of legislative provisions and regulatory decisions but also the strategic and tactical implications of different institutional structures, governmental ideologies and political traditions. For the regulator and the regulated, as well as the analyst, *la verité reste dans les nuances*. Thirdly, in decisions about the location of new media investment complex factors of comparative advantage are involved. Regulatory "burden" is only one of these factors and not necessarily the most crucial. It is unlikely that differences of regulatory "burden" will be so great as to offset the effect of other factors of comparative advantage, like the infrastructure of supporting specialist services, the professionalism of the workforce and the attraction of working in a "media milieu". In so far as a government is confident about its comparative advantage in broadcasting and new media, and with due sensitivity to the importance of perceptions in industry as well as politics, it can afford the "luxury" of a degree of national particularity in policy. Fourthly, the personal image of new media entrepreneurs could prove a "double-edged" sword. Thus Berlusconi and Maxwell were able to exploit their personal image as an asset in countries like France and Spain. By contrast, the senior management of Sky Channel was beginning by 1987 to see its close link with Murdoch as a major handicap in gaining access to major cable systems in Western Europe, hence delaying their achievement of profitability. Such a handicap did not face their new rival, Super Channel. Even so, in 1987 Super Channel chose to shed its "best of British" image by beginning to schedule some Dutch and German programmes (with English sub-titles) and by looking for overseas shareholders. These moves were made in recognition of the fact that 87% of the audience and some 70% of its adver-tising revenue came from abroad.

Finally, and not least, new media policies have not evolved in a historical void. Sectoral characteristics have proved significant. Inherited institutional structures, the working practices of broadcasters themselves (e.g. the way in which news and programmes are put together) and established professional norms in broadcasting remain a central part of the context of policy. Even if they have been on the defensive, public-service broadcasting organisations remain resourceful actors. They possess highly professional staff, some tradition of collaboration, influential political supporters, a developed and respected ideology, "inhouse" programme production capability and extensive programme libraries that constitute major assets. Few of the major public-service broadcasters are not already active in satellite broadcasting. Not least, regulation seems to be moving towards the notion of two pillars or sectors of broadcasting, one public and the other private; and public debate is beginning to focus on the question of whether each sector has a particular function that requires different regulatory conditions for its support. This development is apparent in Britain "post-Peacock", in France with the Chirac government and in West Germany after the ruling of the Federal Constitutional Court in November 1986 and the state treaty of 1987. Institutional heritage is likely to be a powerful ingredient in West European policies towards new media technologies.

Bibliography

BREYER, S. (1982), *Regulation and its reform*, Harvard University Press, Cambridge, Mass.

CERNY, P. and SCHAIN, M. (eds) (1985), *Socialism, the state and public policy in France*, Frances Pinter, London.

DIZARD, W. (1982), *The coming information age*, Longman, London Oxford.

DYSON, K. (1980), *The state tradition in Western Europe*, Martin Robertson, Oxford.

DYSON, K. (1982), Policy style in West Germany, in: J. RICHARDSON (ed.), *Policy styles in Western Europe*, Allen and Unwin, London.

DYSON, K. (1986), West European states and the communications revolution, in: K. DYSON and P. HUMPHREYS (eds), *The politics of the communications revolution in Western Europe*, Frank Cass, London, 10-55.

DYSON, K. and HUMPHREYS, P. (1985), The new media in Britain and France - two versions of heroic muddle?, in: *Rundfunk und Fernsehen*, 3-4, 362-79.

DYSON, K. and HUMPHREYS, P. (1986), Policies for new media in Western Europe: deregulation of broadcasting and multimedia diversification, in: K. DYSON and P. HUMPHREYS (eds), *The politics of the communications revolution in Western Europe*, 98-124.

DYSON, K. and HUMPHREYS, P. (1988), *Broadcasting and new media policies in Western Europe*, Croom Helm, London.

EC COMMISSION (1983), *Realities and tendencies in European television*, EC Commission, Brussels.

HARDEN, I. and LEWIS, N. (1986), *The noble lie*. Hutchinson, London.

HOLLINS, T. (1984), *Beyond broadcasting: into the cable age*, British Film Institute, London.

HOOD, C. (1984), *The tools of government*, Macmillan, London.

HOWKINS, J. (1982), *New technologies, new policies*, British Film Institute, London.

HUNT COMMITTEE (1982), *Report of the inquiry into cable expansion and broadcasting policy*, HMSO, London.

KOMMISSION FÜR DEN AUSBAU DES TECHNISCHEN KOMMUNIKATIONSSYSTEMS (1976), *Telekommunikationsbericht mit acht Anlagebanden*, Verlag Heger, Bonn.

MATTELART, A. and MATTELART, M. (1984), *International image markets*. Marion Boyars, London.

NONET, P. and SELZNICK, P. (1978), *Law and society in transition: towards responsive law*. Harper, New York.

NORA, S. and MINC, A. (1978), *Informatisation de la société. Documentation française*, Paris.

OHMAE, K. (1985), *Triad Power*. Free Press, New York.

PETZMAN, S. (1976), Towards a more general theory of regulation, in: *Journal of Law and Economics*, 19, 211-240.

PRAGNELL, A. (1985), *Television in Europe: quality and values in a time of change*. European Institute for the Media, Manchester.

PRESSMAN, J. and WILDAVSKY, A. (1973), *Implementation*. University of California Press, Berkeley.

RICHARDSON, J. and JORDAN, A. (1979), *Governing under pressure*. Blackwell, Oxford.

SCHILLER, D. (1982), *Telematics and government*. Ablex, New Jersey.

SCHILLER, H. and NORDENSTRENG, C. (eds.) (1981), *National sovereignty and international communication*. Ablex, New Jersey.

SCHRAPE, K. (1987), Fernsehprogrammbedarf und Programmversorgung, in: *Media Perspektiven*, 6, 345-53.

STERLING, C. (1984), *Electronic media*. Praeger, New York.

STIGLER, G. (1975), *The citizen and the state: essays on regulation*. Chicago, University Press.

STREECK, W. and SCHMITTER, Ph.C. (eds) (1985), *Private-interest government: beyond market and state*. Sage, London.

TEUBER, G. (1983), Substantive and reflexive elements in modern law, in: *Law and Society Review*, 2, 239-85.

TOFFLER, A. (1980), *The third wave*. Morrow, New York.

VARIS, T. (1984), The international flow of television programmes, in: *Journal of Communication*, winter.

WENHAM, B. (ed.) (1982), *The third age of broadcasting*. Faber, London.

WILENSKY, H. (1967), *Organizational intelligence*. Basic Books, New York.

ZYSMAN, J. (1977), *Political strategies for industrial order: state, market and industry in France*. University of California Press, Berkeley.

3

Techno-Industrial Innovation and Technology Assessment

The State's Problems
with its New Role

Frieder Naschold[1]

While techno-industrial innovation has characterized economic development, as well as social and industrial change, in an intensive way for at least a decade, the development of technology assessment (TA) as a societal process has emerged only in the last few years. Apart from the USA, other countries such as Sweden, France and the Netherlands have been in the forefront of the institutionalization of TA in recent years. The European Community (EC) held a conference in collaboration with the Dutch Government in 1987 aimed at making TA a more widespread process and procedure. But the most advanced European industrialized country, West Germany, still lags behind its competitors. In November 1986 the German Parliament's Enquête Commission on TA concluded that TA, at that time, was an inadequate evaluative mechanism. However at the

[1] I would like to thank Dr. Ulrich Hilpert for valuable comments on the first draft.

same time, the German Regional Governments of NorthRhine-Westphalia, Hessen and Baden-Württemberg tried to come to terms with TA. Equally, in Japan, two central units and a larger number of commissions with more specific functions are engaged in the development of a long-term scenario for Japan's economy. During 1986 and 1987 UNESCO presented a programme that involved many different aspects of TA and it organized workshops to develop the tools of social technology assessment in developing countries (Naschold et al. 1986; Dierkes et al. 1986).[2]

The enormous changes that are introduced by techno-industrial innovation and the major, new role of the state in these processes, of course, require more information concerning the consequences of innovation and call for greater awareness of the development processes that accompany techno-industrial innovation. TA appears to be a vital tool of qualified and intelligent state policy in this field, and the capacity to develop satisfactory TA appears to be a fundamental requirement for the state's successful performance of its *new role*. Therefore, successful TA will be a condition for continued successful participation in the international division of labour. But the idea that underlies this assumption about the importance of TA is based on the expectations that: firstly, TA can be achieved before political decision-making takes place; and, secondly, TA is undertaken in a way that allows alternative forms of techno-industrial innovation to be developed. Finally, this idea is based on the assumption that TA is more or less a rational process and that there is a depoliticization of policies in techno-industrial innovation. TA gives the state's new role a depoliticized character. So, in dealing with TA and policies on techno-industrial innovation this chapter will also deal with the question: do different politics matter?

1. Via Technology Assessment to the New Role of the State

In technology assessment, as in many other comparable fields of policy, the United States led the way for a long time (Johnson

---

[2] For a more detailed discussion see Naschold et al. 1986.

66

1983; PROGNOS 1983). Like the planning-programming-budgeting system of the 1960s, TA was seen primarily as an instrument for fostering rationality within politico-administrative systems: as an early warning system for the executive and as an instrument of control for the legislative branch. The founding of the Office of Technology Assessment (OTA) in 1973 marks the end of the first period of growing interest in TA. The OTA possesses a distinctive and strong in-house capacity for assessment work. Its main task is to prepare analytic studies, keyed to current decision-making processes. It has found for itself a permanent spot within the process of government of the United States. The OTA, for many years, has represented the dominant model, or at least an essential point of reference, for the development of TA in other countries. As such, the OTA model stands for an orientation towards the centre of the politico-administrative system, a technocratic dominance of the experts and of analytic studies and highly selective consultation with society at large (through centrally appointed advisory boards attached to the individual studies).

In Japan TA already has a long tradition and has to be considered as an integral part of the political planning and steering system. It is largely institutionalized in two central offices, which are attached to the office of the Prime Minister and the Ministry of International Trade and Industry (MITI) respectively, which can be considered to be the two main centres of control in the Japanese political system (European TA Congress 1986). Thus, in Japan TA is not an instrument of parliamentary control, but exclusively an instrument of the government, to support its interventions in the techno-economic process of restructuring the country. These interventions, however, consist mostly of a government-induced coordination and harmonization between economic associations, large enterprises and organized science. The emphasis of TA activities in Japan therefore lies not so much in the production of expert studies, but in the formulation of a common long-term framework of orientation for programmes of action.

The European situation can best be characterized by four development trends. Firstly, in the 1970s and early 1980s we see on the one hand a lot of rather fruitless debate on the institutionalization of TA, but on the other hand the development and actual application of a series of interesting and promising TA instruments. Among these are, for instance, the reports and discussions on the CIM (Computer Integrated Manufacturing) concept, the controversies concerning nuclear energy in West Germany and Sweden and the discussion on telematics in France. Secondly, in sharp contrast with the lack of progress in the 1970s, over the past four years TA has become institutionalized in no less than five European countries. Basically four different variants have come into existence: TA as part of the government apparatus or as a parliamentary institution, as in France and Denmark; independent TA institutes, as in the Netherlands and Austria; and mixed functions, as in Sweden. Thirdly, the importance of the EC level is also undeniably growing: in the stimulating and organizing functions of the Forecasting and Assessment of Science and Technology (FAST) programme, in direct coordination of TA centres in Europe (Rip and van den Belt 1986). Fourthly, in the course of these and other similar activities recent changes in the TA paradigm could become especially important. The traditional TA concept is basically aimed at early warning and emphasizes the dimensions of risks and the consequences of technical change. Recent developments, however, are aimed at a constructive TA, in the sense of the control of technological change, and they place emphasis on the opportunities for democratic influence in the decision-making process, on collective debate and collective learning. Although the success of these programmes is still uncertain, they have at least brought debate considerably beyond the OTA model.

The present state of TA in West Germany is, of course, dominated by the failure of its parliamentary institutionalization. At the end of 1986 an elaborate proposal for the institutionalization of TA was rejected by parliament. This failure can also be considered a considerable setback within the larger European context.[3] Such a comparison, however, should not be limited to the question of a parliamentary institutionalization. Other forms and practices of TA should also be taken into consideration. In this respect, it should be noted that TA has been taking place for

---

[3] A comparison of the international TA conference of 1982 in Bonn, organized by the Ministry of Internal Affairs, with the conference organized in 1987 by the Dutch government together with the EC indicates this point.

many years and indeed has become largely institutionalized within the Ministry of Research and Technology (BMFT). A large number of functionally equivalent TA practices can also be found within the scientific community. From a comparative viewpoint the activities of some of the *Länder* and some other organizations are especially noticeable. *Länder* like NorthRhine-Westphalia, Hessen and Baden-Württemberg have undertaken comparatively detailed programmes, which have been implemented, and other organizations, notably some industrial unions, have a well-known and generally recognized tradition in the field of TA.

Experiences of TA up till now have shown that the field can be characterized by three problem areas, which also constitute the focal points of TA development: the scientific conception and methodology of TA; the institutionalization of TA; and public debate and participation in TA. These problems and corresponding problem definitions have developed into a clear hierarchy: the scientific problems of TA have been generally recognized and delegated to the scientific community to be dealt with according to its routines. The question of the institutionalization of TA is considered to be a central problem area for public debate and a focal point of the political decision-making process. Questions of public debate and participation remain more latent but in the end they may possess the greatest explosive force.

What clearly underpins these recent trends to establish TA is the idea that techno-industrial innovation raises more than purely economic questions and is a matter of particular concern to some interest groups. The investigation of future trends and the importance of the state's policies in supporting and initiating innovation calls for a new activity by the state. The importance of state innovation policies and the growing awareness of their importance with regard to the planning and design of other government programmes has created the new role for the state. The state's growing engagement in TA is an element of this new role and provides evidence of its existence. It is *via* TA that the state can take its active part in initiating techno-industrial innovation when designing state policies.

Frieder Naschold

2. The State and Techno-Industrial Innovation. The Problem of Political Decisions about Future Socio-Economic Development

This role of the state in both participating in and inducing processes of techno-industrial innovation required a more precise and differentiated instrument of analysis; i.e. for a TA that is more competent than the previous synoptic or comprehensive approach. So, in the USA, a highly selective analysis was developed that aimed at the identification of constellations of risks and that still dominates the field. This approach was defined as contingency planning, crisis avoidance and policy options analysis. The current stage of development takes the concept of the identification of constellations of risks as a starting point, but it extends this analysis by making it more comprehensive. This approach increasingly tries to build the processional character of political decision-making into the methodology of its studies. In other words, efforts are made to effectuate a closer connection between the procedural rationality of politics and the substantive rationality of science. But this is based on the idea of an auto-centric development of science that is free from state intervention and that is rarely related directly to socio-economic development. The more science is an instrument of state policy and the more its function is to generate the particular techno-scientific progress that the economy and society require (Hilpert 1983, 1989), then the more the idea of a substantive rationality of science has to be revised. The discussion of TA instead deals with the interrelationship between the rationalities of policy-making and of science. The spreading of this new approach, however, has not in any way stopped the older controversy, whether TA studies should take their starting point in specific technologies, in specific problems, or in concrete technological projects (Paschen 1986). The methodology of TA has therefore been developing from pure risk assessment to policy analysis, towards an integration of the political structures of society into the social and economic structures and relationships. In the course of that development, the corresponding range of alternative courses of action has also been enlarged. The analytical framework of TA consists presently of three more or less standardized components: technology forecast, impact analysis and policy analysis.

However, the types of TA and their fundamental understanding of the relations between technology and society appear to be strongly divergent. They are all based on the same understanding of science and practice, which might be called the prediction-prescription model. It is essentially a three-stage model: the task of scientific analysis is firstly to identify and predict trends in technological and social change; secondly alternatives have to be designed using specific means, based on an analysis of the differences between what has been the predicted state of affairs and what is assumed or (politically) prescribed to be the desirable one. These recommendations, thirdly, then form the essential framework for decision-making and practical action. This indicates the vital role of science in TA and points to the relationship between political issues and the production of scientific knowledge. The dependency of political decision-makers upon scientific knowledge introduces a specific form of scientific analysis that is politically induced. It is important to bear this relationship in mind when the role of science in political decision-making concerning TA is discussed.

Of course, the practice of TA is much more complex than this basic scientific structure would seem to imply. Recent TA studies especially emphasize the importance of alternative scenario's instead of (un)conditional predictions and also the processional character of TA itself in the sense of a series of consecutive TA studies. These new tendencies are clearly visible in the exemplary TA studies that were commissioned by the Investigative Commission. The methodological problems related to the three-stage model are also generally known. Let us mention just three general problems: the problem of prediction, which has gained significance firstly since the abandonment of unidirectional relations between technology and society (IAB 1980) and then more so where principles of causality have been dismissed; the informational control dilemma, which points out that the consequences of a technology only become really visible at a point in time where the technology has already established itself, so that recasting is very difficult and only possible to a limited extent (Collingridge 1980); the problem of aggregation and disaggregation, i.e. the fact that no satisfactory solution so far has been found for the aggregation and transformation of the firm or plant level to macro-economic categories.

The institutionalization of TA itself, of course, requires a more than the pure development of appropriate methods and the availability of the necessary scientific knowledge. If one surveys the relevant positions and arguments within the debate about TA as it has been going on in a number of countries, an impressive and relatively clearly identifiable set of positions can be listed. This can be illustrated by for example the position of those who oppose an institutionalization in principle. This position is basically delineated by four arguments. (i) The gap between analytical claims and practical reality is so large, that institutionalization is neither required nor useful. (ii) The same conclusion can be drawn from the consideration that quantitative as well as qualitative capacities for analysis are sufficiently available. There remains, at most, a problem of the more effective use of available resources. (iii) Institutionalization of TA would mean the creation of one more bureaucratic authority and therefore more red tape and increasing costs of regulation. (iv) An institutionalization of TA would stimulate interventions by organized social groups in the process of technological development and innovation.

Behind these different arguments stands a complex structure of interest with corresponding definitions of the problem. In parliamentary systems, with their functional connection between government and the majority party or parties, an institutionalization which is directly tied to parliament, thus also serving the opposition, is difficult to bring out, or only with severe limitations. Apart from this line of conflict between governments and oppositions, there exists in all parliaments a certain desire to preserve the status quo. The introduction of a parliamentary TA authority would produce unpredictable changes in the network of interests tied up with the existing system of committees. Similarly in the scientific community, damage to existing constellations of interests can be anticipated. In many countries the established organizations of scientists have resisted the introduction of functionally specified TA institutions. Finally, considerable doubts are also usually voiced by the economic associations, emphasizing especially problems of regulation, bureaucracy and public acceptance of new technologies.

Beyond the democratic problem of a public debate and participation, there is the problem of political decision-making on future socio-economic development. It is clear that interest groups play an important role in this process but, equally, it is obvious that the TA debate has a strong tendency towards depoliticization. Interest groups participate in TA debates but the decisions are made primarily on the basis of the role the state plays in the process of techno-industrial innovation and on the information science is able to produce and make available. So, with regard to TA, there is a need for the just-in-time production of scientific knowledge and for a capacity to produce alternative scenarios. State and science therefore are interrelated, and this points to the way politics finally is involved in this process that formally appears to be depoliticized. It points to a twofold dilemma in the state/science relationship.

3. State and Science - The Twofold Dilemma

3.1 The Importance of Scientific Knowledge for the State's New Role

Let us recall once more the intentions of TA. The purpose of the whole TA effort is to obtain a better understanding of the complex processes of technological change and, where possible or necessary, to steer or shape these processes. With that aim the knowledge component of political decision-making processes is to be enlarged and strengthened. This is done by the production of a specific additional knowledge base and a closer connection between science and politics. It is important to see that state policy and the production of scientific knowledge are closely related. The state's activity follows a techno-economic rationality and becomes a key determinant of techno-industrial innovation. But the scientific knowledge is basically important to these state policies. This means that even tough TA in the socio-political system can be achieved only by the means of specific research and *via* the science structure; the political guidelines still predominate. The prediction-prescription model combines predictions of technical change, impact analysis and policy analysis. It couples centralized knowledge production with a centralized political process and, as such, it has become predominant in the concept of TA as well as in TA practice.

This model of TA is certainly adequate to deal with a large number of social problems. However, as mentioned above, the model also has some weaknesses: the problem of prediction and impact analysis in completely new and unstructured situations; the tension between professional dominance and public debate, and participation in processes of evaluation and application; the informational and participative control dilemma; the different demands made by an active, shaping approach to TA versus an approach which concentrated of impact analysis. At several points so far the far-reaching, extraparadigmatic developments in TA have been mentioned.

In the field of production technology, complex and lengthy processes of restructuring are taking place. The available analytical and empirical knowledge about underlying technical trends is extremely limited, and even less is known about the consequences of these trends. The production of additional knowledge is slow and tedious.

On the other hand, an urgent need is felt to influence these developments. The classical TA approach may still be of some use here, but its limits are also becoming all too clear. In West Germany and Sweden this situation has given rise to new TA concepts and activities since the mid-1970s (Naschold 1986). This approach took its starting point in the decentralized innovation processes at the level of the firm or groups of firms. Instead of general statements and predictions, the emphasis is on the development of experimental models and pilot projects. Specific new decentralized forms of organization were built up inside and around the firm on the basis of centrally formulated guidelines. These forms of organization represent a considerably enlarged potential for public debate and participation. The knowledge component is organized through accompanying scientific research: interdisciplinary teams investigate bottlenecks in the development process while it is proceeding and feed their findings back into the ongoing process. Diffusion of these findings does not take the classical form of a generalization of individual findings, but takes place through discussions and learning stimulated by the model project. TA is then a social process, organized in the form of model projects and experiments, with a lot of room for participation and public debate, with definite possibilities for shaping and influencing developments and with a knowledge component in the form of a sequence of accompanying studies.

TA structured as a social process through model experiments and accompanying research has proven to be an effective organizational form for identifying and then investigating, shaping and controlling problems of production organization, production technology and the connected question of costs and productivity. It is much less suitable for dealing with completely new problem areas, especially if we are looking at the general social consequences for the working conditions of groups of workers or for the effects on their conditions of reproduction. Of course, the classical TA approach here is of no use either. Such social problems cannot be investigated within the framework of experimental models. The accompanying research team would not be able to produce valid and reliable findings, because significant structural changes cannot be observed within the short time-span of an experimental model. On the other hand, if the projects were to be drawn out over a much longer period, the socio-technical rationality built up around them would tend to become stabilized and the process of change would become increasingly less malleable. Even though the knowledge would be produced in time the problem of its character would remain. Its political and social definition is unchanged. The production of scientific knowledge is defined by the projects that are undertaken (i.e. science is a politically determined instrument) and it is defined by structural constraints within society (i.e. science is socially finalized) (Hilpert 1983, 1989). One way out of this control dilemma is offered by the instrument of anticipatory or preventive regulation. This can be illustrated by the example of the much-debated problem of tele-work. Negative social consequences are expected of tele-work on two counts: social isolation and uncertainties in employment relations. TA as a process of preventive regulation then takes the following form: reaching an understanding of the possibly critical and unwanted social effects; specification of the minimum acceptable conditions; laying down those minimal conditions in protective regulations. The nucleus of such a process of anticipatory regulation consists of a scientifically based complex of negotiations concerning normative limits on technical change. In view of the control dilemmas described above, this strategy seems to be most fruitful for such hitherto unknown and unexplored situations, more so than either the classical prediction-of-effects approach or the approach using research in pilot projects.

A considerably different kind of problem can be found at the intersection of socio-economic developments in the labour process (i.e. work-related illnesses and questions of industrial safety). The internationally predominant way of processing prob-lems of industrial safety is based on three principles: (i) a scientific knowledge base in the form of threshold values, etc., founded on the conceptions of causality prevailing in laboratory research; (ii) translation of this knowledge through centralized political processes into a hierarchy of abstract regulations, i.e. the system of industrial safety regulations and accident prevention; (iii) application of these regulations to individual plants and work situations as guidelines for action at the plant level. According to this traditional philosophy, problems of industrial safety are essentially problems of scientific measurement, followed by political activities, the interpretation of data and the drawing of suitable conclusions for problems at the firm level. It cannot be denied that this concept can deal effectively with many classical problems of industrial safety. But it does contain, and always did contain, a serious problem: the gap between abstract scientifically based norms and concrete local activities by the affected persons. This problem is becoming radically worse: in the course of techno-economic restructuring new vistas for industrial safety are opening (Kuhn and Schreiber 1986): abstract, informed and complex situations of strain with high and completely unexplored consequences for health; an increase in work-related stress and psychosomatic illness. These con-stellations of problems are very difficult to deal with by the tradi-tional methods of processing problems of industrial safety. Various efforts, based on the traditional approaches to TA, to identify the new problems and to come to grips with their conse-quences produce inadequate results.

Whatever the individual problems of a certain technology may be, primarily, TA is in need of appropriate scientific know-ledge. This is not only a condition for discussing the impacts of new technologies and their application in industry; it is not only a basis for decisions on state policies; but it is, in addition, the basis for the political process of public debate and the interest groups' participation in TA. A continuation of bargaining with interest groups for designing the policy, and achieving a socially accepted innovation, is excluded to the extent that the dilemma of inadequate scientific knowledge cannot be avoided. So, the state is prepared to play its new role in techno-industrial innovation on the basis that scientific knowledge provides the opportunity to introduce this innovative process.

Its decisions, then, do not show a depoliticization based on scientific research. Instead, the dilemma of the lack of timely scientific knowledge which is essential for TA means that policies are the product of the politics of the Government and the general role of the state in techno-industrial innovation. The similarity of the different national strategies therefore is primarily a question of convergences in politics, but it also indicates a convergence in techno-scientific knowledge and the common lack of the scientific knowledge that forms the basis for TA. It is this uneven availability of types of scientific knowledge (the opportunity to introduce techno-industrial innovation versus the inability to realize a full TA) that illustrates the specific new role of the state.

3.2 The Political Dimension of the Scientific Production of Knowledge

The outstanding importance of scientific knowledge, beyond the dilemma of timeliness, is clearly indicated by the problem of achieving adequate TA. One may have the impression that the situation characterized above is purely a problem of time and management. Little attention is paid to the question of whether science in current form in Western industrialized countries is capable of producing the scientific knowledge needed for TA. Supposing the timeliness dilemma could be avoided, would it mean that there are alternatives designed by science that could form the basis for a full TA? This question brings us to the more general and theoretical problem of the relationship between the scientific production of knowledge and the society within which this process takes place. It gives us an idea of the limits of TA and, therefore, an idea of the limits of political decision-making and alternative directions of development. Three problems may enable us to look at the political dimension of the scientific production of knowledge: (i) instrumentalization, (ii) finalization, and (iii) functionalization of science.

It has been shown above that TA requires specific forms of scientific knowledge and that science, in principle, is prepared to produce. However it is not only the scarcity of this knowledge that has to be kept in mind but also its genesis. The knowledge that is produced concerns a specific interest, a specific need and a specific application. Scientific knowledge is produced with reference to this initial situation. The use of certain methods and the engagement of scientifically qualified personnel may give us an idea of the quality of the knowledge, but it does not imply anything regarding the general applicability of this knowledge in different situations and with regard to different interests.

The opportunity to produce alternative approaches that may form the basis for TA is quite narrow. On the one hand, the knowledge that is produced in certain research projects concerns the economic interests of potential producers and consumers of the innovative product. Little attention is given to non-economic or non-technological questions. Even publicly funded academic research is organized as an instrument for techno-industrial innovation (Hilpert 1983, 1989). Alternatives here are limited to the application of the particular findings of the research and they do not include the generation of general alternatives suggesting new routes and strategies for development. On the other hand, apart from this project orientation in the generation of scientific knowledge, the institutional organization of academic science is hardly structured to avoid this problem. Particular support is given to those parts of science that tend to have potential importance for techno-industrial innovation. The close relationship between basic research and applied research, indeed the growing difficulty in differentiating them, indicates the importance of science for future competitive positions and the narrow limits that exist for the formulation of alternative approaches.

This organizational aspect of the instrumentalization of science leads us to a discussion of its finalization. This problem, which is evidenced by the external definition of the aims of scientific investigation, lies at the heart of the development of theoretical understanding within science. In contrast to direct instrumentalization, this problem does not concern the focus of particular research projects but determines the directions in which science develops, and hence its fundamental structure (Böhme et al. 1973). As a consequence the production of scientific knowledge and its application in the development of technologies does not allow any opportunities for fundamentally divergent alternatives to be pursued (Böhme et al. 1972). The institutionalization of particular scientific disciplines, the promotion of certain fields of science, discrimination against others, and the organization of a science that produces knowledge corresponding to certain economic and social needs for techno-scientific progress, demonstrates that pure scientific knowledge no longer exists. This finalization of science makes it politically acceptable (Daele and Weingart 1975), but the politicized character of such science is not made apparent by the depoliticized form of presentation which is used to express and explain scientific knowledge.

The current international competition in science-based products requires more than the finalization of science. Whilst a very limited number of alternative development approaches is possible under these competitive relations, they nevertheless necessitate a clear orientation towards certain products and applications. This means that, in addition to the finalized (and still theoretically oriented) development of science, the instrumentalization of scientific investigation has to ensure that particular aims, concerning the acquisition of useful scientific knowledge, are achieved within a short and calculable span of time. On the congruent relationship between the socio-economic system and science, that occurs with the finalization of science, is focused an extrascientific definition of the aims of scientific investigation i.e. the functionalization of science (Hilpert 1983, 1989). Scientific knowledge that is produced in this context is geared to the optimization of technology development, but is of hardly any use for TA. To the extent that TA questions the products of the functionalized science, it takes the form of a relatively irrational attempt to oppose the 'true' findings of pure science. Nothing of the political genesis of this scientific knowledge is either visible or acknowledged.

So, beyond the timeliness dilemma that hinders the continuation of bargaining and participation of interest groups, the development of adequate TA faces major problems. The genesis of new technologies and the economic decisions that are made about them often occur decades before the necessary knowledge for an adequate TA is available. The transformation of political decisions into scientific knowledge and techno-scientific progress disguises their political dimension. But this political dimension is a fundamental feature of modern functionalized science. So, even though the timeliness dilemma could be managed, scientific knowledge still contains an alternative implicit dilemma: the politically determined transcendence of science's capacity to generate fundamental alternatives.

4. On the Importance of the State for the Achievement of Techno-Industrial Innovation

When analysing TA it is interesting that the concepts of public debate and interest group participation are of declining significance, while the roles of the state and of science receive closer attention. Indeed the timeliness dilemma has shown the problems that stand in the way of the continuation of corporatist policy-making in the field of TA. But the alternative dilemma has shown that the idea of science-based decision-making is a complete misperception and that the presentation of TA as a depoliticized process (because it refers to pure scientific knowledge) is a chimera. The political dimension is involved in two ways: (i) the way in which scientific knowledge is produced (as mentioned above); and (ii) the way that techno-industrial innovation, as it takes place in Western countries, is regarded as a matter beyond discussion. It is, in particular, this second form of politicization that characterizes the role of the state and the way it deals with TA. Although the capitalist economy, and the way in which it functions, is the basis for the processes of techno-industrial innovation, increasing international competition and the national socio-economic consequences, once again it is regarded as a matter beyond discussion. This presents the appearance of a depoliticization treatment of the problem, even though such an apparent treatment serves very specific economic and social interests.

But the way the state deals with TA is characterized by the attempt to harmonize socio-economic development with techno-industrial innovation. This harmonization is regarded as both necessary and inevitable, and is induced or supported by state policy. There are, of course, problems in achieving TA, but the fact that the state tries to achieve it and the importance that is ascribed to it shows that state policies are fundamental to future development. The results of TA or the activities that follow from it (no matter whether or not it is fully achieved) are a key determinant of the ways in which techno-industrial innovation is realized in different countries. No doubt every country tries to do it. State policies are appropriate instruments to bring about economic optimization and may try to deal with problems in the field of social, regional, ecological, policies, etc. But they are also appropriate to reduce the social and ecological costs of innovation and they may harmonize social and industrial development. Finally, TA is concerned with more than the choice between the full realization of economic opportunities and risk avoidance. State policies can determine future socio-economic development and the ways in which techno-industrial innovation can be used within a specific national situation in order to achieve optimum results.

The twofold dilemma with regard to TA has shown the decline in significance of corporatist decision-making and it has also transcended the specifically Marxist view of the state as serving concrete capitalist interests. The state can introduce techno-industrial innovation and can also make decisions on its national application. Within the limits of the capitalist economy, and because of the problems of TA, this new role of the state is closely related to the politics of the party that forms the government. So, the state's problems with TA indicate its new role in techno-industrial innovation and that differences in political behaviour and institutional forms have a direct influence on policy.

Frieder Naschold

Bibliography

BÖHME, Gernot, DAELE, Wolfgang van den, and KROHN, Wolfgang (1972), Alternativen in der Wissenschaft, in: *Zeitschrift für Soziologie*, 1, 302-316.

BÖHME, Gernot, DAELE, Wolfgang van den, and KROHN, Wolfgang (1973), Die Finalisierung der Wissenschaft, in: *Zeitschrift für Soziologie*, 2, 128-144.

COLLINGRIDGE, David (1980), *The Social Control of Technology*, London.

DAELE, Wolfgang van den, and WEINGART, Peter (1975), Resistenz und Rezeptivität der Wissenschaft - Zu den Entstehungsbedingungen neuer Disziplinen durch wissenschaftspolitische Steuerung, in: *Zeitschrift für Soziologie*, 4, 146-164.

DIERKES, Meinolf, PETERMANN, Thomas, and VON THIENEN, Volker (eds.) (1986), *Technik und Parlament*.

EUROPEAN TA CONGRESS (1986), Draft Paper, September.

HILPERT, Ulrich (1983), *Zur Funktionalisierung der Wissenschaft in hochindustrialisierten Gesellschaften - Am Beispiel der Wirkung staatlicher Wissenschafts- und Technologiepolitiken auf die Energieforschung in der Bundesrepublik Deutschland*, Ph.D. Dissertation, University of Constance, 728p.

HILPERT, Ulrich (1989), *Staatliche Forschungs- und Technologiepolitik und offizielle Wissenschaft - Wissenschaftlich-technischer Fortschritt als Instrument politisch vermittelter technologisch-industrieller Innovation*. Opladen: Westdeutscher Verlag, 295p.

IAB (1980), *Das prognostizierte Jahrzehnt*. Stuttgart. 3.

JOHNSON, Chalmers (1983), *MITI and the Japanese Miracle*. Basel.

KUHN, Karl, and SCHREIBER, Paul (1986), Arbeitsschutz und neue Technologien, in: *Der Bundesminister für Arbeit*, Forschungsbericht 114. Dortmund.

NASCHOLD, Frieder (1986), Politik und Produktion, in: HARTWICH, H.-H. (1986), *Politik und die Macht der Technik*. Köln.

NASCHOLD, Frieder et al. (1986), *Social Technology Assessment*. Nairobi and Paris.

PASCHEN, Herbert (1986), Technology Assessment - Ein strategisches Rahmenkonzept für die Bewertung von Technologien, in: DIERKES et al. 1986.

PROGNOS (1983), *Das Forschungs- und Technologiesystem in Japan*. Basel.

RIP, Arie, and VAN DEN BELT, Henk (1986), *Constructive Technology Assessment*. Zoetermeer, ms.

Part II

Small Internal Markets and the Relevance of State Capabilities: Is Techno-Industrial Innovation State-Introduced?

4

Economic Adjustment by Techno-Industrial Innovation and the Role of the State

Solar Technology and Biotechnology in France and West Germany

Ulrich Hilpert

The global change in the international division of labour introduced by the emergence of newly industrialized countries (NICs) and their participation in the world market, has led to a number of particular attempts at economic adjustment in the Western industrialized countries. The unavoidable decline of old industries, and perhaps even their disappearance, is calling for new forms of industrial development, economic adjustment and of policy. It is important to be aware of the field in which the NICs have achieved economic success: in the Fordist industries and mass-production industries in general. Low wages created advantages in these countries, and legislation (e.g. on labour conditions, environmental protection, waste disposal) added additional attractions for older industries. Given the leading industrialized countries' inability to compete in these fields, they had to develop their own advantages that could not be counter-balanced by the NICs. This introduced the importance of science-based products, because the general weakness of NICs in research and development, and the still significant brain drain to the industrialized countries, created advantages for such countries. The need of mature industries for advanced technological equipment (e.g. microelectronic products) to remain innovative provided the opportunity not merely for the continuation of participation in international markets but also to claim an enhanced position when competing with other industrialized countries.

Techno-industrial innovation offered the opportunity to manage economic adjustment to the changing international division of labour and to participate progressively in the economic development that takes place in all industrialized and industrializing countries. But investments and risks are extremely high and the national markets of the West European countries usually are inadequate to guarantee the amortization of investment costs. In addition to this market problem there is the need for effective research structures that can produce the techno-scientific progress required, and there is also the question of whether there are industrial structures that are appropriate to form the basis of the new, innovative industries. The realization of techno-industrial innovation, therefore, requires more than the support of industries and firms it requires a state policy for innovation. It is interesting to see how countries such as France and West Germany, that are very differently organized with regard to their politico-administrative structures, respond to this situation. The divergent conditions of techno-industrial innovation based on infrastructure technologies, as against those based on innovative products and methods of production, moreover, indicate the role of the state and the congruence of state policies with the international division of labour and national opportunities made available by the presence of initial conditions within the nation's industry and science. The examples of solar technology, (an infrastructure technology that requires large external markets) and of biotechnology (an innovative means of production and source of new products) can indicate the role of the state and the aims of state innovation policy rather than differences due simply to variations in national circumstances.

continue international cooperation (A.F.M.E. 1982). In this way A.F.M.E. has a political aim for the industry that is much more than the promotion of research in the industry, which was carried out by the COMES (Desprairies 1980). Moreover, to improve export opportunities the A.F.M.E. promotes the early presentation of French energy technologies and materials (A.F.M.E. 1982).

The main contribution to innovation to meet new needs in the solar energy industry is the responsibility of the C.N.R.S. There 500 engineers are working in the field of solar reserarch, which is half of all scientists engaged in this field in France (Rodot et al. 1980). The C.N.R.S. carries out the PIRDES (Programme Industrielle de la Recherche et du Développement) which is intended to achieve a strongly organized programme of industrial research. It also cooperates with the nationalized French enterprise E.D.F. to plan and build solar thermal technology installations (Hoez 1978). From this collaboration emerges the demand for a market-oriented structure in the field of solar thermal research. The C.N.R.S. plays an important part in the CETHEL group, which was created as a result of this demand by state organizations for a centre for the development of the French solar industry.

The orientation of the French solar industry on the Franc Zone is a consequence of French policy. During decolonization and the period in which the young African states won their independence France introduced a new form of connection based on contracts of cooperation (Adamelobun 1978). In this way the French state was able to continue the existing relationship of dependence and reserve the market of the Franc Zone for its own dominant economy. So in France not only is the organization of the industry achieved by state policy but also the organization of the market. This centring on the state and its orientation towards former colonies has an effect on the circumstances of innovation within the industrial structure, and as a result the French solar industry reveals an R&D orientation on technologies which are needed in the countries of the Franc Zone.

The French programme "Sahel Energie Nouvelle" takes the combination of market and innovation into account. Here the aims are regional research, the adjustment of the technologies to the need of the Sahel countries, demonstration of the working characteristics of the technologies in the use of renewable energies, and the offering of these concepts for rural development in the Sahel countries (Desprairies 1980). The main point of the Sahel programme is the promotion of solar technologies. On the basis of solar thermal processes 123 pumps, irrigation and electrification stations have been erected, which are normally limited on the kW scale. Using solar cells, 15 such stations have been built (Desprairies 1980). In addition to the Sahel programme there is cooperation with countries from the extended Franc Zone (Desprairies 1980).

Supplementary to these activities the institution TRANS-ENERG was established by the Ministry for Cooperation (Desprairies 1980). Its task is the solving of concrete problems in developing countries. It is interesting that it is exclusively made up of nationalized enterprises and state institutions, which have to analyse the actual and future energy resources, to prepare programmes for the development and planning of all types of energy, to calculate the financial needs for the achievement of these aims, and to educate qualified personnel (Desprairies 1980). In this way a situation is created in which a reserved and dependent market for French solar technologies exists. The nationalized enterprises and state institutions analyse the needs, and the state creates programmes to build up a solar industry that is, at least for the near future, oriented on this zone. Because of the economic dependence of the Franc Zone, which leads to the concentration on French technologies, the solar programme is consequently oriented on technologies that are important for the French solar industry. Cooperation with developing countries is relatively rare and limited to the field of industrial collaboration, but there is no endeavour to cooperate with consumers in the field of R&D.

Within the scope of solar technologies French policies aim at the substitution of traditional sources of energy; however, an expansion of demand and of need for the technology by assisting general regional development processes is not included in these activities. Because of the limitation of the programme to energy substitution there is a lack of rapidly expanding demand for the technology, and the orientation on the Franc Zone, with its need for middle- and small-scale solar technologies (like pumps and irrigation stations and electric power generators), forms too narrow a setting for the solar industry. The extraordinary importance of the French state for the French economy and orientation towards the Franc Zone are leading to innovations in industrial structure introduced by the Third World's need for solar technology, but its effects are limited by the demand structures in the countries of the Franc Zone, which are concentrated on the less attractive solar technologies in the lower and middle scale of power generation. But because of cooperation with industrialized countries, like West Germany, advanced and threshold countries, it can be expected that these countries, producing on low wages, will become competitors in the less complicated areas of solar technology. So the limitation of the French solar industry to the market of the Franc Zone will be perpetuated at least in the case of these particular technologies.

In France technological and industrial innovation in the solar energy industry is done in the context of a protected market with structures that are significantly different from the world market. The resulting policies for the development of the solar industry contain structural problems. The research and production capacity of France is absorbed by technologies of little economic relevance. Equally the innovations made by the French industry are made substantially outside the world market for solar technologies. This is the case with regard to the supply of technologies as well as the conditions of production and development. Because of the orientation on the protected market of the Franc Zone competitiveness is of little importance and the all-embracing dominance of the state leads to a development of the solar industry that depends on internal and external state policies (Papon 1975; Cavard and Criqui 1979) and on the resultant economic planning process (Papon 1973, 1979).

The importance of the developments in the Franc Zone for the innovations in the French industrial structure is clearly reflected in the French policies for the setting up of the national solar industry. The solar technologies, as well as the form of the relationship with the market of the Franc Zone both reflect the neo-colonial structure of this relationship. But more than anything they point to the tight economic and technological constraints which arise for industrialized countries like France, if they do not develop market demand in potential consumer countries, and if the lack of cooperation hinders the dynamic development of the need for large-scale technologies.

2.2 The German Concept: Promotion of Technological Development and of Demand in the Third World

The German industry's orientation towards the world market, the policies of the German state, and the open market for solar technologies of economic relevance have led to a close relationship between development in the Third World and the innovations in German industrial structure. The central elements connecting the development of demand with technological and industrial innovation are the competitiveness of German high technology enterprises and their established positions in the world market. The industrial policies of the German state are based on this favourable situation and can promote tendencies likely to be successful in the future.

It is essential that policies in the solar energy field can utilize an established industrial structure with a limited number of participating enterprises, which are engaged in solar research themselves. In the market of photovoltaics the firms Siemens and AEG, which have a long-standing experience in producing solar cells for the American NASA space expeditions, are involved. The silicon production for these technologies is done exclusively by Wacker. In the domain of solar thermal technologies there was an early involvement of MAN and MBB but it is only Dornier that participates in R&D. These enterprises have been guided exclusively by the profitability and diversification of their activities using innovative technologies in an attractive market. So the state is in a position to limit its activities to the promotion of innovative technologies and of adequate activities by the firms concerned.

The "Programm Energieforschung und Energietechnologien" (Programme for the promotion of energy research and energy technologies), which started in 1974 and has continued since, promotes the structures of industrial innovation and of adjustment to the technological needs of the countries that make up the world market. Thus, of the financial means given to private enterprises, a share of 74% is given to AEG and a share of 13% to Siemens. Likewise, in the domain of the solar thermal technologies, the relationship between innovation in the industrial structure and developments in the Third World is promoted. Here the heavily involved firms MAN and MBB receive 39% and 24.5% respectively and Dornier has a share of 18.5% of the financial resources given to private firms. The promotion of those firms particularly commited to innovation is also a support of the development of technologies for the Third World and a support of an industrial sector oriented towards this region.

At the same time the German state comes to agreements on cooperation with consumer countries. Scientific and technological cooperation forms an essential precondition for technological and industrial innovation that results from setting up a national solar industry. It is the increasing energy need and the present shortage of natural and non-renewable sources of energy in developing countries and rapid industrialization in Third World countries which lead the German government to predict a large potential market for energy technologies (BMFT 1979, 1979a). In this context the government is trying to open up these "interesting export opportunities for the German economy" (BMFT 1979b), because in "practically all cases the expensive production of solar energy systems depends on the opening up of large and substantial markets, capable of leading to high production capacities" (BMFT 1979b). In this way the German state tries to integrate the consumption of the Third World into its policies for the development of solar industry and to initiate technological and industrial innovation. Existing close economic links with the industrializing developing countries and the established positions in the world market of enterprises in the solar energy industry (Siemens, AEG, MBB, MAN) make possible the production of state policies that are able to open the markets necessary for the development of the solar energy industry.

In particular the links with industrializing developing countries contain the potential for a dynamic expansion of trade. Economic relations with India, Egypt, Mexico, Brazil, Argentina, and Indonesia include the important parts of the world market for solar technologies. There the applicability of solar technology is possible and because of the intensive processes of industrialization, increase of population, and urbanization, conurbations are created which lead to a progressively increasing demand for large-scale technologies to supply the urban regions with high energy demand densities. For the near future, above all, the German government expects a considerable demand for the solar-tower technology (BMFT 1979b).

This future demand for large-scale solar technologies is confronted by a current actual demand for small-scale technologies adequate for the existing decentralized supply situation. Because the consumer countries cannot develop and produce technologies appropriate to these needs, they are interested in the transfer of suitable technologies and the assistance of industrialized countries in setting up national productive capacities for less complicated small-scale energy technologies. These interests of the industrializing Third World countries are met by the policy of the German state and its offer of bilateral scientific and technological cooperation. The cooperation with countries which have large markets but lack industrial potential is integrated in the strategies of the German government to open several national markets to risky large-scale technologies (BMFT 1979c, 1979a) and subsitutes not only for the lack of an internal market but also reserves large parts of future markets for the German solar industry at an early stage.

In the domain of solar research West Germany signed contracts for scientific and technological cooperation with Egypt, India, Mexico, Brazil, Argentina, and Indonesia, to mention only those countries with large markets. In these cases cooperation continues existing relations and develops them in the domain of the solar technologies. Above all the cooperation is appropriately designed to assist the developing processes in the developing countries and in this way to lead to an expansion of the demand for large-scale solar technologies to meet the needs of the increasing industrialization and urbanization. So scientific and technological cooperation not only opens new markets for the German solar industry, but the division of labour involved leads to an interlinking of the consumer market and the German solar industry. Therefore policies for the opening of markets lead to a connection of the solar industry with the dynamic processes in the industrializing developing countries. The growth of the solar industry is decisively promoted by state activities.

The industrial division of labour between West Germany and threshold countries, and scientific and technological cooperation, lead to innovations in the West German industrial structure, which are characterized by a concentration on complicated solar technologies, such as solar cells and large-scale solar technologies. In this way West Germany is successfully utilizing the developments of the industrializing developing countries and their increasing competition in the production of traditional mass-products by meeting the resultant growing energy need with the development of an innovative solar industry; so the competition with countries producing on the basis of low wages can be partially countered by innovation in the industrial structure. This organization of the production of solar technologies additionally promotes developments in the consumer country and leads to an increasing demand for large-scale technologies. So the German policy concept has no fixed limitation of the innovation, but it is linked with the dynamic development of the world market and the market that has already been opened up. Here the developments in the Third World lead to innovations in the West German industrial structure that protects and enlarges its technological advantage, but on the other hand they also assist the developments of the consumer economy which is advancing towards industrial partnership, although it is a partnership at different levels.

3. The Example of Science-Based Production: How to Induce Techno-Scientific Progress and its Industrial Application

3.1 The German Concept: Organizing Techno-Scientific Progress

Biotechnology provides opportunities for basic innovations in the chemical and pharmaceutical industries. In contrast to solar technology, it does not require organized sizable markets, but it forms the path that established industries can take to avoid a ruinous competition with products from NICs and demonstrates how they can transform themselves into a science-based industry. Existing chemicals and pharmaceutical products can be manufactured in a new way. High demand products can be manufactured in greater quantity. Finally there is the development of new products that offer attractive new uses that have not been known before but find a huge demand. So biotechnology forms the basis for innovative processes within existing markets or creates new markets simply by its appearance. The participation in these innovative processes is based on the generation and application of techno-scientific progress and, in addition, upon appropriate industrial structures.

But engagement in biotechnological research is extremely expensive and risky. Besides, it needs available scientists, who are experienced in this field, and developed research and science structures that are able to generate the scientific progress that may form a basis for innovation. Because of these initial conditions, it is not very surprising that the German chemical and pharmaceutical industry did not partake of this opportunity (Hack and Hack 1985). On the one hand, the long lead times from first engagement in research until final application require enormous funds and the pay-offs are uncertain at that early stage. On the other hand, a very small number of scientists were engaged or educated in the field and so no functionalization of academic research or technology transfer was possible. This created a situation where the appropriate industrial structure was established and the organization of markets was not required, but the innovation could not take place. Here, granting state subsidies could not introduce the innovations. Financial incentives are an inappropriate policy instrument to counterbalance the lack of techno-scientific progress.

German state policy, consequently, started to increase the number of scientists engaged in biotechnological research from a low level of about 30 in 1968 to some 300 in the early 70s (Buchholz 1979). This formed an important basis from which to follow the biotechnological path of innovation. Now techno-scientific progress could be generated that fitted with the requirement and opportunities of the German chemical and pharmaceutical industry. Here one has to bear in mind that the big German enterprises are involved with different types of products and different parts of the markets. The fields of application of biotechnological progress, therefore, are intimately related to the involvement of particular large enterprises. Designing a state policy on biotechnology therefore requires close attention to the national industrial structure as well as to the available new world markets for these innovative products.

The German chemical and pharmaceutical industry is organized in a complementary rather than a competitive way. While Hoechst concentrates on pharmaceutical products, Bayer is engaged mainly in pesticides and herbicides. BASF produce predominantly synthetic materials and basic chemicals (Spangenberg 1986). In addition, this German industry is well established in international markets. Its share in the world market for chemical products in 1981 was 16.6% (OECD 1988), although production units for mass production had been transferred to the NICs. Export sales still count for more than 50% of the total sales. The continuation of national industrial development, focusing on more advanced products, and the avoidance of competition with the NICs in mass products, calls for a policy that transforms this industry into an advanced science-based industry. The well-established position of particular firms in particular international markets clearly forms the basis for their orientation in biotechnology. A successful export-oriented political strategy for techno-industrial innovation can be designed to the extent that it fits with the industrial structure and the opportunities in particular world markets.

The German biotechnology programme consists of seven parts:[1] (i) bio-processing and enzyme techniques; (ii) techniques dealing with cell cultures and cell fusion; (iii) genetic engineering; (iv) biological safety and substitution of animal tests; (v) breeding of plants and plant protection; (vi) promoting big science centres on genetic engineering; and (vii) new fields of research and interlinking questions. It is interesting that besides the last two parts of the programme the proportion of state funds given to the industry dominates, in particular, the fields of genetic engineering, biological safety, breeding of plants and plant protection, where large enterprises received from 70 to 80% of the funds that are spent to promote industrial research. This maintains the existing industrial structure and makes use of its position in international markets.

But even more interesting is the large share that is given to academic research. Although in the first five parts of the programme, industry receives between a half and two-thirds of

---

[1]   This and the following calculations of ours are based on BMFT 1987 and 1988.

the funds, academic science accounts for 56% of the total programme. This again indicates the enormous importance that is given to the research capacities outside industrial research and that are publicly established and funded. The high research component of these new products and the global race in techno-industrial innovation require increasing techno-scientific progress that industrial research is neither able to produce nor prepared to produce because it lacks the roots in basic research and because of the high risks involved in heavy investment at a very early stage.

Genetic engineering in this programme is a good example of the importance of coordinating non-industrial capabilities with opportunities for techno-industrial innovation. In parts (iii) and (v), about 40% of the programme's funds is spent altogether. While the money given to the industry accounts only for about one-third of the total, academic science here claims about twice as much of the funding. It is in particular genetic engineering's very early stage of development that adds importance to this case. The process of techno-industrial innovation and, in particular, the state policies that aim at such development rely heavily on the functionalization of academic research. The importance of this extra-industrial sphere and the German state's responsibility for non-industrial research calls for the utilization of this instrument and for the political organization of the production of techno-scientific progress that matches the industry's opportunities in international markets.

Compared with the other parts of this programme, the research infrastructure in genetic engineering is the least developed one. Academic research can provide its contribution to techno-industrial innovation only insofar as it develops an appropriate capacity and structure. So part (vi) of the programme shows a concentration of 83% of the funds given to academic research going to only five institutes. But the need for such concentration is less necessary when industrial research is already prepared to involve and to correspond with the existing academic research units. Part (iii) of the programme, the industrial application of genetic engineering, consequently shows a concentration of less than one-third of the funds given to academic research. The other parts of the programme, again, indicate a growing organization of the academic research infrastructure where there is less extensive participation by large enterprises and vice versa.

This clearly shows the outstanding importance of academic research for introducing techno-industrial innovation and it also draws attention to the particular situation in which this instrument is used. The whole programme, but the case of genetic engineering in particular, shows that in a situation that offers opportunities for techno-industrial innovation the state fosters the generation of techno-scientific progress and the organization of an appropriate and capable research structure. Without any particular instrument for intervening in enterprises' decisions, the state can induce a certain process of techno-industrial innovation by ensuring so far as possible the availability of techno-scientific progress that meets the needs of the industrial structure and its opportunities in world markets. The utilization of the research infrastructure and supply of techno-scientific progress can provides the incentives necessary to influence privately owned firms.[2]

3.2 The French Concept: State-Organized Generation and Application of Techno-Scientific Progress

French biotechnological innovation takes place in a situation that is characterized by overall dominance of the state in both industrial decision-making and fields of academic research. But, first of all, it has to be borne in mind that, in contrast to the American, the Japanese or the German activities, this is a strategy for catching up with international standards and for holding onto the domestic market rather than a strategy that is appropriate to penetrate international markets, in particular the key markets of the United States and Japan. The programme itself also reflects French needs and opportunities. Nevertheless, the French government aims at a share of 10% of the world

---

[2]   It should be mentioned that there is, of course, the case where it fails. In 1981 Hoechst did a deal with Harvard Medical School accounting to $50 million because they regarded German academic research to be incapable. Nevertheless, Hoechst denied a contract with Biosyntech in 1976 and collaborations with other German researchers; these were more successful and much faster in R&D when smaller firms entered the field (*Wirtschaftswoche* April 27, 1987).

biotechnology market by 1990 (Ministère de la Recherche et de l'Industrie 1982). But its current position in the world markets for chemical and pharmaceutical products is, in general, rather weak and very uneven. The overall market share was 9.3% in 1981, but the really strong positions exist in perfumes and cosmetics (37.5%) and in synthetic rubber (18.9%) (OECD 1988).

Even more significant is the low level of investment in R&D that prevents a competitive position in the global market and opens the domestic market to foreign penetration. The pharmaceutical industry, which forms a key sector for the application of biotechnology, is an impressive example: although this industry ranks third in export sales it invested only FFr. 4.3 billion in R&D and lags far behind the U.S. (FFr. 19.3 billion), Japan (FFr. 7.3 billion), West Germany (FFr. 7.0 billion) and the U.K. (FFr. 6.0 billion) (Projet de Loi de Finances Pour 1986). So it is not surprising that the French position is weakest in pharmaceuticals and that there is a lack of experience in fermentation techniques when expertise in antibiotics, steroids and cephalosporin is possessed by the multinationals (Barlet 1981).

The French industry in this sector is dominated by the nationalized enterprises Rhône-Poulenc, Pechiney-Ugine-Kuhlmann (less involved in biotechnology), Roussel-Uclaf (60% Hoechst, 40% state-owned) and ELF-Aquitaine (through its subsidiary Sanofi that engages in biotechnology). But even though the three major corporate groups are tooling up and have expanded their R&D efforts (annually FFr. 450 million) they still have to catch up with the competition. The nationalized ELF-Aquitaine is the strongest enterprise, because of its petroleum revenues. According to government policy it has engaged in biotechnology *via* the activities of its firm Sanofi. This firm's activities in R&D are, of course, strongly related to the oil business. About 30% of its R&D is in this field. A rapid growth has taken place in its perfumes and beauty products with high increases in sales abroad. It has also consolidated its activities in the agrofood sector and focuses on developing high nutrition animal feeds, and on the application of molecular and cell biology to plant and animal breeding. Particular attention is also given to its pharmaceutical business. But, although the firm is achieving 50.5% of its sales outside France, it has only minor access to the important markets for pharmaceutical products in the U.S.

Bibliography

ADAMELOBUN, Lapido (1978), Co-operation or Neocolonialism - Francophone Africa, in: *Africa Quarterly*, XVIII, 1, July, 34-50.

A.F.M.E. (Agence Française pour la Maitrise de l'Energie) (1982), *Le Programme à moyen terme de l'A.F.M.E. 1983-1985*, November, 35p.

BARLET, A. (1981), Quantifier les marches de la bioindustrie, in: *Revue d'Economie Industrielle*, No. 18.

BMFT (Bundesministerium für Forschung und Technologie) (1979), *Zwischenbilanz in der Energiediskussion*, Bonn.

BMFT (1979a), *Programm Energieforschung und Energietechnologien 1977-1980*, Bonn.

BMFT (1979b), *Programm Technologien zur Nutzung der Sonnenenergie 1977-1980*, Bonn, 4th edition.

BMFT (1979c), *Forschungsbericht IV*, Bonn.

BMFT (1987), *Zusammenstellung der bisherigen direkten Projektförderung durch den BMFT aus dem Förderbereich K "Biotechnologie"*. Bonn.

BMFT (1988), *Förderungskatalog*. Bonn.

BUCHHOLZ, Klaus (1979), Die gezielte Forschung und Entwicklung der Biotechnologie, in: DAELE, W./KROHN, W./WEINGART, P. (eds.), (1979).

CANTLEY, M.F. (1983), *Plan by Objective: Biotechnology*. European Commission FAST Project XII/37/83/EN, Brussels: Commission of the European Communities.

CAVARD, Denise, and CRIQUI, Patrick (1979), La Strategie des Pays Industrialisés en Matière de Développement de l'Energie Solaire: Etude Comparée Etats-Unis/France, in: KAHN, Philippe (ed.), 337-384.

DAELE, Wolfgang/KROHN, W./WEINGART, P. (eds.), (1979), *Geplante Forschung - vergleichende Studien über den Einfluß politischer Probleme und Wissenschaftsentwicklung*, Frankfurt/M.

DESPRAIRIES, M. (1980), *New and Renewable Energies - Their Contribution to Growth and Development*. French Government Paper for the United Nations Conference on New and Renewable Energy Sources (UNCNRS), Nairobi, August 1981. COMES, December.

GERWIN, Robert (1980), *Die Welt-Energieperspektive - Analyse bis zum Jahr 2030 nach dem IIASA-Forschungsbericht* - vorgelegt von der Max-Planck-Gesellschaft, Stuttgart: DVA, 3rd Edition, 224p.

HACK, Lothar, and HACK, Irmgard (1985), Kritische Massen. Zum akademisch - industriellen Komplex im Bereich der Mikrobiologie/Gentechnologie, in: *Technik und Gesellschaft*, Heft 3.

HÄFELE, W., and SASSIN, W. (1977), Contrasting Views of the Future and the Influence on our Technological Horizons for Energy, in: *Oak Ridge Associated Universities*, 195-227.

HOEZ, D. (1978), Le marché prometteur de l'energie solaire, in: *L'Usine nouvelle*, edition mensuelle, March, 88-92.

JANSEN, P.J. (1982), Energy Strategies, in: THIELHEIM, Klaus O. (ed.), 359-368.

JUNNE, Gerd (1984), *Auswirkungen der Biotechnologie auf den Welthandel und die internationale Arbeitsteilung*. Studie für die Friedrich-Ebert-Stiftung, Oktober.

KAHN, Philippe (ed.) (1979), *De l'Energie Nucléaire aux Nouvelle Sources d'Energie vers un Nouvel Ordre Enérgetique International*. Travaux de Centre de Recherche sur le Droit des marchés et des Investissements Internationaux. Paris: Librairies Techniques.

MINISTÈRE DE LA RECHERCHE ET DE L'INDUSTRIE (1982), *Programme mobilisateur: l'essor des Biotechnologies.*

MONSAN, Pierre F. (1985), *The Industrialization of Biotechnology in France: Recent Developments.* Abstract prepared for the 1st International Conference of Biotechnology, Osaka, Japan, November 5-8.

OECD (1988), *Biotechnology and the Changing Role of Government.* Paris.

PAPON, Pierre (1973), Research Planning in French Science Policy: An Assessment, in: *Research Policy*, 2, 226-244.

PAPON, Pierre (1975), The State and Technological Competition in France or Colbertism in the 20th Century, in: *Research Policy*, 4, 214-244.

PAPON, Pierre (1979), Centres of Decisions in French Science Policy: The Contrasting Influences of Scientific Experts and Administrators, in: *Research Policy*, 8, 384-398.

PELISSOLO, J. (1980), *La biotechnologie demain.* Paris: Documentation Française.

RODOT, Michel et al. (1980), Les centrales solaires, in: *La Recherche sur les énergies nouvelle.* Paris, 226-250.

ROUSSEL-UCLAF (1985), *Annual Report.*

SALOMON, Jean Jacques (1985), *La Gaulois, Le Cowboy et le Samurai.* Rapport sur la politique française de la technologie. Centre de prospective et d'evaluation. Paris, July.

SANOFI (1984), *Annual Report.*

SHARP, Margaret (1985), *The New Biotechnology: European Governments in Search of a Strategy.* Sussex European Paper No. 15, Brighton: SPRU.

SPANGENBERG, Joachim (1986), *Chemische Industrie in NRW - Biotechnologien als Zukunftshoffnung?*, unpublished ms.

SPANGENBERG, Joachim (1988), *Chemische-industrielle Umwandlung durch genetisch manipulierte Mikroorganismen*, unpublished paper.

THIELHEIM, Klaus O. (ed.) (1982), *Primary Energy - Present Status and Future Perspectives.* Berlin, Heidelberg & New York, 371p.

TRUSCHEIT, Ernst (1986), Die Bedeutung der Gentechnologie für die pharmazeutische Industrie, in: *Pharmazeutische Industrie*, vol. 48.

UN WORLD POPULATION CONFERENCE (1974), Bukarest, 19-30 August. New York. United Nations, 147p.

U.S. DEPARTMENT OF COMMERCE (1987), *Biotechnology in Western Europe*, Washington, D.C.

WIRTSCHAFTSWOCHE April 27, 1987.

WORLD ENERGY CONFERENCE (1978a), *World Energy Resources 1985-2020 - Renewable Energy Resource.* New York: IPC Science and Technology Press.

WORLD ENERGY CONFERENCE (1978b), *World Energy: Looking ahead to 2020.* Report by the Conservation Commission of the WEC. New York: IPC Science and Technology Press.

5

The State and Telecommunications Modernization in Britain, France and West Germany

Peter Humphreys

Telecommunications is an old industry which is currently experiencing very dramatic change as a result of rapid developments in technology ("technology push"), new patterns of consumer demand ("demand pull") and the internationalisation of the markets themselves. At the heart of the upheaval are the diffusion of computers, the resultant demand for new data transmission facilities, the application of computer technology to telecommunications and, more generally, no less than the dramatic and wholesale technological "convergence" of the data processing and communications sectors. As a consequence of technological advance, the scope of telecommunications has expanded from that of the "plain old telephone service" to include a proliferation of new transmission methods and services - for which the term "tele-matics" has been coined.

Rapid technological advance has been made in all three main areas of telecommunications operation: transmission (with the advance of fibre-optic cable, satellite technology, and semiconductors), switching (with the change-over from electro-mechanical to fully electronic, "digital" switching technology) and terminals (with the ubiquitous microprocessor facilitating "intelligent" terminals). Convergence and technological innovation are opening up telecommunications markets to new entrants. With the collapse of barriers between the telecommunications, office automation and data processing sectors, computer and business automation firms (like IBM) have been able to enter the field, while telecommunications firms (like AT & T) have entered into data processing. Satellites are bringing in aerospace manufacturers and optical fibre the glass and laser makers. Thus firms belonging to previously separate, distinct and typically far less regulated industrial sectors are coming into competition with one another (OECD 1983).

The historically entrenched common West European institutional framework for the telecommunications sector itself has been that of a highly regulated, discrete telecommunications industry, dominated by major public sector monopoly providers of the telephone network - and the postal services. In turn, these state monopolies have sustained oligopolies of large national equipment suppliers protected from outside competition. Through typically nationalistic procurement, industrial, network attachment approval and standardisation policies there has existed a very close relationship between the public sector monopoly service providers (the PTTs) and these generally private sector national equipment suppliers. As a result, the latter have benefited from sufficiently large, protected and profitable domestic bases for them to thrive in their respective, comparatively small domestic markets, and between them to maintain a firm hold on the wider European market.

1. The Deregulation and Liberalisation Debate

With the proliferation of new telematic services the telecommunications market is fast becoming highly diversified and complex where it was previously unified and simple. As a result, it is no longer an obvious case of natural monopoly. With telecommunications no longer confined to telephony and simple telex, unity of the network is no longer at a premium and, arguably, competition will be more responsive to the opportunities provided by technology. Moreover, there is a growing awareness that the future requirements of the "information economy" might be better served by introducing competition from new private commercial value added carriers and suppliers of switching systems, terminals, network services and interconnect systems (OECD 1987).

By the early 1980s many new suppliers were already seizing the opportunities to supply new private markets and business demands with their innovations. However, delays in approval by the PTTs were causing mounting frustration and fuelling pressure for deregulation and liberalisation. In addition, "convergence" (of sectors) was undermining the rationale for the high degree of regulation to which the telecommunications - but as suggested not the data processing or the office automation - sector had been traditionally subject. Also by the 1980s new export markets were opening up as large, lucrative telecommunications contracts started to emerge from the OECD countries. In Western Europe, reliance on comparatively small, fragmented and protected national markets was now increasingly perceived as a handicap to growth, efficiency and competitiveness. Similarly, European firms began to appear decidedly small in stature. Competition from giant US and Japanese producers, which benefited from large domestic markets and economies of scale, was growing fast. The dismantling of the AT & T monopoly in the United States and the potential threat of both AT & T and IBM to the European market now acted as a spur to European governments to act to modernize their domestic telecommunications industries (Tunstall 1986). Increasingly vocally during the 1980s, critics of the telecommunications monopoly argued that it had created a "...closed, inert marketplace...(which had) tended to limit technological innovation and...(had) led to serious delays in the provision of services and equipment by the PTTs" (the Yankee Group 1983a). They argued that the "quasi-vertical" links between the PTTs and national manufacturers had led to the virtual "capture" of the former by the latter, with the result that prices were over high and quality often suffered. For example, in Europe switching equipment was estimated to cost at least 35-

50% more than in the United States.[1] Furthermore, industry remained too oriented to the domestic market and not to exports and innovation was too attuned to PTT technological requirements and not to international ones. Finally, restrictive and nationalistic PTT certification procedures appeared to be a barrier to innovation. For increasingly many, the solution was to liberalise and introduce competition into the market.

The disadvantages of the existing situation seemed to have been dramatically demonstrated by both the British and West German efforts to replace electro-mechanical with fully electronic switching. Both the EWS-A system offered by Siemens and the System X offered by GEC, Plessey and STC had led to grave disappointments and delays. Overreliance on national firms seemed to invite complacency and inefficiency. In both cases, the chosen remedy was to open up the provision of the new exchanges to greater competition: in the British case, under pressure from the government BT took action to expose the domestic suppliers to competition from the Swedish company Ericsson (with Thorn EMI); and in West Germany, the Bundespost decided to give the American firm ITT access to the German switching market through its subsidiary SEL (Nguyen 1983).

2. The State and the Organisation of Telecommunications Markets

Against this turbulent and uncertain background, West European states became increasingly concerned to adopt policies that would secure and, if possible, promote their countries' ranking among the advanced industrial economies. Since the late 1970s, there had been growing common recognition that telecommunications was a "strategic" sector. Firstly, it was an - increasingly embattled - sector, in which the West Europeans had so far managed to maintain a better position in competition with the US and Japan than they had achieved in other areas of IT. Secondly, governments fastened on to the key importance of

---

[1] The Yankee Group *Report on European Telecommunications*. Volume One p. 16. The organisation for economic co-operation and development (OECD) *Trends of c ange in telecommunications policy* puts this differential between Western Europe and the United States at 60-100%.

telecommunications modernization programmes for national economic modernization. Increasingly, telecommunications modernization was viewed as a vital competitive factor right across the whole economy, with an important contribution to very many business sectors. A series of government reports in all three countries made this point with varying force and urgency. Most notably, the influential Nora/Minc Report, commissioned by the French government of Giscard d'Estaing and published in 1978, emphatically characterised telecommunications as a "strategic industry". It warned about the danger of loss of national sovereignty (mainly to IBM), and called for a national strategy to meet the challenge of American domination in "telematics" (A.C.A.R.D. 1980a,b and 1982; KtK 1976; Nora and Minc 1980).

Yet, the "appropriate" direction of state action was not immediately evident. On the one hand, state action might best be employed to open up national markets to competition, as the new wisdom suggested, in order to reap in full the rewards of technological innovation, new market niches and general economic competitiveness. On the other hand, the long-term competitive position of national telecommunications suppliers might thus be threatened by a too sudden dose of exposure to competition with more efficient overseas producers, especially if it was not reciprocated. Moreover, precisely such a policy raised the risk of dependence on foreign supply and the attendant threat to national security (Grewelich 1987). Instead, the state might be better employed in engaging heavily in consolidation, rationalisation and investment programmes aimed at the domestic producers.

In Britain, the former option was seized with unprecedented and unmatched enthusiasm. Under the Conservative governments since 1979, the introduction of deregulation and liberalisation in telecommunications amounted to a dramatic example of state action. Here, however, the state acted to "disengage the state" and "liberate the market". No other Western European state went so far down the road of liberalisation, dismantling its own monopoly of the telecommunications network - by introducing Mercury Communications as a competitor for BT - or privatising its national carrier. Whilst the effects should not be exaggerated, they were considerable. The 1981 and 1984 Acts resulted in a certain dilution of the monopoly although on nothing like the scale in the US. More importantly there was an un-doubted large increase in competition and freedom in the supplier market. BT's procurement was opened up and regula-tory restrictions were relaxed. Moreover, business users from all over Europe soon came to appreciate the new British competi-tiveness in services, and a host of foreign multinationals chose Britain as the main location for their European operations (Morgan and Webber 1986).

Largely through deregulation and liberalisation though sig-nificantly not through tax-incentives or subsidies, the Thatcher government sought to create a favourable environment for a market-led, decentralised and innovative development of cable systems, and also, with far more success, for exploitation of the vast potential for private LANs, VANs and PABX systems. As will be seen, private sector, market-led and wholly unsubsidised cable development was disappointing (Humphreys 1986a, 1985). By contrast, the previously very small private VANs market expanded enormously. In fact, it developed much more vigor-ously in Britain than elsewhere in Western Europe, where it generally remained within the PTT's orbit. In addition to the public videotex system (Prestel), over 700 VANs were licensed in the period 1981-86 (Dyson and Humphreys 1986). Similarly, two competing privately owned networks for cellular radio, Cellnet (BT) and Vodafone (Racal), were established in 1985. With over 200,000 subscribers in 1987 and no less than 500,000 predicted for 1990, their success outstripped by far PTT-led programmes in France (25,520) and West Germany (36,900) (Thomas 1987). However, the cost of liberalisation was a substantial penetration of foreign firms into British markets.

As suggested, an alternative avenue of possible state action was that of direct state intervention, through nationalisations and planning, to co-ordinate and encourage rationalisation and colla-boration between national producers in the various "converging" sectors. This strategy was based on the premise that domestic firms would be able to pool their resources constructively and benefit from new economies of scale. This had become particu-larly important since the development costs of the new technol-ogy products were so high (particularly for the new digital exchanges, fibre optics, satellites etc.). Moreover, firms might also be able to benefit thereby from the new complementarity of their different areas of excellence, and the synergies between them in the domestic market. The state might further seek to sustain these companies and help them to establish a firm base for an "assault" on international markets by developing large-scale, ambitious and centralised *grand projects* for development and diffusion of their products in the internal market. Such a "strategy" reflected a growing belief that in the near future the European market would only merit three telecommunications giants: the appropriate role for the state in such a high stakes race became to promote "national champions".

The French case, under the Socialist governments 1981-86, offers the best example in Western Europe of this latter approach. In contrast to the British Conservative government, but no less dramatically, the French Socialist government stepped in, in this case in order to involve the state closer in the new telecommunications markets. Largely as a result of the impact of the Nora/Minc Report, the telecommunications industry was given a central role in a highly *étatiste* national plan for the *filière électronique*, which in turn was given a key place in the ninth Five-Year Plan (1984-88). Accordingly, the DGT (the French telecommunications administration) was given the task of leading the electronics *filière* towards greater international competiveness and the leading firms in the *filière* were nationalised (notably CGE, Thomson and CGCT). The explicit aim was to "reconquer" domestic markets and develop an "economic strike force" in order to attack foreign markets (Humphreys 1986a). In line with this aggressive international strategy, in 1983 the French Socialists merged the telecommunications operations of Thomson into CIT-Alcatel (the telecommunications subsidiary of Compagnie Générale d'Électricité, CGE) in order to consolidate and rationalise national resources and to give France a major presence on the international markets. Thus merged, these firms' capacities ranked fifth instead of ninth and tenth respectively in the worldwide supply of electronic switching equipment (in 1984) (Turnbull and Hug 1984).

Even under the French Socialists and despite the retention of the traditional role of the PTT in France, the pressure of new industrial requirements did in the end lead to some significant modifications in the direction of privatisation and liberalisation. For example, a number of separate subsidiaries were established with private participation to provide new services such as Transpac, the world's largest public packet switching network established to cope with high density data traffic. It was also somewhat ironic that the above-mentioned industrial rationalisation and reorganisation ultimately led to an element of de facto liberalisation of the domestic market since it raised the problem of finding a second source for the public switching market. It had originally been hoped that the rationalisation would increase output enough to cover more or less domestic demand. However, it turned out that the giant CIT-Alcatel was unable to meet this goal. For its part, the DGT had always been bitterly opposed to becoming reliant upon a single supplier. Consequently, between 1984 and 1987 the successive governments of Laurent Fabius (Socialist) and Jacques Chirac (RPR/UDF) were compelled to struggle with the delicate political business of choosing a suitable foreign firm for this second source. The question soon became which of three powerful foreign bidders - AT & T/Philips (US), Siemens (FRG) and Ericsson (Sweden) - should the French state allow to buy Compagnie Generale de Constructions Téléphoniques (CGCT), an ailing nationalised French telecommunications firm which carried access to 16% of the French public switching market. Yet here too, the French state played the key role (even after the RPR/UDF coalition replaced the Socialists). In late 1987 the government sold CGCT for FFr 500 million to a consortium of the French firm Matra and Ericsson. Very interestingly, Ericsson was allowed to gain management control but the new "neo-liberal" government's privatisation laws still only granted the foreign firm a maximum stake of 20%. There was, in fact, a greater degree of continuity in policy between the French Socialists and the new Gaullist-led government than might have been expected from the latter's "new right" rhetoric. There was first of all a pragmatic explanation.

By choosing Ericsson, the French government was able to avoid a major trade confrontation with either the US or West Germany, each of which would have seen a decision in favour of the other's national champion as an affront meriting trade reprisals. However, just as importantly, the government's choice was clearly dictated by the same "strategic" concern as the Socialists before them, namely to strengthen French markets and gain technology access. Indeed, the decision dramatically reinforced an already conspicuous trend towards French dominance in European markets. In fact, this trend had been started under the Giscard d'Estaing government, carried an important stage further by the French Socialist government and was now clearly being adopted too by the RPR/UDF government of Jacques Chirac. Ericsson was credited to be both innovative and internationally oriented. It had captured dozens of Third World markets and was already the second largest supplier of public switching equipment in Europe (next to CIT-Alcatel). It had formidable expertise in those very markets which would best consolidate French strengths (public switching) and give technology access in the case of French weaknesses (radiotelephony). Thus, in the CGCT sell-off, the prime role of the French state in managing telecommunications markets in the national interest was once again strikingly evident. At a stroke, the CGCT deal relegated all other European producers into the second division of switch manufacturers (Oxford Analytica 1987; Thomas 1987).

3. Constraints on State Action to Modernize Telecommunications

The "strategic" goals may be broadly clear, but it remains obvious that the real test is in policy implementation. State action is invariably constrained by political variables (political culture, national ideologies, bureaucratic politics, institutional structures, "distributional coalitions" in society). The success of state action to deregulate and liberalise the national telecommunications markets depends upon the balance of forces for and against change and the state's ability to act "autonomously". On the other hand, there are financial constraints on state "interventionism": direct state action to promote domestic industry is constrained by finite financial limits.

Thus, despite the similar commitment of the British Conservatives (since 1979) and the West German "Christian Liberal" coalition (CDU/CSU/FDP) (since 1982) to a disengagement of the state in the economy and a rejuvenation of the free-market economy, the telecommunications policies of these governments turned out to be strikingly different. A number of analysts have pointed to a combination of obstacles to reorganisation of the telecommunications sector in West Germany. Most notably, these were: the fragmented nature of the state and the divided nature of the ruling coalition, the autonomy of the Bundespost, the entrenched institutional position of the unions (the strength of the post and telecommunications union, the DPG), the characteristically West German *Sozialstaat* or "social state" ideology with its enduring commitment to public-service values, and the status quo orientation of powerful "insider" manufacturers like Siemens (Morgan and Webber 1986; Humphreys 1987; Grande 1987). Douglas Webber was able to suggest (in 1986) that "...among the major advanced capitalist states, the FRG stands out as an island of stability (meaning "no-change") in terms of its telecommunications regime" (Morgan and Webber 1986).

However, even in West Germany, by the mid-1980s there was growing concern about the costs of this failure to reorganise telecommunications. With respect to innovation, it was becoming clear to many policy-makers, especially in the Research and Technology and Economics Ministries, that West German "insider" suppliers like Siemens had become far too oriented to the requirements of the PTT. This had entailed a certain inability to exploit high technology and gain foreign high-technology markets. Somewhat brutally, the Bundespost has been described as having a "post-war reconstruction mentality" (the Yankee Group 1983b). As a result, according to one leading telecommunications analyst, the Germans have the "highest-quality old technology network in the world".[2] In fact, during the 1980s there arose a vocal internal "coalition for change" including the neoliberal FDP, innovative "outsider" manufacturers like Nixdorf and the business-user lobby, reinforced by external pressure mainly from the US, France and the EC (Morgan and Webber 1986; Humphreys 1987).

In 1987, the government-commissioned Witte report did recommend a considerable degree of liberalisation (Neuordnung der Telekommunikation 1987). However, the constraints endured. In particular, the "sectorised nature of policy-making" in West Germany meant that policy initiative remained with the Bundespostminister, Christian Schwarz-Schilling. He quickly

---

2   Economist Telecommunications survey November 23, 1985, p.25. It quotes the words of Mr Ross, a Wiesbaden-based analyst for A.D. Little.

indicated that change would be moderate rather than dramatic (Humphreys 1987). Moreover, in the 1980s, rather than "disengaging", the West German state intervened increasingly directly to promote innovation. In 1984, the Technology Ministry launched a comprehensive DM 3 billion IT (information technology) support programme for the period 1984-88, which focused large sums on the telecommunications sector. Also, Siemens benefited from very large investment by the Bundespost to strengthen its position as the "national champion" in both telecommunications and computer markets. Therefore it could be safely predicted that deregulation and liberalisation in West Germany would be most unlikely indeed to entail a future "disengagement of the state" (BMFT 1984; Humphreys 1987).

The French case is highly illustrative of both the financial limits to state interventionism and the political constraints on following a neo-liberal course. After 1983, with the "U-turn" towards *rigeur* ("austerity"), the Socialist government became much less enthusiastic about *étatisme* and voluntarist industrial policies. By the end of the Socialists' period of office the notion of the primacy of the firm was being introduced; Laurent Fabius himself was actually recommending a degree of denationalisation. Mitterrand summed up the new mood by announcing *"...c'est l'entreprise qui crée la richesse"*. Socialist spending programmes were revealed to be far too ambitious and had to be reined in. Furthermore, the DGT had become the "milch" cow of the *filière électronique* (nearly three and a half billions FFr. and also the state budget amounting to two FFr billions. Moreover, as will be seen, the Socialists' interventionism registered some successes but also some dramatic failures (Humphreys 1986b; Morgan and Webber 1986).

Under the Socialists, as seen, the state's major contribution was undoubtedly its coordinating role in building French national champions and consolidating their place in international markets (a process actually commenced by the previous Giscard d'Estaing government). Interestingly, over the subsequent period 1986-88, the Chirac government's radical rhetoric in favour of a neo-liberal strategy hardly materialised at all. Despite much discussion about a law to liberate and reorganize the French telecommunications sector, there was a certain degree of continuity in the actual implementation of policy. The constraints

factor in that competition between them had entailed pernicious rather than productive effects and was a handicap to international competitiveness (Turnbull and Hug 1984). If indeed applicable, these factors would suggest that state action to rationalise switch production capacity and support domestic industry more (along the lines of the French grand strategy) might well have led to much greater success. The irony is that in October 1987 GEC and Plessey suddenly announced the merger of their telecommunications businesses into a 50:50 joint venture to produce belatedly a single British supplier operation with the economies of scale required by international competition (previously the monopolies and mergers commission had prevented a simple merger, reflecting government doubts over the diminishing of domestic competition). Between them, GEC and Plessey would rank ninth, instead of tenth and twelfth respectively, in the league of world telecommunications manufacturers (Large 1987).

Nevertheless, by 1987, France was "streets ahead" of both Britain and West Germany in the digitalisation of its network, with 50% of its local exchanges and 60% of its long-distance ones fully digitalised. Britain was at last installing System X at a significant rate, years later than originally planned, and West Germany had hardly commenced, although a huge Bundespost programme had been launched. Without a doubt, Frances's lead reflected the state's huge commitment and "strategic" approach (Telecommunications survey 1987).

Videotex: Another dramatic illustration of the efficacy of direct state action is given by the French videotex programme. Videotex is one telecommunications application in which Europeans have so far led the world. It is an "interactive" communications system which uses the television set and the telephone line to enable the user to key into large data bases or computer systems. It is also noteworthy for being a public sector initiative and everywhere its development has been characterised by "technology push". The British actually pioneered videotex R&D, but BT misjudged its pricing strategy by falsely assuming the pre-existence of a mass market and basing its prices on actual user levels. The West German approach was even less successful not so much because of overreliance on a market-led approach, but more due to technological and political problems (notably a dispute over regulatory competence between the federation and the states). Subscriber numbers (40,000) were even lower than in Britain (80,000) in 1987.[4]

By contrast, the French state pursued a unique, centralised and highly voluntaristic programme designed to establish an early world lead in this technology. Originally, the DGT was to spend no less than FFr 46 billion over a period of 12 years: the bold strategy was simply to supply videotex terminals to French homes *en masse* and without charge in order to create the mass demand for its services. Although subsequently *rigeur* reduced the ambitious timetable of the ambitious programme, by 1988 nearly 3 million had been supplied. In 1987 alone Télétel had boosted the use of the French telephone network by more than fourty million hours. Consequently, the DGT was recouping at least some of its massive investment costs (Telecommunications survey 1987). At the same time, French telecommunications producers were benefiting from massive state contracts and from a large domestic base for an assault on foreign markets. In this way, the French state acted to create both an industry and a market for videotex services. However, there were two major questions beside videotex, namely: whether it was as well adapted to business-user requirements as private systems (VANs, as seen already flourishing in the British regulatory environment); and also whether it would soon be seen as an outdated technology in view of the opportunities presented by more versatile and high-performance broadband "interactive" systems provided by satellite and cable. Was there, therefore, a foreign market?

Satellites: In fact, in response to the increasing demand for high-speed, integrated (voice, image and data) telecommunications services and new broadcasting channels in the 1980s, all European PTTs were devoting considerable resources to the develop-

---

[4] For a very useful background to videotext developments see: G. Nguyen and E. Arnold Videotext: much ado about nothing, in: M. Sharp (ed.)(1983), *Europe and the new technologies.* However, this account was overoptimistic about the development of the West German system and it completely underrated the success of the French system.

ment of high bandwidth ("broadband") networks: notably in the area of satellite communications and fibre optics. Once again, the French state was particularly active in the development of telecommunications satellites. After all, had not the Nora/Minc report suggested that "...satellites (were) at the heart of telematics" and that if they were "...eliminated from the satellite race, the European nations would lose an element of their sovereignty" (Nora and Minc 1980).

During the early 1980s, the DGT invested heavily in, and the CNET conducted much of the R&D for, the development of the Télécom 1 "medium-powered" satellite (built by the French firm Matra). Launched in 1984, it was designed mainly for high data rate links, in conjunction with packet switching circuits like the innovative French Transpac system. Almost immediately, both the Bundespost and British Telecom rented transmission capacity on Télécom 1 for high-speed data purposes. French leadership in this fast developing field, due to very heavy state investment, was duly further rewarded, in May 1986, when a lucrative £146 million contract for the construction of three new "medium-powered" ECS (European communications satellites) was awarded by Eutelsat to a consortium led by France's Aerospatiale (SNIAS). Towards the end of the 1980s, the commercial prospects for "medium-powered" satellites appeared to be very considerable indeed. The West German state was also becoming an active player in the field of telecommunications satellites, with the development of the DFS Kopernikus "medium-powered" tele-communications satellite by the Bundespost, due to be launched in 1988.

Agreement between the West German and the French states in 1980 also led to industrial collaboration and the largely state-financed joint development of a direct broadcasting satellite (DBS) series: two French and two West German satellites (the first of which was successfully launched in November 1987, but seriously malfunctioning in early 1988). In the late 1970s, the commercial prospects of DBS had appeared to be exciting. Consequently, there had seemed to be a clear role for state-led development of a new industry (Humphreys 1988). However, in contrast to, and largely because of, the technological development of "medium-powered" telecommunications satellites and improved reception equipment, there soon arose considerable doubts about the economic and innovative potential of DBS satellites. Such "high-powered" satellites, with a television channel capacity of only five, had entailed massive state investment; in the French case the massive sum of FFr 1.14 billion in direct state subsidies and capital grants for the TDF programme (Betts 1986). However, at the very same time technology was making it possible to employ more versatile "medium-powered" satellites for DBS. Moreover, the commercial viability of DBS had yet to be proven (Dyson and Humphreys 1988).

By contrast, lack of commitment by the British state meant that British initiatives in the commercial satellite field either failed completely due to lack of private sector interest (notably, the abortive UNISAT project for a British DBS satellite, which collapsed in May 1985) or were part shares in joint projects (e.g. the OTS satellite for ESA or ECS satellites). With the government's reluctance to invest more, the possibility existed that Britain was squandering its sophisticated industrial base and past excellence in space communications (Eberle and Wallace 1987). On the other hand, Britain's commitment to space communications remained very high in the field of satellite services (e.g. BT's sophisticated "Satstream" service on the ECS system or its "project universe" system to connect LANs by satellite link) and determined by safer commercial (rather than risky industrial) considerations. Moreover, it seemed highly unlikely that the British state would regret its failure to invest in the development of a DBS satellite.

Broadband Cable: Meanwhile, the risks and disappointments of overcommitment of the state to grand programmes (*grand projets*) had been fulsomely illustrated, in different ways, by the West German and French national cable programmes. In 1982 the West German state (under the SPD/FDP government) had begun the installation of a series of networks known as BIGFON (*breitbandiges integriertes Glasfaser-Fernemeldeortsnetz* or "broadband integrated fibre-optic local telecommunications networks). By 1987 the BIGFON fibre-optic programme had been the focus of around DM 700 million investment by the Bundespost and the Research and Technology Ministry (Dodsworth 1987). However, after the change-of-power in 1982 the new CDU Bundespost

Minister, Christian Schwarz-Schilling, suddenly gave priority to a national cable programme, which utilised less costly and more readily available "old" copper coaxial technology rather than "new" fibre-optic technology. This choice was dictated by reasons relating to the new government's broadcasting policy rather than technology or telecommunications policy (namely, the most rapid possible promotion of a commercial cable television sector). Between 1983 and 1986 the Bundespost invested DM 1,000 million per annum in this copper coaxial cable programme; and in 1986 the figure was raised to no less than DM 1,500 million. However, by 1987 this programme had engendered much criticism on account of its economics and the fact that it appeared to be an expensive "white elephant" (Humphreys 1985).

By contrast, the French approach had been to back the "vanguard technology", namely fibre-optic cable. Towards the end of the presidency of Giscard d'Estaing, the French state had begun to invest heavily in a futuristic fibre-optic experiment at Biarritz in order to create an integrated multi-service network (including videophone and cable television). After 1982 the Socialists launched a far more ambitious FFr 50 billion Plan Câble to cable France with the most advanced fibre-optic cable by the turn of the century; no less than one-third of French homes were to be cabled in this way by 1992. The cable plan was to be France's chosen route to the ISDN (integrated services digital network) and the project was to be largely financed by the state.

However, implementation of the cable plan quickly encountered grave problems of a technical, financial and politico-administrative nature (Humphreys 1985; Dyson and Humphreys 1985). French industry seemed ill-equipped to supply the technology and the DGT's finances were becoming overstretched by 1983 as it became the milch cow of the rest of the *filière électronique*. At the same time, the French Socialists' spending programmes were running out of control and the budget of the DGT was even raided in order to bail out their social expenditure programmes. As a result, the French cable plan turned into an expensive fiasco. By 1987 it had been estimated that expenditure on the "fibre-optic cabling of France" amounted to around FFr 1,500 million, which was a very modest sum indeed in comparison with the original grandiose aims of the cable plan. Worse still, despite this expenditure, construction on new systems had hardly commenced by 1988. Nevertheless, the French state somehow contrived to maintain a high level of "myth" about French process in fibre-optic cabling (Dodsworth 1987).

In fact, during 1987 Britain led the field by far in fibre-optic cabling. Interestingly, this lead appeared to have been achieved in spite of, rather than because of, the British Conservative government's "neo-liberal" strategy. In the period 1982-84, restrictions on cable services had been lifted as part of the government's deregulation and liberalisation programme. This had been supposed to bring about an "entertainment-led" high-technology cabling of Britain. A host of entrepreneurs had been expected suddenly to leap to exploit the new technologies and the new opportunities thus created. However, no state support at all had been ventured. Indeed, as a result of compartmentalism of government and the Treasury's insensitivity to the concerns of the DTI in particular, capital allowances were withdrawn in line with the government's overall policy of financial restraint (reduction of the PSBR). As a result of the removal of this incentive to invest, the market-led British cable plan soon encountered great disappointment (Negrine 1988).

However, in the meantime both BT and Mercury had been conducting their own highly successful infrastructural programmes for fibre-optic cabling. In 1987, BT was well on the way to fulfilling its aim of replacing half its old telephone trunk lines with fibre-optic cable by 1991 and Mercury had made good progress towards constructing its own 1,300 km fibre-optic network. Very significantly, since 1982 the Conservative government had targeted very considerable state industrial aid on this designated key technology. By 1985 direct government funding to promote R&D had amounted to £55 million (Office of telecommunications 1984). This vital stimulus had led BT and Mercury between them to invest no less than $370 million in the cabling of trunk lines by 1987 (Dodsworth 1987). In other words, rather than reflect government strategy, it seemed that the British lead in fibre-optic cabling reflected a mixture of accumulated British expertise in the field, the fulfilment of a long-range goal of the previously public sector BT and, not least, an untypical measure of state commitment to industrial aid. However, surprisingly, at the end of 1988 the Thatcher government indicated that it might withdraw state support for a national fibre-optic network. This provoked speculation and apprehension that Britain might squander its lead in this field as a result of the government's overzealous commitment to its "neo-liberal" ideology.

The picture of the state's role in the promotion of specific technologies and technology programmes is therefore very mixed. In some cases, the state's intervention would appear to have been a vital prerequisite to the very creation of a domestic industry, as with videotex, or to the development of a promising growth industry, as in the case of "medium-powered" multi-purpose telecommunications satellites (an area dominated by the Americans until the mid 1980s). In other cases, however, it would appear that the state could make highly expensive mistakes, as was very likely with the French and West German joint programme to build "high-powered" DBS satellites. Similarly, the Bundespost's coppercoaxial cable programme was certain to be seen as an expensive anomaly since it was largely incapable of serving the future requirements of the telecommunications industry. Yet, backing the "correct" technology appeared to be no guarantee of success, and as already suggested, nor did simple commitment by the state. There were material - technological, industrial and financial - limitations on state action, as indicated dramatically by the French Socialist's failed Plan Câble.

5. Conclusions

The following broad conclusions might be drawn from this rather messy picture. In the first place, the overall rate of introduction and adoption of the new telecommunications techniques and systems seems unquestionably to reflect the character of state action: that is, whether the state forces the pace of development by heavy investment in switching systems, cable networks, fibre optics, videotex and satellites etc.; and, equally, whether the state provides incentives for private sector involvement and new entrepreneurial activism and innovation. This chapter suggests that the state has an important role both in industrial support and the creation of new markets. Deregulation and liberalisation by themselves are hardly likely to be the panacea. The disappointments of the "entrepreneurialled" development of British cable and the failure of the British (so far) to produce a modern multi-purpose "medium-powered" telecommunications satellite suggest that further incentives are often required (i.e. fiscal measures, subsidies, R&D support etc.) in order to foster the growth of nascent industries and stimulate technological innovation.

Generally, though, all three countries studied were investing heavily in the modernization and digitalisation of their networks, the replacement of coppercoaxial cable with fibre-optic cable, the introduction of new networks and services etc. At the same time, there appeared to be important differences in the character and mix of state/private sector involvement and action. While Britain appeared to be pursuing the path of disengagement of the state and deregulation and liberalisation most consistently, France and West Germany eschewed making a stark choice between disengagement, deregulation and liberalisation and continued regulation, monopoly and protection. They appeared to be attempting to discover a "middle way": gradually relaxing monopoly control and partially opening up their markets to competition, while at the same time retaining institutional structures that were well suited to maintenance of the options of PTT-led R&D, industrial and protectionist procurement and certification policies.

Nevertheless, it is possible to detect a steady, seemingly inexorable shift in government policy away from a tradition of public-service monopoly and strict regulation towards the promotion of competition. Both the French and West German telecommunications authorities were adapting their institutional structures and liberalising to varying degrees the regulation of the sale of subscriber equipment, though not yet generally liberalising network services. At the same time, the French approach illustrates most clearly how the state can still play a key interventionist role in restructuring the domestic industry, by co-ordinating the rationalisation of domestic producers' capacities and encouraging greater collaboration between them, and between them and strong foreign producers, in order to strengthen their position in international markets and to gain technology access.

Moreover, state action would seem to have an important role beyond that of forcing changes in the marketplace. Long lead times, the speculative nature of the commercial returns and the early stage of market definition all point to the need for public investment. The rapid pace of technological innovation and

the fierceness of international competition make state investment an increasingly vital factor for maintaining comparative
advantage. The French case again demonstrates most clearly the
state's continued role in the promotion of specific technologies.
The modernization of the French telephone network is an
example of where state action - in the shape of a *grand projet* -
demonstrably contributed to very major success. Again the
commitment of the French state to promoting "medium-
powered" satellite developments may well turn out to be the success story of the 1990s. The French state-led videotex programme is a good example of how government intervention can
go a long way towards creating an entirely new industrial activity.
The disappointing experience of state-led cable development as
in France and West Germany, on the other hand, graphically
demonstrates the limitations and risks of "heroic" state action. As
Margaret Sharp has commented recently, of the "heroic"
approach of the French state to techno-industrial innovation,
"...the costs may be very high and the pay-offs uncertain" (Sharp
1983).

Bibliography

A.C.A.R.D. (Advisory Council for Applied Research and Development)
(1980a), *Information technology*. London: HMSO.

A.C.A.R.D. (Advisory Council for Applied Research and Development)
(1980b), *Technological change - threats and opportunities for the United
Kingdom*. London: HMSO.

A.C.A.R.D. (Advisory Council for Applied Research and Development) (1982),
*Cabinet Office/Information technology advisory panel (I.T.A.P.) Cable
systems*. London: HMSO.

BETTS, Paul (1986), French agree financing for television, in: *Financial Times*,
Friday, March 14.

BETTS, Paul (1987), Catching up with the rhetoric of change, in: *Financial Times
World Telecommunications*, FT, October 19, 1987.

BMFT (Der Bundesminister fuer Forschung und Technologie) (1984), *Konzep-
tion der Bundesregierung zur Förderung der Mikroelektronik, der Informa-
tions- und Kommunikationstechniken*. Bonn: BMFT.

DODSWORTH, T. (1987), Fibre optics in vogue, in: *Financial Times World telecommunications*, FT, October 19.

DODSWORTH, T., and THOMAS, D. (1987), The Ericsson/CGCT deal: an inspired
piece of commercial politics, in: *Financial Times*, Friday, April 24, p.24.

DYSON, Kenneth, and HUMPHREYS, Peter (1985), The new media in Britain and
in France - two versions of heroic muddle?, in: *Rundfunk und Fernsehen*,
33 Jahrgang 1985/3-4.

DYSON, Kenneth, and HUMPHREYS, Peter (1986), *Introduction* to Kenneth DYSON and Peter HUMPHREYS (eds.), *The politics of the communications revolution in Western Europe*. London: Frank Cass.

DYSON, Kenneth, and HUMPHREYS, Peter (1988), *Broadcasting and new media policies in Western Europe: a comparative study of technological change and public policy*. London: Croom Helm.

EBERLE, J., and WALLACE, H. (1987), *British space policy and international collaboration*. London: The Royal Institute of International Affairs/ Routledge & Kegan Paul.

ECONOMIST TELECOMMUNICATIONS SURVEY (1987), October 17.

GRANDE, Edgar (1987), *Telecommunications policy in West Germany and Britain - a comparative analysis of political configurations*. Paper presented at the Political Studies Association Annual Conference (Aberdeen, April 7-9).

GREWELICH, K.W. (1987), Telecommunications in European perspective, in: S. WILKS, and M. WRIGHT (eds.), *Comparative government industry relations*. Oxford: Clarendon Press.

HUMPHREYS, Peter (1985), Cable; the heroic French experiment examined and compared with the British and German cases, in: *Journal of area studies*, no.12, Autumn.

HUMPHREYS, Peter (1986a), Satellite and cable television, in: *European Intelligence Unit (EUI) European trends*, no.4.

HUMPHREYS, Peter (1986b), "Legitimating the communications revolution, in: K. DYSON, and P. HUMPHREYS (eds.), *The politics of the communications revolution in Western Europe*. London: Frank Cass. 170-71.

HUMPHREYS, Peter (1987), *West German public policies for technological and industrial change*. Paper presented at the Association for the study of German politics (ASGP) workshop on public policy (Warwick University, December 5, 1987).

HUMPHREYS, Peter (1988), Satellite broadcasting policy in West Germany, in: R. NEGRINE (ed.), *Satellite broadcasting*. London: Croom Helm.

KTK (1976), *Telekommunikationsbericht mit acht Anlagenbaenden*. Bonn: Verlag Heger.

LARGE, P. (1987), GEC announces phone link-up with Plessey, in: *Guardian*, October 2.

MORGAN, Kevin, and WEBBER, Douglas (1986), Divergent paths: political strategies for telecommunications in Britain, France and West Germany, in: Kenneth DYSON and Peter HUMPHREYS (eds.), *The politics of the communications revolution in Western Europe*. London: Frank Cass.

NEGRINE, R. (1988), New media in Britain: is there a policy?, in: K. DYSON and P. HUMPHREYS (1988).

NEUORDNUNG DER TELEKOMMUNIKATION (1987), *Bericht der Regierungskommission Fernmeldewesen* (Vorsitz: E. Witte). Heidelberg: R. v. Decker's Verlag.

NGUYEN, Godefroy Dang (1983), Telecommunications, in: M. SHARP (ed.) *Europe and the new technologies*. London: Frances Pinter.

NORA, Simon, and MINC, Alain (1980), *The Computerisation of Society*. MIT Press, Cambridge, Mass. (*Informatisation de la Societé*. Paris: Documentation Francaise, 1978).

OECD (Organisation for economic co-operation and development) (1983), *Telecommunications: pressures and policies for change*. Paris: OECD.

OECD (Organisation for economic co-operation and development) (1987), *Trends of change in telecommunications policy*. Paris: OECD.

OFFICE OF TELECOMMUNICATIONS (1984), *International trade administration. United States department of commerce: a competitive assessment of the US fibre optic industry*. Washington, D.C.: US government printing office, September 1984.

OXFORD ANALYTICA DAILY BRIEF (1987), April 23.

SHARP; Margaret (1983), Conclusions, in: M. SHARP (ed.) *Europe and the new technologies*. London: Frances Pinter.

THOMAS, D. (1987), Cellular telephone services: a highly-priced business, in: *Financial Times World telecommunications*, FT, October 19.

TUNSTALL, J. (1986), *Communications deregulation. The unleashing of America's communications industry*. Oxford: Basil Blackwell.

TURNBULL, Peter W, and HUG, Fiona (1984), The telecommunications industry: technology, supply and market structures, in: *UMIST Occasional Paper no. 8408*, 58-59.

THE YANKEE GROUP (1983a), *Report on European telecommunications*. Volume One. Rickmansworth: the Yankee group.

THE YANKEE GROUP (1983b), *Report on European telecommunications*, Volume Two. Rickmansworth: the Yankee group.

6

Government Policies for Techno-Industrial Innovation in Weaker Economies

The Case of Biotechnology in the United Kingdom and in Italy

Wendy Faulkner and Luigi Orsenigo[1]

This chapter explores government policies for industrial innovation in two European countries: Italy and the United Kingdom (UK). In doing so it seeks to highlight issues surrounding state support for innovative activities in relation to two considerations, namely: the position of economically weaker industrialised countries; and the requirements of a particular technology, i.e. biotechnology.

On the first point, it is widely recognised that governments play a fundamental part in the promotion of industrial innovation, although their intervention takes remarkably different forms over time and across countries and is motivated by a variety of objectives. The role of the state is, *a fortiori*, crucial in weak economies with limited markets where the scientific and industrial systems are unable to generate autonomously high

[1] The authors wish to thank Ilaria Galimberti, Carlo Gola, Jacqueline Senker and Margaret Sharp for their comments and advice on this chapter.

rates of innovative activities on the technological frontier. In these conditions, however, governments usually face severe problems in terms of the resources available for allocation to science and technology policies; of their ability to mobilise the political and economic support for new and risky industrial activities; and to design and implement a coherent set of measures in a context characterised by intrinsic uncertainty and conflicting interests. The case of Biotechnology epitomises these problems and raises some further issues about public policies for innovation.

1. Biotechnology: Some General Considerations

Biotechnology is a generic technology with a long history encompassing the centuries-old practice of using fermentation to process foods and drinks; the large-scale production of antibiotics following the second world war; and the development of "genetic engineering" in the mid-1970s. These latter techniques represent a discontinuity in the development of biotechnology, which should in principle improve the economics of biological production processes and thus open up whole new areas of innovative activity. New applications are envisaged in health care (both therapeutics and diagnostics), foods, chemicals and the extraction industries, and - perhaps of greatest significance in the long-term - in agriculture. So far, the number of products spawned by the new biotechnology is unimpressive. Its more widespread application will depend on some major technological breakthroughs at the research frontiers. It is inevitable that there should be substantial uncertainty concerning likely targets and time frames.

These considerations highlight the importance of policy measures geared to encouraging the enormous potential of biotechnology. However, a number of further features bear mention. First, the new technology has been characterised by science-push: the key breakthroughs, and much of the impetus for their development, have emanated from the public research system. Second, these breakthroughs are essentially research techniques capable of stimulating both scientific and technological advance: discovery and invention are extremely proximate activities in this field. Third, the key discipline underpinning the new biotechnology - molecular biology - was virtually absent from industrial R&D prior to the development of genetic engineering; academia remains the centre of gravity for research in the field.

Developments to date suggest that success with the new biotechnology will depend crucially on the utilisation and exploitation of public sector R&D. In the United States, which saw much of the early interest and activity around genetic engineering, this came mainly because of the opportunities offered by this technology to large established corporations associated with frontier research in academia (Kenney 1986). These new companies have layed an important role in the generation and transfer of technology to large established corporations associated with older forms of biotechnology, performing as "bridging institutions" or specialised suppliers of research inputs (Orsenigo 1988; Teece et al. 1987). Large companies, in order to develop capability in the science and techniques of the new biotechnology, have been obliged to collaborate closely both with the research start ups and with academic researchers (Faulkner 1986a; 1986b and 1986c). Indeed, linkage between academic and industrial research has been a recurring feature in the commercialisation of this technology.

In short, the new biotechnology is a strongly knowledge-based technology. This indicates a major role for government in the development of biotechnology - one commensurate to the need to enhance the flow of knowledge from the public research system into the productive sector. It also means that governments have to operate in an environment characterised by considerable uncertainty about the future technological developments and by conflict between the diverging expectations and interest of scientists, industrialists and the public.

2. The UK Case

2.1 The Emergence of UK Policy for Biotechnology

The event which brought biotechnology into the public arena was the publication, in March 1980, of the "Spinks Report". This report was the product of a committee which uniquely drew together representatives of the UK research establishment - from the Research Councils and the Royal Society - alongside representatives of major industrial R&D concerns - from the Advisory Committee on Applied Research and Development (ACARD). The final report contained a measured assessment of the technology and concluded that despite the country's research strength in the field British industry had yet to recognise and exploit its full potential. It called for: more funding for research, encompassing training, centres of excellence and industry/academia collaboration; a public-sponsored company; and administrative coordination between relevant government departments.

Such measures were anathema to the Conservative government which under a year earlier had been elected on a ticket of reducing both public expenditure and government intervention in industry. Indeed, the government's response to the Spinks Report - a White Paper published a full year later in March 1981 - rehearsed the government's belief that the task of growing a new industry should be left to the private sector and that any sizeable increase in public funding of academic research would have to await more prosperous times. Needless to say, UK policy for biotechnology has emerged largely in spite of rather than because of the government in power (Sharp 1985).

In terms of practical support, the White Paper offered only two substantive measures. First of these was the launch, in late 1980, of the new biotechnology firm Celltech. This venture emanated from the National Enterprise Board (now amalgamated with the NRDC as part of the British Technology Group (BTG)) which, since the establishment of the government-funded semiconductor firm Inmos in 1978, had built up a portfolio of investments in biotechnology many of them geared to exploiting university research. It was hoped that as with Inmos (and in the United States) these new ventures would stimulate the established companies to enter the field.

Celltech was initially given preferential commercial rights to exploit research from Medical Research Council (MRC) laboratories (including the Laboratory of Molecular Biology). The government stake in the new firm was a minority one, worth £4.4 million, which has since been sold off. In 1984 the BTG launched the "country cousin" of Celltech, the Agricultural Genetic Company, which has links with the Agricultural and Food Research Council (AFRC) and received a government stake of £3.75

million. Government financing of other new ventures has been considerably more modest: between 1978 and 1987 the BTG has invested a total of approximately £10 million, in ten new biotechnology firms. In line with the previous role of the NRDC, another £10 million has been spent in a "seed corn" capacity: on the development and licencing of over 100 biotechnology inventions emanating from the public research system (BTG, personal communication).

The second initiative announced in the White Paper was the Science and Engineering Research Council (SERC) Biotechnology Directorate launched in November 1981 as a result of earlier moves from within the Research Council. Following the model set up by previous directorates in engineering fields, the Biotechnology Directorate had two aims: to channel funding for research and post-graduate studentships into areas seen to have potential commercial application, these often crossing disciplines; and to encourage collaboration between industry and academia. It was a modest initiative, with a starting budget of £1 million rising to £2.5 million over three years, intended originally to have a life of five years.

The White Paper was a resounding disappointment to all concerned. Scientists were especially voluble in this regard. Not only were they in a unique position to grasp the potential of the new techniques: there was also by that time widespread concern that dwindling public expenditure on universities and science budgets in general would erode the UK's comparative (intellectual) advantage in biotechnology. During 1982 prominent members of the scientific community engaged in an orchestrated lobby campaign within Parliament focusing on Select Committee hearings of the Department of Education and Science. As a result of these efforts an additional £1.4 million was released for biotechnology research at specified university centres.

Also in the wake of this episode, the (now) Department of Trade and Industry (DTI) began to take a lead in biotechnology, with the establishment of an interdepartmental committee chaired by the Government Chemist. In November 1982 the Department launched a programme with a budget worth £16 million over the first three years. Like earlier initiatives in electronics, this essentially provided a mechanism for targeting already available support on a specific sector. Half of the funding was earmarked for specified government laboratories; the remainder was allocated to encourage firms to move into biotechnology by offering financial support for R&D and, on a smaller scale, consultancy work for feasibility studies and the like. In 1983 a Biotechnology Unit, assisted by a small team of specialist advisors from industry, was established to undertake this work.

The DTI's emphasis on encouraging R&D is seen as consistent with the long time frames in biotechnology. Department policy regarding the most appropriate sectoral targets for funding has evolved over time; the involvement of industrial secondees has been particularly helpful here as well as in advising firms. By June 1987, some £25 million had been committed by the Unit, annual spend being around £6 million. £14 million had been spent on the existing "Support for Innovation" scheme, resourcing a total of 85 projects in 68 companies across sectors. (The projects range in size between £0.1 million to £1 million.) In that time, over £0.5 million was spent on support for consultancy (50%) in 78 firms. This scheme is seen as providing companies with a "route in" to the technology and has been deemed a success in that over half of the companies involved have moved into biotechnology as a result of the studies commissioned (DTI, personal communication).

In 1986 the DTI launched a new programme "SMART" in the biotechnology and instruments sector. It is aimed at helping the very small new firm through the "finance gap", by awarding (on a competitive basis) grants of 75% for R&D (to a maximum of £50million) in year one, the proportion declining to 50% in year two and progressively thereafter. In 1987 the Department set up a Biotechnology Equipment Unit, along similar lines to the Biotechnology Unit, but intended to concentrate efforts on the (still weak) process engineering and equipment sectors in biotechnology (Dietz 1986).

To summarise, there are three main aspects of UK policy for biotechnology:

(i) support for public sector (and collaborative) research funded through the Research Councils;

(ii) support for industrial (and collaborative) R&D both in government corporate laboratories funded through the Department for Trade and Industry; and

(iii) investment in new ventures and inventions through the British Technology Group.

All of these measures are geared by varying means to stimulate the transfer of new technology from academia into the commercial arena. In spite of this apparent coherence, however, it should be appreciated that British policy for biotechnology is fundamentally fragmented and lacking in coordination.

Total government expenditure on R&D in biotechnology is indicated in table 1. Only a fraction of the overall funding indicated here has been spent on measures which are specifically targeted on biotechnology. Thus, in addition to the SERC, both the Agricultural and Food and the Medical Research Councils (AFRC and MRC) fund a great deal of research which is at least nominaly related to the new techniques, although neither have any policy for biotechnology. Moreover, little of this is new expenditure: DTI funding for the Biotechnology Unit, though new to the sector, was found from within pre-existing budgets, whilst Research Council funding of biotechnology essentially protected existing levels of funding within a declining overall budget.

Many would argue that the resourcing of biotechnology in the UK is wholly inadequate to the task at hand and, further, that the failure to coordinate the efforts mounted has resulted in

Table 1: UK Government Funding of Biotechnology R&D, 1986-87

Source	Amount (£ million)
Medical Research Council	27
Agricultural and Food Research Council	21
Scientific and Engineering Research Council	3
National Environment Research Council	1
University Grants Commission	3
Department of Trade and Industry	6
Ministry of Agriculture, Fisheries and Food	4
Other Government Departments	2
Total	67

Source: Department of Trade and Industry

the inefficient use of those resources which have been allocated. These weaknesses reflect a genuine ambivalence evident in the current government. The adherence to prevailing anti-interventionist orthodoxies runs counter to the de facto interest of government ministers, especially the Prime Minister, in the high technology sectors. In this context, the approval (eventually) given to the establishment of Celltech was perhaps not such a surprising achievement for the interventionists (Sharp, personal communication). Importantly though, both Celltech and the SERC Directorate were initiated independently of the cabinet. Throughout the development of UK policy for biotechnology, government has in effect reacted to initiatives of other institutions - and interest groups - rather than taking a proactive stance. As a result, the UK lost the opportunity to take an early lead in the field.

2.2 The Role of Collaborative Research and Technology Transfer

In order to build up innovative capability in the new biotechnology, companies have to establish new and often unusually close linkages with the public research system. This aspect was examined in a recent study of the major British pharmaceutical companies (Faulkner 1986a and 1986b). The funding of collaborative research in academia, and the use of consultants and of networks of informal links with public sector institutions, are a relatively routine feature of pharmaceutical R&D. However, these activities have been especially intense in the area of research related to genetic engineering. Amongst the more progressive firms (those which made the earlier and greater commitment to the new technology), new contacts and new collaborations have been pursued in a particularly purposeful fashion. It seems likely that strong communications with the external research community will have a considerable bearing on companies' success with the new techniques.

Companies' motivation for "plugging in" to academic research is related in large measure to the science-based character of the field. It is interesting that the role of linkage here has changed significantly as the technology has developed. In the mid-1970s the major emphasis was on picking up expertise in the new techniques; by the early 1980s, when these techniques had become standardised and companies had had time to establish their own in-house teams, the emphasis was firmly on "getting a window" on the relevant research frontiers. The resulting inputs enable companies to "hedge their bets" in terms of potential targets, and to ensure that their own research efforts in specific areas are underpinned by the latest knowledge available. Some companies are now reporting that their research is closer to the state of the art than is that in academia - if only because the universities can no longer afford to keep up to date in terms of research equipment. Whilst this may hold in some specific areas there remains a general need for companies active in biotechnology currently to draw on the breadth of expertise available in academia.

The encouragement of industry/academia collaboration has of course been a recurrent theme in UK policy for biotechnology. Between 1981 and 1986 inclusive, 34 out of the 235 research grants awarded by the SERC Directorate, and 87 of the 182 studentships, have been cooperative with industrial companies. The private sector contribution to Directorate research grants totals approximately £3.5 million in cash and perhaps another £1 million "in kind" (SERC, personal communication). By this measure, the Biotechnology Directorate has been more successful than any of its predecessors in other technologies.[2]

Collaborative research has been the hallmark of DTI funding as with the SERC. Where initially the emphasis was on competitive research (where the firms were the prime movers), DTI Biotechnology Unit has moved progressively towards more basic - or so-called "strategic" - research. As a result there is now considerable overlap with the types of studies funded by the Biotechnology Directorate.

A novel element in both the SERC and DTI efforts has been the establishment of "research clubs". Through this mechanism, groups of interested industrial concerns have been involved cooperatively in funding programmes of pre-competitive re-

---

[2] This record has now been superseded by the UK's response to fifth generation computing - the Alvey Programme - which, as in Japan and other countries, is founded on the promotion of large-scale collaborative and cooperative research programmes.

search in designated government or university laboratories. The precedent for this approach was set by the Leicester Biocentre, an independent initiative opened in September 1982 with subscriptions from five established companies (three have subsequently pulled out). Similar clubs have since been launched - not all of them associated with a specific facility - in protein engineering, antibiotics and in rDNA, animal cell biotechnology, molecular recognition, bioreactor technology and downstream processing, and genetic engineering in plants.

In the latter case, which started in the Autumn of 1986, the club centres around a three year research programme to be conducted in four research institutes jointly at a total cost of some £3 million. Half of this cost is to be borne by the DTI, the other half being shared by 11 companies each paying around £50,000 a year for access to and control over club research. Numerous benefits are claimed from such arrangements: industry gets a high ratio of research value to cost, as well as an "inside track" in an area of rapid scientific advance and the option of progressing specific pieces of research to a one-to-one contract basis; academia in turn benefits from additional funding and the interaction with industrial scientists which ensues.

Technology transfer can take place through the "spin out" of new companies from academia, as well as through collaborative research linkages. There is some evidence of this in the UK, as in the US; even amongst those new biotechnology firms whose origins lay elsewhere, many enjoy extremely close links with academia (Faulkner 1986c). Both Celltech and the Agricultural Genetic Company were unique in the arrangements made for them to benefit directly from the inventions and discoveries emanating from public sector research. Celltech's special link with the MRC undoubtedly gave it a competitive advantage: it meant the company had two products on the market within its first year of operation.

Some of the other research-based start ups rely heavily on contracting their expertise to the large established companies in order to generate revenues with which to fund more long term development and build up capabilities in production and marketing. The success of these strategies will of course depend on the value which large companies place on the "intellectual birthright" of the new biotechnology firms. A second group of companies are already manufacturing products. In some cases - Cambridge Life Sciences is an early example - these products have their origins in the public research system and are subsequently marketed by established concerns. In many others, the products themselves are inputs to research related to the new techniques - reagents and instrumentation. Such companies form an important part of the complex of R&D activity which is spanning science and technology in the new biotechnology.

2.3 The Erosion of the UK's Research Base in Biotechnology

Collaborative research and technology transfer are arguably the areas in which UK policy for biotechnology has made the greatest inroads. Of course, the value of these activities will depend utlimately on the strength of public sector research in basic science. Perhaps the most damning criticism of UK government in this field is that by limiting the resources allocated to basic research it has not only failed to build on Britain's research advantage, it has all but lost that advantage - as the research scientists warned it would.

It is difficult to measure the extent of the problem. However some indication is provided by bibliometric comparisons internationally (Stankiewicz 1986), and by data on the "brain drain" in biotechnology. In the early 1980s, the UK was losing on averager thirty scientists qualified (mostly to post-doctorate level) in the new biotechnology to the US and elsewhere (Pearson and Parsons 1983). The extent of the flow had diminished (at least in relative terms) by 1986, in part because of increasing employment opportunities in UK companies (Bevan et al. 1987). However, it is notable that the single most commonly cited motivation for scientists leaving the UK is the lack of employment and career opportunities in the new biotechnology - especially in the public sector.

The SERC Biotechnology Directorate is of course the only body with specific responsibility for funding public sector research in biotechnology. An independent investigative study suggests that in spite of resource limitations the Directorate has gone some way to meeting its objectives: it has channelled resources into relevant research and in the process brought previously disparate disciplines together; and it has had notable successes in the area of industry/academia links (Senker and Sharp 1988). This notwithstanding, the Directorate's achievements have been constrained not only by the derisory budget it was allocated, but also by the wider failure to link and coordinate all of the UK's considerable research resources.

In fact the SERC Biotechnology Directorate has made efforts to coordinate research funding by the three Research Councils involved. These efforts have floundered in part on inter-agency jealousies. In addition, the Directorate was seen to challenge some of the more entrenched traditions surrounding Research Council funding. Thus, the emphasis on "strategic" research, the efforts to foster industry-academia collaboration and, related to these features, the involvement of industrialists on the management committee of the Directorate have all fuelled suspicion of it within the Research Councils.

In particular there were fears that research proposals were being judged on commercial rather than scientific criteria. These fears are not substantiated (Sharp and Senker, forthcoming). Indeed it is notable that when in 1984 the Biotechnology Directorate decided on a shift in the topic focus of funding - away from process technologies towards more fundamental techniques in genetic engineering, biocatalysis and cell culture - it was the industrialists on the management committee who were largely responsible for this move. The need to secure Britain's basic research strength in biotechnology is the one issue over which industry is united in its condemnation of government policy (Sharp 1985), though this may be more a large company than a small company concern (Yanchinski 1984).

It will be remembered that the Spinks Report identified a major weakness in the response of British industry to recent developments in biotechnology. To this extent, the impact of the government's efforts on the industrial side might be measured by the level of activity which has been stimulated in the private sector. Industrial involvement in biotechnology has increased in all sectors since 1980. However, whilst some companies now have considerable R&D capability in the new techniques, some of the moves have been largely cosmetic - the renaming of existing research departments for instance. Moreover, in the crucial area of bioreactor technology and downstream processing, which has received the largest share of SERC funding, the UK continues to be weak.

There has been a tendency for involvement in the research clubs to be dominated by a core of the large established companies along with Celltech. There have been complaints that these companies have also received a disproportionate share of the DTI's funding for specific studies. Certainly some have received major grants, but the issue is complex. It seems to have been difficult to persuade established UK companies (as opposed to overseas interests) to enter into collaborative research initiatives. There may also be genuine difficulties associated with meeting the requirement to show that a project is both commercially feasible and would not be undertaken without government backing, though this problem is by no means unique to biotechnology. Perhaps most importantly, there is a sense that many of the established companies are still not willing to take responsibility for the support of basic and applied research strategic to the establishment of innovative capability in the new technology (Margaret Sharp, personal communication).

3. Italian Policy for Innovation in Biotechnology

3.1. *Innovation Activities and the Formation of Public Policies in Italy*

The history of the new biotechnology in Italy is very short indeed. Both industrial activities and government policies began much later than in other European countries and, as yet, the commitment to the new technology is rather small. Italy entered biotechnology from a position of relative weakness. Italian biological research has a long tradition and some centres did perform research in areas related to biotechnology. Only a few of them were conducting frontier research in the new biotechnology, and overall Italy lags significantly behind the other European countries with respect to its scientific base in biotechnology (table 2). On the industrial side, the chemical industry - most notably the two largest companies, Montedison and ENI - had accumulated good technological capabilities in some older areas of biotechnology. Yet, the reaction to the new opportunities opened by genetic engineering was very slow, with no significant involvement in innovative activities occurring before 1982-83. Moreover, apart from Montedison and ENI, only some medium-sized pharmaceutical companies showed any concerned interest in biotechnology.[3]

Table 2: Country Shares of Scientific Publications and US Patents in Biotechnology

	Scientific Publications (1982-83)	US Patents (1) (1980-84)
USA	32.2	55.4
JAPAN	13.9	42.3
UK	9.9	7.5
GERMANY	4.8	17.4
FRANCE	4.1	6.4
ITALY	1.2	4.4

(1) The US share is calculated over the total number of patents. The share of the other countries is calculated over the total number of foreign patents.

Sources: Federchimica (1986) and Orsenigo (1988) (OTAF/SPRU Data base)

An important factor which has so far hindered the emergence of consistent innovative activities in biotechnology in Italy is certainly the absence of a focused and conscious government intervention. Public involvement in biotechnology could be justified on a number of specific grounds, as well as on the conventional arguments for public support of a generic pre-competitive technology.[4] Biotechnology is potentially capable of influencing the performance of many economically and politically important industries. Moreover, biotechnology affects and is being developed by industries and firms which already have a prominent position in the national economies (chemicals above all) and can therefore exert a substantial political pressure on the government. In addition, biotechnology raises wider social issues (e.g. public health and safety, energy, food policy, etc.). In the case of

---

[3] In general, technological capabilities in biotechnology appear to be relatively higher in areas such as enzyme production and fermentation and purification techniques. Some pharmaceutical companies have also developed capabilities in enzyme immobilisation. The Italian industry is instead virtually absent in fields like cell fusion, cell culture and in the technologies related to agricultural applications (Federchimica 1986).

[4] See Sharp (1985) and Orsenigo (1988) for a more complete discussion.

Italy, the relative weakness of the scientific base, the economic and political weight of the chemical industry, and the low rates of innovative activities in the private sector constitute further compelling motives for a strong and coherent government intervention. Yet, the Italian government has been the last among the European countries to respond.

One reason for this delay lies in the insufficient and belated demand for policy expressed by industry itself. As in most European countries, the emergence of public policies was contingent on the formation of industrial and scientific lobbies to press for government intervention and participate in the process of policy formulation (Sharp 1985; Orsenigo 1988). As a result of the relative backwardness of the scientific and industrial base, such initiatives did not emerge before. If anything, it was scientists who took a more active role. Biologists (and in particular molecular biologists) had traditionally had little interaction with industry; but because of the strategic importance of scientific knowledge in the development of biotechnology, they had strong interest at stake and acquired a key economic and political position.

The Italian biotechnology lobby emerged around the Federation of Technical and Scientific Associations (FAST), composed of scientists, technologists and industrialists. In 1984, FAST published the first Italian report on biotechnology (FAST 1984). It provided information about the ongoing activities within university and industry and described briefly the experiences of other countries. It emphasised the need to support and coordinate both basic research and industry-university ties, as well as the lack of finance for new innovative ventures, but did not propose specific policy measures.

The biotechnology lobby subsequently gathered within Federchimica, the Chemical Industrial Association which formed a group to elaborate a new report on biotechnology and a policy proposal. Much as in the case of Germany (Jasanoff 1985), the pressure of the chemical industry eventually provided the stimulus for government action. The Federchimica Report was published in 1986 and it emphasised the need of a comprehensive policy broadly inspired on the British experience (Federchimica 1986).

A final source of pressure on the government was the EEC - and, more generally, the mechanism of international imitation in

National Plan for Biotechnology. The Committee asked for 400 billion lire to be allocated (over an unspecified time-frame) to the support for applied industrial research, emphasising the need of closer industry-university ties. Priorities were identified in the biomedical applications of biotechnology which are closer to commercialisation and to agricultural and food applications in the longer run.

Table 4: Public Support to Biotechnology ($ M.) 1983*

USA	550
JAPAN	35
GERMANY**	49
FRANCE	31
UK	36
ITALY	44

* Data are refered to a "narrow" definition of biotechnology.
** Federal Support only.

Source: Orsenigo (1988)

The National Plan for Biotechnology was eventually passed in 1987. The original approach was maintained but funding was cut to around 200 billion lire. Half of this is allocated (according to the procedures of the Law 46) to eight research projects in the biomedical field and half to 11 projects covering bioprocesses in the chemical, energy and environment application fields on the one hand and to agriculture on the other. Whilst the National Plan focuses on applied research, support for basic research and industry-university collaboration is provided through a new CNR "Finalised Project" for biotechnology launched at the end of 1987, which allocates 87 billion lire in five years mainly to biomedical research. Further initiatives include government participation in the foundation of an international research centre in Trieste promoted by UNIDO. In addition, the National Agency for Alternative Energy (ENEA) created, in 1986, a re-search division for agricultural biotechnology with the task of promoting technology transfer in this field.

In sum, a coherent policy for biotechnology is gradually emerging in Italy. Its structure reflects the needs raised by the specific features of biotechnology. To this extent it is similar to the approach taken in most European countries, in the emphasis on the generalised support of basic and applied research, to the fostering of industry-university links and more generally to technology transfer and collaborative generic research in industry. No specific trajectory of innovative activities is targeted as a priority, and only some very broad areas of research are indicated as being of a particular interest for the future of Italian industry, although it is recognised that support has to concentrate on relatively few selected projects in order to generate a critical mass.

3.3 The Structure and Problems of Government Intervention

The Italian government was thus under some pressure to design and implement a coherent set of policy measures for biotechnology. However, whilst not being ideologically opposed to an active intervention, it lacked both the necessary experience and the administrative structure.

As in all countries, a number of technology-specific factors had to be dealth with: the strongly science-based and pervasive nature of biotechnology; the traditional separation of biologists from industrial research; the number and the heterogeneity of the agents involved[6]; the difficulty of selecting priorities in an uncertain and fast developing technology with an absence of products; and the lack of relevance of some traditional instruments of intervention (public procurements, import controls etc.). Rather, policy had to focus primarily on the support and coordination of basic and applied research, on industry-university links, on the regulation of experiments, on patent laws. In many countries, including Italy, these aspects had rarely been consciously and systematically incorporated into the policies for industrial innovation.

Government support for innovation has traditionally been weak in Italy, both in terms of total public expenditure and of the

---

[6] Scientists, companies active in different industries, etc. Similarly, many government agencies were involved in the process of formation of public policies: in Italy they were Departments of Scientific Research, Industry, Agriculture, the National Research Council, other bridging institutions like ENEA, and many others.

array of instruments which had been used.[7] During the early
1980s, the whole set of science and technology policies under-
went a reappraisal. In 1982 a new law (the Law 46) was passed in
order to reorganise and increase public expenditure on applied
research. This significantly improved the level and the efficiency
of public support for industrial innovation. However, the absence
of a well-functioning structure capable of monitoring and assessing technological developments, to support and target and bridge
effectively basic and applied research, continued to be one of the
major weaknesses of the Italian innovation policies (Momigliano
1986).

An assessment of the adequacy and consistency of these
policies is obviously premature. However, both the size and the
structure of these measures seem to compare unfavourably with
other European countries, especially if account is taken of the
relative weakness of the Italian scientific and industrial base in
this field. Moreover, government action seems to lack initiative
in some crucial areas, namely: (i) the encouragement of new
firm formation; (ii) the definition of research guidelines and
(iii) the adaptation of patent laws.

The first aspect reflects the objective obstacles to the emergence of new high technology ventures in Italy: primarily the
absence of sufficiently high and differentiated capabilities within
the academic system and industry, which provide the seedbed
and the opportunities to engage in new risky ventures operating
on the technological frontiers. The structure of the financial
system, which is characterised by the underdevelopment of the
stock market and the virtual absence of venture capital, represents a further constraint hindering the birth and growth of new
"Schumpeterian" companies. In this context, any reliance on new
small firms as engines of significant innovation processes is likely
to be misplaced, innovative activities being mainly driven by the
existing companies.

---

7   See Malerba and Orsenigo (1987) and Momigliano (1986) for a discussion
of this issue. Public support for innovative activities was mainly based on
the supply of financial incentives to R&D. Bureaucratic inefficiencies related to the complexity of the administrative procedures required to get access to the funds had further weakened the effectiveness of such instruments.

The absence of initiative in the regulatory field is an even more serious drawback, which reflects a structural failure to understand the complexity of long term science and technology policies and the related weaknesses in the capacity to exert an autonomous influence on the innovative strategies of the private sector. This failure is clearly particularly serious in a context characterised by a weak industrial involvement in innovative activities, where the government should provide consistent support and coordination and where the uncertainty on the future developments of the technology precludes the choice of well-defined priorities. On the other hand, the weakness of the industrial base represents itself as a further constraint on the ability to design and implement public policy for technological development.

4. Conclusions

The recent emergence of government policy for biotechnology in Italy and the UK provides many interesting contrasts. Italy started with a comparatively weak base in terms of both public research and industrial R&D in the new technology. It also lagged behind most of Europe in the formulation of policy. The UK government was essentially reactive on this front, being ideologically opposed to the level of intervention required: most of those measures which have been implemented emanated from within pre-existing institutions. Whilst in Italy there was no ideological constraint on the development of policy for biotechnology, there was a lack of institutions with the requisite tradition of support for industrial innovation in an advanced technology.

The result in Italy appears to be a policy which, though it has increased the level of funding in biotechnology, is weak in targeting this research funding and in the promotion of collaborative research and technology transfer between academia and industry. Also, Italy has not seen any significant start up activity around the new technology. These are all areas in which the UK can claim some success - albeit on a very limited scale. This being said, UK policy for biotechnology has been lacking both in the level of resources allocated and the level of coordination achieved, with the result that the country appears to have lost its initial research advantage. In short, neither country has been particularly "dirigiste" in its efforts over biotechnology, though for different reasons.

In spite of these differences, there are important areas of commonality in the experiences of the UK and Italy - notably in the prominence of scientists as a political interest group, and in the emphasis on the resourcing, utilisation and exploitation of public sector research. Here we have confirmation that the promotion of a strongly science-based technology such as biotechnology requires attention to the funding of basic and applied research, as well as industry-academia research linkages and technology transfer.

To the extent that this demands intervention in the public research system, some progress has been made in the development of appropriate measures - witness, for example, the UK's research clubs. Problems still remain to be resolved - finding the right balance between basic and applied research, easing the institutional barriers between academia and industry and so forth - but in principle none of these need be intractible, given some imagination and adequate resourcing and coordination.

However, in the area of economic and industrial intervention, the prescriptions are less clear. Government policy in both Italy and the UK has as yet had only limited impact on the growth of innovative capability in the private sector. Indeed, this represents a second important area of commonality: in both countries there continues to be a marked reluctance on the part of industry to commit resources to R&D, especially strategic research, in biotechnology.

In effect, industry - with few notable exceptions - looks to government to underpin the risk involved in developing a new and dynamic technology in which targets remain uncertain and time frames long term. The reasons for this are complex and entrenched including, in Italy, the fragmented and narrow base of the industrial structure and, in the UK, the risk-averse and anti-technical tradition of management. In short, the real problems are quite intractable and thus not particularly amenable to short term policy measures.

Such considerations highlight a problem: the weaker the country's position in a new technology, the greater proportionately will be the effort required to compete in the areas of innovation it opens up. The cases of the UK and Italy reveal a number of problems which may be generalised. First, there is the sheer scale of resources required in order to maintain the public research system of sufficient weight in basic science to underpin the development of an advanced technology. Second, since the targets for intervention span both science policy and industry policy it is crucial that government efforts to promote growth in an advanced technology such as biotechnology be both coherent and coordinated. Third, the type of policy objectives pursued in such cases demand many new and imaginative instruments. The absence of the state playing an active part increases the problem of participating in the global race in techno-industrial innovation and in attractive new world markets.

Bibliography

ADVISORY COUNCIL FOR APPLIED RESEARCH AND DEVELOPMENT (1980), with the Advisory Board for the Research Councils and the Royal Society, *Biotechnology: Report of a Joint Working Party (The Spinks Report)*, London: Her Majesty's Stationery Office.

ADVISORY COUNCIL FOR APPLIED RESEARCH AND DEVELOPMENT (1983), with the Advisory Board for the Research Councils, *Improving Research Links Between Higher Education and Industry*, London: Her Majesty's Stationery Office.

BEVAN, S., PARSONS, D., and PEARSON, R. (1987), *Monitoring the Biotechnology Labour Market*. A report prepared by the Institute of Manpower Studies, Swindon: Science and Engineering Research Council.

COLEMAN, R. (1984), Biotechnology demands a special strategy, in: *New Scientist*, 9 February, 26-28.

DIETZ, R. (1986), Biotechnology - the equipment challenge, in: *Engineering*, 225:16-21, January.

DUNNILL, P. and RUDD, M. (1984), *Biotechnology and British Industry: A Report to the Biotechnology Directorate of the UK Science and Engineering Research Council*, Swindon: Science and Engineering Research Council.

FAST (1984), *Le biotechnologie in Italia*, Franco Angeli, Milano.

FAULKNER, W. (1986a), *Linkage between industrial and academic research: The case of biotechnological research in the pharmaceutical industry*. D Phil thesis, Brighton: Science Policy Research Unit, University of Sussex.

FAULKNER, W. (1986b), *Linkage between academic and industrial research in the new biotechnology*. Presented to a European symposium on The Utilisation of the Results of Public or Publically-funded Research and Development, Luxembourg: Commission of the European Community, 23-25 September.

FAULKNER, W. (1986c), *The new firm phenomenon in biotechnology*. Presented to the Ninth National Small Firm Policy and Research Conference, Gleneagles: Scottish Enterprise Foundation, 20-22 November.

Wendy Faulkner and Luigi Orsenigo

FAULKNER, W., OAKEY, R., COOPER, S., and WALSH, V. (forthcoming research report), *Innovation and growth in biotechnology*, Edinburgh: Heriot-Watt University.

FEDERCHIMICA (1986), *Le biotechnologie in Italia: una opportunità di sviluppo industriale*, Milano, Sviluppo Chimica.

GEORGHIOU, L., GUY, K., CAMERON, H., HOBDAY, M., RAE, T. and QUINTAS, P. (1988), *The evaluation of the Alvey Programme Interim Report*, London: Her Majesty's Stationery Office, March.

HOUSE OF COMMONS (1982), *Biotechnology: Interim Report on the Protection of the Research Base in Biotechnology*, Sixth report from the Education, Science and Art Committee, Session 1981-82, London: Her Majesty's Stationery Office, July.

JASANOFF, S. (1985), Technological Innovation in a Corporatist State: the case of Biotechnology in the Federal Republic of Germany, in: *Research Policy*, 14, 1985, 23-38.

JUNNE, Gerd (1985), *International Interaction between National Industrial Policies. The Case of Biotechnology.* Paper presented at the World Conference of the International Political Science Association, Paris, 15-20 July.

KENNEY, M. (1986), *Biotechnology: The university industry complex*, New Haven, CT: Yale University Press.

MALERBA, F., and ORSENIGO, L. (1987), *Technological Capabilities and Innovative Activities in the Evolution of the Italian Industry*, Università L. Bocconi, Milano.

MEDICAL RESEARCH COUNCIL (1982 onwards), *Inter-Research Council Coordinating Committee on Biotechnology Reports to Heads of Research Councils,* London: Medical Research Council.

MOMIGLIANO, F. (ed.) (1986), *La legislazione sulla politica industriale: obiettivi, strumenti e risultati.* Rapporto CER-IRS sull'industria e la politica industriale italiana. Il Mulino: Bologna.

OFFICE OF TECHNOLOGY ASSESSMENT (1984), *Commercial Biotechnology: An International Analysis*, Washington DC: Government Printing Office.

ORSENIGO, L. (1988), *Institutions and Markets in the Dynamics of Industrial Innovation. The Theory and the Case of Biotechnology.* PhD dissertation, Brighton, SPRU, University of Sussex.

PEARSON, R., and PARSONS, D.J. (1983), *The Biotechnology Brain Drain.* A report prepared by the Institute of Manpower Studies, Swindon: Science and Engineering Research Council.

ROTHMAN, H., and TOWALSKI, Z. (1984), British Biotechnology Policy, in: GOLDSMITH, M. (ed), *UK Science Policy: A Critical Review of Policies for Publically Funded Research*, London: Longman.

SCIENCE AND ENGINEERING RESEARCH COUNCIL (1982 onwards), *Directory of Research in Biotechnology*, Swindon: Science and Engineering Research Council.

SCIENCE AND ENGINEERING RESEARCH COUNCIL (1986), *Report of the Biotechnology Review Panel*, Swindon: Science and Engineering Research Council.

SENKER, J., and SHARP, M. (1988), *The Biotechnology Directorate of the SERC: Report and Evaluation of its Achievements, 1981-1987*, Brighton: Science Policy Research Unit, University of Sussex.

SHARP, M. (1985), *The New Biotechnology: European Governments in Search of a Strategy*, Sussex European Paper No 15, Brighton: SPRU.

STANKIEWICZ, R. (1986), *Genetic engineering - international R&D trends*, paper presented at the International Symposium on Japanese Technology, 4th Meeting of the Japanese - Sweden - German Crosscountry Study on Long-Term Technological R&D, Urawa, Saitama, Japan 17-19 September 1986.

TEECE, D., PISANO, G.P., and SHAN, W. (1987), *Joint Ventures and Collaboration in Biotec nology*. International Business Working Paper No.1B-8, Berkeley Business School, University of California, Berkeley.

UK GOVERNMENT (1981), *Biotec nology: A W ite Paper* (Cmnd 8177), London: Her Majesty's Stationery Office.

YANCHINSKI, S. (1984), Industry wants a role for government, in: *New Scientist*, 9 February, 29-30.

7

The State and New Forms of Communication

The Introduction of Videotex in Europe and North America

Volker Schneider, Thierry Vedel and James Miller

This chapter presents a comparative analysis of the introduction of videotex in several industrialized Western ountries.[1] While much has been written about videotex - often highly partisan, descriptive or journalistic - there have been relatively few published analyses, theoretically based, that attempt a critical, comparative study. Our central question is: Was the role of the state the predominant factor in videotex "success" or "failure" in Britain, Canada, France, Germany and the United States?

---

[1]   The European part of this article is based on a research project which was initiated by Prof. Renate Mayntz in 1985 and was carried out by research teams from the CNRS in Paris, the Max-Planck-Institut für Gesellschaftsforschung in Cologne and the SPRU at the University of Sussex. We thank our colleagues Jean-Marie Charon, Ian Miles and Graham Thomas for providing us with valuable information and helpful comments.

Videotex, as discussed below, is a novel form of telecommunications,[2] an advanced form of information transmission which incorporates characteristics shared by the telephone, video technologies and computers. It is a very recent development, with origins in the mid-1970s, expensive, complicated and often referred to as a leading example of Information Age communications. For all these reasons it has been the object of high-technology policy - state and corporate - in most major Western nations. Its development has been exceptionally uneven, and the same may be said of its prospects. Videotex is therefore an apt choice as a case study in state attempts to guide the sputtering economies of advanced industrial nations into the promised land of post-industrial society.

This paper has several goals. First, there is a desire to locate interventions by the state on behalf of videotex in the larger context of industrial policy. Videotex may be a special case of this, with ties to high-technology policy and even cultural policy as well. Second, the paper selectively documents the historical record of videotex development for each country, with special emphasis on actions by the state and other powerful actors who possess legitimate policy authority, and the consequences of their actions. Next, a comparison along specific dimensions suggests how and why certain forms of state intervention may have been more fruitful than others. Lastly, the paper offers some generali-

---

2   The term videotex denotes both a technology and a service, but in this context it is used for a technological system which in turn makes available certain services. It is known by multiple names (viewdata or videotex; Prestel, Télétel, Bildschirmtext, Telidon, etc.), but today's common, internationally accepted generic term is videotex. Videotex refers to an interactive technology that permits the exchange of visually displayed information between points equipped with video screens and keypads. These points tend to be connected by telephone lines or by coaxial or fibre-optic cable. Generally there is some central source, such as a database stored in a computer, and many user locations which can communicate with one another, as well as with the central source. The displayed information appears as letter and numerical characters and as graphic and pictorial images. By sending encoded messages that they type into keypads, users make their way through hierarchically arranged data at the central source, for example information on flight schedules. Users can also in the same way send information to each other, as in an electronic messaging service.

zations drawn from the videotex experience regarding the efficacy of state power, and forecasts the likely outcomes of similar future programmes of high-technology industrial planning in the communications realm.

As intimated above, in carrying out this analysis we discovered that the role-of-the-state question may not be adequate to the problems under investigation. It may be more that functions identified with the state are important, not whether those tasks are actually carried out by authorities who are said to be politically accountable. In order to develop a technological innovation like videotex, it may be necessary to possess a high degree of expert knowledge, to have access to great wealth, to enjoy the luxury of patience and, especially, to wield the power of fairly centralized, over-arching control. These conditions may apply to the state, to transnational corporations, or to some mix of both. Whatever, they may be *sine qua non* in determining the fate of videotex, and by extension the fates of other "technologies of the future". Some states, for some technologies, in some instances, are better situated this way than others. This is a theme the paper returns to in the final section.

1. Videotex Policies in Advanced Industrial Countries

Videotex policies can be understood as cases of high-technology policy. It may illustrate new forms of state intervention, by which the state initiates, promotes, guides, administrates and regulates the development of new technology. When interactive videotex was developed in the mid-1970s by the British Post Office, many believed that this could be a new "technology system" by which the emergence of a whole information industry could be triggered. The French government with its Télétel programme deliberately decided to promote the development of its national telecommunications and information industry. In Canada and the UK, videotex was also believed to be a strategic element of the new "information society". Fedida and Malik (1979), for instance, considered videotex "as critical to the development of the 'third' industrial revolution as were the steam engine to the first and the internal combustion engine to the second".

1.1 The North American Policy Scene for Videotex

Telidon in Canada: To understand the fate of videotex in Canada, it is necessary to see it in terms of high-technology industrial policy and telecommunications regulatory traditions. Telidon, it can be argued, resulted from elements common to both, not least a particular sense of Canadian nationalism.

State authority over telecommunications in Canada is complex and somewhat uncertain. Critics have cited the fragmented power among and within policy agencies, and suggested that recent attempts to consolidate and exercise national policy planning authority have been decidedly mixed. Three Canadian provinces own and regulate their own systems. Two large telephone companies are federally regulated, although between them they serve just two provinces. A major US telecommunications firm owns several Canadian phone companies. The national satellite service, begun by the state, is now owned by federally regulated common carriers.

Jurisdictional disputes between provincial and federal authorities have historically been settled in court. Generally speaking, the notion that telecommunications (and broadcasting) are or need to be technologically integrated systems on a country-wide scale has frequently been decisive. In addition there is often expressed an essential need to contribute to nation-building, to an elusive Canadian identity and unity. During the last quarter century this has tended to argue for an accretion of federal political power of all kinds, including telecommunications policy planning.

Canada regulates with one agency and ostensibly plans with another. The Canadian Radio-Television and Telecommunications Commission (CRTC) administers laws passed by Parliament concerning broadcasting and telecommunications. Like many regulatory bodies, its discretion is considerable, and in assigning licences or setting rates or establishing rules governing ownership, the CRTC actually determines important national policy positions. The federal Department of Communications (DOC), headed by a cabinet minister, conducts research of a mostly technical nature, but increasingly it has become oriented to cultural issues. How and whether these authorities interact with each other and with their provincial counterparts clearly has significant consequences for national policy.

If towards telecommunications the Canadian State can be said to take a somewhat awkward stance, one whose authority is questioned and not uniform, whose capacity to plan is doubted, then federal industrial policy provides a sharp contrast. The continuing subject of an often favourable debate, national industrial policy came to identify the information/telecommunications/ broadcasting sector as having some of the greatest potential to reward Canada economically during the final years of the century. This in turn offered the DOC a special opportunity to promote videotex.

Canada often has been described as having a "branch plant" economy, especially weak in high-technology design and production, except as foreign-owned firms (mostly American) produce or adapt such goods and services on Canadian soil. During the 1970s, analysts called for national policy to foster Canada's "technological sovereignty". That is, through state support of various kinds, including direct financial and research assistance, creation of government markets for Canadian products, and export assistance, Canadian high-technology industries would grow larger and richer, permitting Canada a measure of independence (and self-respect) in strategically important sectors like communications and information.

Telidon, the Canadian videotex, was announced by DOC scientists in 1978. It had grown out of work done on military applications of computer graphics, just at a time when Prestel and Télétel were establishing themselves in Europe. Its promise, as a "second generation videotex", was that it would become an instrument of technological sovereignty: Canadian videotex for Canadians. Equally important, Telidon's superior graphics capability would, planners believed, make it the videotex of choice for all of North America, the US having not set a national standard. The DOC Telidon programme ran until 1985. Fifty to 60 million Canadian dollars in federal money were expended, and observers estimate that industry may have spent four times that amount. Some fourty field trials took place in Canada and the US. In 1981 AT&T accepted a modified version of Telidon (NAPLPS) as its own standard. A DOC official happily announced that Telidon had "moved from a promising but still controversial technology in search of a market to the threshold of mass use and general recognition as the world's leading videotex system" (Parkhill 1981). Governmental forecasts were extremely optimistic, predicting more than half a million subscribers by 1986 and a direct employment of 8,400 persons in the Canadian videotex industry. For 1985 planners envisioned services in all major Canadian cities and most rural areas, reaching a principally residential market. The DOC termed Telidon a "prime example of technology transfer through government-industry cooperation". (DOC 1982-83).

However, the enthusiasm of the early 1980s soon vanished, and today the two Canadian videotex industry associations no longer exist. State involvement is invisible, and there are but a handful of videotex services available in Canada. There is little to show for all the money of the early 1980s. Even as an international standard Telidon appears to have been superceded by others. Perhaps the one bright spot was a 1988-89 field trial by Bell Canada in Montreal of a primarily residential service called Alex, which was closely modeled on the French Télétel system. Canadian policy planners clearly misjudged Telidon's capacity to achieve such multiple and weighty goals as introducing the so-called Information Age at home, reducing Canada's economic and cultural dependencies, and asserting Canada's position in expanding global markets.

Videotex in the United States: The US, "with the largest mass market for electronics in the world, with the highest concentration of telephones, televisions, computers and other telecommunications devices" (Mosco 1982), is the one place where videotex might be expected to flourish. Yet paradoxically it has not, and state authorities there have approached videotex with indifference, taking tentative policy steps only in the late 1980s. A significant part of the explanation is the deregulatory posture at the Federal Communications Commission (FCC), which regulates the telecommunications and broadcasting industries, in Congress, which passes laws administered by the FCC, and at the executive branch policy planning National Telecommunications and Information Administration (NTIA). Dating back to the early 1970s, deregulatory policies for telecommunications and broadcasting have steadily found favor in the US, trading federal policy authority for corporate decision making as the key determinant of US communications and information industries.

Perhaps the single most prominent state involvement in US videotex has been a negative one. As part of the agreement that divested AT&T of its Bell subsidiaries (now seven regional holding companies and 22 operating firms), a federal court barred AT&T and the Bell companies from offering enhanced forms of information services like videotex. The purpose of this prohibition was presumably to limit the exercise of exceptional market power in the information sector by the local telephone monopolies.

The unwillingness, under deregulation, of US federal authorities to set technical standards, establish industrial policy goals or coordinate the appropriate infrastructure for videotex has led to a series of expensive trials, carried out by corporations, most of which have been unsuccessful. The future for US videotex is far from certain and, as far as can be seen, hardly revolutionary.

There are, in rough terms, three broad categories of videotex use in the US. The first chronologically was to provide the news. Initially, the corporations with the greatest interest in videotex were major communications conglomerates, who of course feared the potential encroachment of the new technology into their established domains of radio and television, newspapers and magazines, and cable. Thus NBC, CBS and Time, Inc. were active early on. The most elaborate videotex trials were carried out by two firms best known for their newspaper publishing, but which also own broadcasting and cable properties. Both of these attempts at "electronic publishing" were considered failures. Knight-Ridder, second largest owner of US newspapers, ended in 1986 its three-year Viewtron trial. Serving households primarily in Florida, it garnered only about half the expected subscribers, and the entire project lost an estimated $50 million.[3] The Times-Mirror company's (fourth in newspapers) Gateway, offered in Los Angeles at approximately the same time, experienced a similar lack of interest, and lost some $30 million.

---

3   Interestingly, Knight-Ridder noted the popularity among subscribers of "conversing" with one another on the system as in France, not an intended or expected use of videotex.

A second, and continuing, category of US videotex use comprises essentially time-sharing services, many of them offering financial news to investors. CompuServe is the biggest and best known, with about 350,000 international users. Others, at quite expensive rates, provide research data, as does Knight-Ridder's Vu/Text for about $100/hour. Subscribers to these videotex services constitute a special class of users - often corporate - and lacking an advanced graphics capability, the technology is something less than videotex in the usual sense. A third category is really a catch-all for new videotex applications. Most of these concern the sale of retail merchandise. A consortium called Trintex which involves Sears and IBM (and originally CBS, though the parent company of American Airlines has been rumored as its replacement) began trials of Prodigy. Shopping transactions, travel and financial information and electronic messaging are planned. Another collaboration yet to begin field trials, Covidea, includes Chemical Bank, Bank of America and AT&T. Lastly, in addition to these shop-at-home services, videotex technology is being used ever more frequently to provide directory information at shopping malls and opportunities to make impulse purchases of selected merchandise at places like airports. These latter applications are known in the industry as "public access" videotex (Sloan and Talarzyk 1988). As of 1988 there are surely no more than 2.5 million videotex subscribers in the US, and that is a very generous figure, including users of all information services.

The US is distinctive in having no public policy objectives for videotex. The search for private profit has dictated nearly all events thus far. Overall videotex is unavailable to most Americans and probably unknown to them as well. The evolving applications of this new technology that generate sufficient profit to interest corporations have a disappointingly familiar ring to them: used either as a mundane device to sell conventional retail goods and services, or as a means to provide specialized, high-cost information to already existing centers of societal wealth and power. The future of videotex in the US may be shaped by corporations not usually considered as being in the information business, but which in fact possess the essential infrastructure. For example, banks and others circulate financial information routinely, and already operate their own extensive international telecommunications systems: American Airlines owns one of the largest computer-reservation systems, and clearly has ready access to travel information; Sears owns an investment house and has long been the nation's leading retailer. Videotex, especially in a situation where state authority is indifferent, is sometimes described as a technology seeking a market. If this is so, then videotex in the US is likely to find its function under the guidance of one of the transnational commercial giants mentioned above, and not through the exercise of state control.

1.2. The European Policy Scene for Videotex

The European experience in videotex development shows an interesting contrast to the North American case. In all the three European countries under discussion, it was a public telecommunications agency - the PTT - which played the leading role. Yet, significant differences appear in the scope, intensity and style of state intervention in videotex.

Prestel in the United Kingdom:[4] Prestel was the first mature videotex system in the world and was originally developed by the British Post Office (B.P.O.) research center. Although the first studies treated videotex as a business service, the B.P.O. marketing staff aimed more at the residential market. At a time when telephone saturation was foreseeable, it was expected that this technology would create a new business area alongside telephony. Since videotex used the telephone network as its transmission medium, it also promised extra traffic at off-peak periods, and thus a more optimal use of the telephone network.

The system was technically designed and implemented by the first British telecom- and computer producer, GEC, a company which traditionally had a close relationship with the B.P.O. The system consisted of centralized databases, and gateways to privately owned computers did not exist within the early version. This 'closed system' character and its centralization made the system extremely rigid and difficult to adapt to innovations and more sophisticated demands.

---

4   This section draws heavily from Graham Thomas (1988).

In the early terminal philosophy, the TV set occupied a central place. It was believed that by this strategy the terminal costs could be kept low. Potential problems raised by this approach, such as loss of control over the terminal marketing and distribution process, were thought to be offset by the beneficial effects of coupling Prestel subscription growth with the TV replacement cycle and incorporating TV manufacturers into a coalition with an interest in making Prestel a success. The idea was that the TV manufacturers, under increasing pressure by market saturation and the challenge of Far-East competition, would seize this opportunity for new markets. However, this approach had the disadvantage for consumers of requiring them to buy or rent new TV sets. It also made the development of Prestel critically dependent upon the response of TV manufacturers to the challenge of producing an adequate supply of cheap, new terminals.

In the British videotex approach, the information industry was planned to be completely private, and the B.P.O. decided to limit its role to that of a "common carrier". It would not own and operate the information services, but would merely act as a "transporter" and "storage device" of information provided and controlled by others. By this approach the B.P.O. hoped that information providers from existing media would be encouraged to join the new venture rather than oppose it.

This strategy of avoiding opposition was successful, and the B.P.O. was able to get the service up and running rapidly, without political hindrance. A first field trial was begun in 1978 on a modest scale with about 1,400 people participants. Its primary objectives were marketing research and not, as in German field trials, technology and legal assessment. Speedy implementation was so important because there was fear that international competitors could imitate the innovation. In a climate where state ownership and intervention were increasingly coming under criticism, the B.P.O. attempted to show that a nationalized industry could be innovative and could acquire a significant technological lead.

While Britain experienced some successes in exporting its videotex technology, its service at home, Prestel, was a failure. It started in London in autumn 1979 and began nationwide operation in March 1980. By December of that year it had only 7,262 registered users, 6,351 of these in businesses and only 911 in homes. At the end of 1981 the number of subscribers had risen to around 16,000 - only a tenth of the users which had been predicted for that time. The most crucial reasons for this slow growth were generally seen in the late delivery and high prices of the TV-set terminals. Other reasons for the slow take-up were uncoordinated marketing, lack of thorough market research, the indifferent quality of the databases of many information providers, too expensive and confusing tariffs and a too hasty expansion of the system from the pilot trial to the full-blown service. The B.P.O. reacted by cutting back on the scale of the service and by redefining its purpose and target markets: it closed computer centers, postponed a planned expansion of the database and concentrated future marketing efforts in specific business areas such as the travel trade. Since the early 1980s the system has no longer been seen as a flagship enterprise for the B.P.O., now the privatized British Telecom (BT). From this point on, BT has been wary of developing new services for residential customers.

A reorientation along the lines of the "French model" was unlikely in the British climate of liberalization and increasing market competition from private videotex systems. Several years before the privatization of BT, developments around Prestel had anticipated liberalization. In 1977 the users of videotex terminals were allowed to dial directly into private systems over the public switched telephone network. After further liberalization of the British telecom sector in the early 1980s a large number of competing computer-communications services emerged. Organizations were allowed to carry third-party value-added services on their own leased-line telecommunications networks, and particularly in the travel and financial sectors sizeable new networks and services arose which competed directly with Prestel. Although British Telecom was responding strategically by abandoning the common carrier approach and becoming the major service provider on Prestel, this did not push the slow growth of Prestel much further.

Télétel in France: The development of videotex in France has occurred as part of a larger movement to introduce new information technologies and services into that country. However, the videotex programme, known as Télétel, has been by far the most successful: at the end of 1988, there were over 4 million terminals in use.

The history of videotex in France has had four main periods: The first period witnessed the transformation of technological capabilities into a public policy. As early as 1971-73, researchers at the Centre national d'études des télécommunications (CNET), the public telecommunications laboratory, experimented with transmitting data over telephone lines. These experiments resulted in a device known as Tic-Tac and later in the setting up of a videotex standard, Antiope. Meanwhile, Direction Générale des Télécommunications (DGT) officials were concerned about finding new market opportunities for the domestic telecommunications industry, which was faced with a near-saturation of telephone equipment. In the beginning of 1978, the Nora/Minc report, which called on France to meet the IBM challenge and develop its own information-age infrastructure, helped create a political environment receptive to the lauching of affirmative industrial policies in this realm. The DGT proposed a plan to create an electronic telephone directory and to offer a "dumb" terminal free to every telephone user. This plan, which was intended to foster a strong French electronics industry, was officially endorsed by the government on December 6, 1978.

From 1978 to 1981 was the second phase, a time of experimentation. Several field trials were undertaken either under the sole responsibility of the DGT - as in Velizy - or in cooperation with local communities. During the preparation of these trials, it soon became clear that the DGT intended to develop, beyond a mere electronic directory, a nationwide information retrieval system. In response, newspaper publishers, fearful of a potential loss of advertising revenue to this emerging new medium, began to lobby against the videotex programme. Backed by some politicians and various social groups, this opposition opened a public debate over the social usefulness of videotex in the French society, which virtually blocked the Télétel programme on the eve of the 1981 presidential election.

The third period followed the election of a Socialist president and parliamentary majority. In an attempt to continue the industrial objectives of the videotex programme while managing any opposition to it, the new PTT minister adopted a compromise solution. The use of the electronic directory service would now be entirely voluntary. The local press and elected authorities would have to give their approval before service was begun in their region. Professional or community services would be given priority. The 1982 communication law was also favourable to the publishers by giving them a temporary monopoly on classified advertising in videotex services. By mid-1982, a more favorable climate allowed the DGT to take operational steps - especially the establishment of the kiosk function, explained below - to implement its Télétel system. In February 1983, the electronic directory made its debut.

The fourth period, which began around 1984, was marked by the take-off of videotex among the general public. The number of terminals grew from 90,000 in December 1983 to about half a million just one year later. The number of services increased regularly as well. Contrary to the expectations of the DGT, which initially stressed applications between man and machine, the services involving some modes of interpersonal communication, for instance electronic messaging, proved to be more popular. Today a videotex industry - information providers, consulting firms, equipment manufacturers, specialized publications, professional associations - has emerged in France. And its annual revenues are now above those of the French motion picture industry.

Several factors are responsible for the successful diffusion of videotex in France. The first are structural or environmental. Because of the DGT's monopoly, the development of videotex in France was not fragmented among numerous actors. Although the DGT had to cooperate with other partners, it was in the position of centralizing the design, implementation and regulation of videotex. Another factor that helped to structure a favourable response to videotex was the low number of personal computers (PCs) in France. This allowed the Minitel terminal, although a dumb one, to diffuse quickly while in other countries PCs served as the primary device to access videotex.

Other factors have to do with the strategy followed by the DGT. One of the unique elements of the Télétel programme was to associate the development of videotex with an end product, the electronic directory. This strategy permitted the administrative and political legitimation of the Télétel programme. Since the electronic directory was to rationalize an existing service, the

and were very sensitive to the importance of designing an effective communications infrastructure. In 1974 a commission was charged to investigate the improvement of German telecommunications. It recommended the introduction of several new telecommunications services, and suggested a "careful observation and promotion" of videotex technology. In reaction to this report the Bundespost decided to introduce a videotex system as a "means to increase the use of the already existing narrow-band telephone network".

However, Bildschirmtext development was not only influenced by a telecommunications rationality. Media policy makers engaged in a battle around the legal definition of BTX. The government explicitly stated in 1976 that Bildschirmtext should not be treated as broadcast communication but merely as a form of individual telecommunications. This definition had far-ranging consequences because it meant that the German *Länder* (federal states) would be excluded from any authority over this medium. In the German system of telecommunications, broadcasting and the printed press are regulated very differently. Telecommunications have always been a state monopoly, operated at the federal level. Following the Nazi period, the broadcasting system was reconstructed as a federalized one. The press is entirely market driven, with the state intervening only as a "watchdog".

Within this context the *Länder* and broadcasters perceived BTX as a Trojan horse in the public broadcasting domain. They feared that private market forces could use BTX as an instrument for tapping TV advertising. Conversely, the press viewed the defensive strategy of the broadcasters as an attempt to widen their regulatory responsibilities into the area of new forms of telecommunication.

The media policy aspect of Bildschirmtext also explained the great importance attributed to the public field trials, which took place in Berlin and Düsseldorf. Initially the DBP planned a short trial with the rather limited objective of gathering information about the public acceptance of BTX. Conflict with media policy makers led to a swelling of the scope and length of the trials. In the end they turned into a large-scale "technology assessment procedure" which cost the DBP more than 100 millions of DM. Although the decision to implement BTX was to be linked to positive results from the field trials, pressure from information providers and TV producers lead the government to introduce BTX in 1981 before the trials ended. The field tests, however, greatly influenced the legal regulation of the system.

The technical design of the BTX system was primarily determined by the DBP, although there had been much information exchange and accommodation of interest among the DBP, equipment manufacturers and information providers (in 1978 formal working groups had been established). The DBP was interested in a fully developed, workable version which would allow quick implementation of the service more than in any industrial policy considerations. In late 1981 IBM was given the commission to set up the national computer network instead of SEL, a traditional court supplier in telecommunications, which was offering a decentralized system. The disadvantage of the IBM concept is its overcomplexity and the relatively closed system architecture which makes gateways to the non-IBM computer world rather expensive.

As in Britain, the fact that TV sets were chosen as the main terminal excluded the DBP from the control of the terminal domain since the TV market was always exclusively private. Compared to France this had important implications. By providing only the infrastructure for BTX, the Bundespost had very limited instruments to "steer" the general development of BTX. It could influence the terminal provision only indirectly by financial support in research and development or by the licensing policy. The strategy of the Bundespost was to charge a big producer with the development of a highly integrated chip, the EUROM, which would be used by the biggest German TV manufacturer for large-scale production. Enormous economies of scale were expected to lead to cheap terminals. However, the complex standard and continuous modifications due to the international standardization process hampered this strategy. The chip producer had immense problems, and the Bundespost was forced to swap horses in the midst of the race. Only Loewe Opta, a medium-sized but highly innovative TV producer, made it possible that at least some CEPT-standard decoders were on the market for the official start of the system. Despite the heavy support of Bildschirmtext by the Bundespost, none of the initial goals were achieved. In 1986 there were only about 50,000 subscribers instead of the million which had been predicted in the early 1980's. The residential information market was virtually non-existent, although the whole BTX system initially had been tailored for this target group. Bildschirmtext, which had originally been thought of as a solution, became itself a problem. However, in contrast to the British, the Bundespost adapted its strategies upward and tried to give a second push to Bildschirmtext. First, it reoriented its marketing strategy toward the professional domain. Second, it entered the terminal market itself with the so-called Multitel, which could be rented for a reasonable fee. In taking these steps, the Bundespost might be able to reverse the trend of declining growth rates but the service is still behind the initial expectations.

2. The Role of the State in Videotex Development

The story of videotex in the various countries reveals some important differences with respect to the role of the state. While in the US videotex development was left to the marketplace and the state limited its role to regulating this technology - which it did in a restrictive way - in Western Europe and in Canada the state played a very active role. In these countries, the typical pattern of state intervention encompassed four main functions (besides the legal regulation of videotex, which is a sovereign prerogative of the state):

1. The state performed a planning function by creating the ideological - as opposed to material - conditions for videotex. In Canada, France and Germany, various governmental commissions or task forces underlined the strategic importance of videotex and helped to put the issue on the public agenda. In these countries, videotex was sold in the wrapping of national programmes aimed at restructuring parts of the economy.

2. The state also played an active role in supporting research and development activities through public research centers or subsidies. In Germany and Canada this can be explained by the willingness of public authorities to compensate private firms' reluctance to get into a risky and uncertain market. Therefore either a technological transfer from public centers to private entrepreneurs had to be organized, or private centers had to be subsidized.

3. A third task performed by the state concerned the launching and support of pilot trials. The trials were not only a substitute for market research of private firms which doubted the existence of a demand for videotex. They also were a means for the public authorities a) to legitimize the pertinence of going into videotex b) to pretend they were assessing the social impact of videotex. In most cases, this assessment was merely symbolic. But at least public authorities could show they were taking into account concerns from various groups and acting in the public interest.

4. A fourth function performed by the state is the promotion of videotex exportation. Through their representatives in international committees, such as the CCITT or the CEPT, public authorities tried to orient the definition of standards so as to benefit their domestic industry. In some instances, public authorities also supported experiments using their national technology or public relations campaigns in foreign countries.

However, despite this common pattern of state intervention with respect to the initiation of the development process of videotex, important national variations appear at the level of the practical implementation of videotex systems. The strategies followed to design and organize the Telidon, Prestel, BTX or Télétel systems differed sometimes radically. Different technical or policy options were chosen, especially with respect to two critical points: the conditions of information provision and those of terminal diffusion.

(i) In some countries public agencies supported the information industry in the offering of applications or services. This was especially the case in Canada, but also in West Germany the information providers received much public assistance. In France, the PTTs initially tried to coordinate government agencies' service provision - which was not very successful - and subsidized the development of applications by private firms, in particular a handful of newspapers. But eventually the information provision was entirely left to the private sector with the exception of the electronic directory. The B.P.O. first followed a common carrier approach and tried to stay out of the provision and regulation of information content. However, when growth problems emerged and Prestel met increasing competition from similar or identical private services, the B.P.O. and later BT started to get directly involved in information services.

In some countries, the PTTs were in charge of the storage of information. In Britain, the first country to confront the design of a nationwide system at a time when packet data switching facilities were not universally available, this occurred for technical reasons. In Germany, this was more a political decision, since there was the belief that private databases would favour the big, wealthy information providers and hamper pluralism and equity in access to information provision. In France, by contrast, information storage was left to private firms very early on. This seems surprising, given the French tradition of state centralization. It may be that the PTT officials found it more efficient, both technically and financially, to do it this way. As they were having difficulties developing the electronic directory database, they may have realized that they were not familiar enough with computers. Eventually, this decision proved to be very beneficial both in political and marketing terms.

(ii) In the terminal policy dramatic contrasts in state strategies appear between France and the other countries. In the latter, although the technical specifications were defined by the PTTs or public research centers, terminal provision was left to the marketplace. Following a completely different path, the French PTT gave terminals away free of charge to all telephone subscribers willing to take them. France was thus able to control the key elements of videotex development, whereas in other countries the PTTs were dependent on a number of other partners which they could only influence indirectly. Whether this diffusion strategy - which played a decisive role in creating a critical mass of videotex users - is a form of state subsidization or not will be discussed below.

The terminal concept had important implications. In Britain and Germany, the terminal policy was based on the use of the regular TV set as a monitor. It was believed that in this way it would be easier to reach a mass market. As TVs traditionally had been produced for the "private market" (as compared to public purchases), this implied a different relationship between PTT and the TV industry from that in telecommunications. In France, where dedicated, simple, compact terminals with integrated modems were developed, the PTT could apply its traditional terminal provision policy, which, moreover, was justified by the electronic directory project. Terminals were simply thought to replace the printed book.

How can we explain these differences in state involvement? As the previous section illustrates, the differences in the forms and degree of state intervention are linked both to technical and political factors. The initial technical options assigned the public authorities a specific role. These technical options were to some extent more determined by engineers' visions - what seemed feasible to them - than by philosophical stands - what the state should do. Eventually, numerous problems were experienced in implementing these technical options which again led to adjustments of the role of the state. There is no one single direction to these adaptations and they encompassed both more and less state intervention. For example, in the Prestel case, the exclusive centralized storage of information by BT was given up, but BT also got directly involved in information provision.

State involvement in videotex development was not only technology-driven, but also shaped by the institutional and social configurations of each country. The balance of power among private and public actors involved in videotex, the traditions and beliefs regarding the state's role as well changing conceptions about this role, the degree of bureaucratic fragmentation: all these factors structured the degree of freedom of state interventionism. For example, it was due to the German institutional structures that an agreement between the federal authorities and the *Länder* had to be worked out regarding the legal definition of videotex. In Britain, BT chose to implement a common carrier policy as a means "to get allies and to avoid enemies". In France, the bureaucratic rivalry between the DGT and TDF - the public agency in charge of broadcasting transmission - is one of the reasons that the option of the TV decoder was not favoured.

3. Are We Really Talking about the State?

Videotex projects in Europe were indeed initiated and to some extent governed by PTTs. But can we confuse PTTs - undoubtedly state-run organizations - with the state? In other words, did the PTTs, when developing videotex programmes, perform functions which are the proper domain of the state (the use of state privileges or sovereign prerogatives)? Or did they simply act as big public corporations with the benefits of a monopoly position?

This question can be examined from two perspectives. Seen from the side of objectives, European videotex programmes were clearly governed by an internal rationality of PTTs: the goal of increasing traffic revenues, the willingness to meet new and profitable needs in telecommunications services, the modernization of services in order to save money. Videotex programmes were conceived as a means for PTTs to grow or to survive as big corporations.

However, videotex programmes were also part of public policies aimed at various societal goals: protection or promotion of the domestic industry, provision of an infrastructure to enable people to take part in the information age, promotion of sovereignty (France and Canada) etc. These latter objectives may just have been rhethoric for PTTs. But even so, they gave videotex programmes a dimension extending beyond simple corporate strategies by legitimizing them in the name of the public or general interest.

A further perspective concerns implementation. As state agencies, the PTTs could avoid some problems in implementing their videotex programmes, whereas it would have been much more difficult for private firms. The telecommunications monopoly certainly helped the diffusion of videotex. On the one hand it did so by preventing the emergence of competing standards, and on the other by giving a national dimension to the systems. The amortization of research and development costs is generally approached in different ways by state agencies and private firms. The latter have to recoup their investments quite quickly, while the former may see an investment not just as an opportunity for immediate profit, but also, for example, as providing positive externalities to the whole society or to specific groups (the idea of technology transfer in the Canadian case). However, it should not be forgotten that most PTTs do have financial constraints, since their resources come from revenues and not from taxes. In the British case, Prestel's accounting unit was even turned into a profit center. This means that there was not state subsidization of videotex, although PTTs could take on their own revenues to help videotex development as an internal strategic option.

It is often asserted that the "free distribution of terminals" strategy - which was so instrumental in the growth of Télétel - indicates that videotex success is a consequence of state intervention. This has to be evaluated more carefully. First, the free distribution of terminals was only one element in the success of Télétel, which must be placed alongside such other choices as the early opening of gateways, the implementation of the kiosk system or the decentralized design of the Télétel network. Second, it is conceivable that this strategy could have been followed by any private big company bound to solve a chicken-and-egg dilemma in the market where it operates. Indeed, DGT officials claim that they do not subsidize Minitels and that they are acting as managers concerned about the revenues of their "company". There is a series of other historical examples of such a strategy: Kodak selling inexpensive cameras and reaping large profits from selling films; companies selling inexpensive shaving razors while earning large profits on razor blades; Rockefeller giving away free oil lamps and selling the oil. In this respect, state intervention is only one way to solve the chicken-and-egg dilemma or critical mass problem. Another way would be vertical integration and central coordination by a big private firm. If this pattern did not occur, it was because of restrictive regulations or because the big corporations did not expect a sufficient demand for videotex.

More crucial than the mere fact of state intervention is the "quality" of state intervention. The apparent success of videotex in France and its failure in other countries underline the importance of a central mechanism of coordination by which the different components of a videotex system (information services, network, terminals) are developed in a coherent and balanced way. Wherever one of the components fell back (generally because of a lack of control by a supervising authority), videotex experienced serious difficulties.

Modern states may well be best placed to perform this coordination function. Not only do they have the technical abilities, through their PTT agencies, to master the different components of a videotex system. They are the legitimate authorities which define the rules of the game, which in turn influence the resources and strategies that actors in a social system may use. They also have powerful legitimization capabilities to justify their policies. Morever, a state coordination may be preferred to a coordination by a big corporation because the state is an actor which is ostensibly politically accountable.

On the other hand, state coordination may be criticized for various reasons. By technically involving itself in information provision, the state gains potential control over information content. In France and Germany this potential danger raised important concerns and political conflicts, which were solved by the state's commitment to limit its role in information provision. Another argument against state coordination is the inability of state agencies to meet the actual demand or to adapt to unexpected usage patterns because of their rigid structures. Indeed, in most countries, PTTs made incorrect assumptions about users' needs.

There are now some hands-off attempts to achieve the coordination required for videotex to develop. In Britain, state regulatory agencies now limit their role to a few functions. They set the ground rules for fair competition and equality of access for existing and new service providers and promote the adoption of standards through which it becomes possible for different videotex services suppliers to interconnect their systems and run them across a variety of networks. It is hoped that the critical mass can be reached through the aggregation of smaller systems rather than through the development of a single, universal system. The problem here is whether this strategy can work in the context of fiercely competing economic actors whose previous success has been founded on the supply of incompatible proprietary solutions. In the US, there is currently a move to let the regional telephone companies perform, in their respective territories, the functions performed in Europe by the PTTs. The problem here is that these companies may be less public-minded than European PTTs and will be tempted to take unfair advantage of their central position. Of course, such activities can be controlled by government regulation. As the French say: *Quand on met l'état dehors par la porte, il revient par la fenêtre* (When one ushers the state out of the door, it returns through the window).

Bibliography

ARNOLD, Eric, and DANG-NGUYEN, Godefroy (1983), Videotex: Much a Do about Nothing?, in: SHARP, Margaret (ed.), *Europe and the New Technologies*. London: Frances Pinter.

AUMENTE, Jerome (1987), *New Electronic Pathways. Videotex, Teletext, and On-line Databases*. London and Beverly Hills: Sage.

BAER, Walter S., and GREENBERGER, Martin (1987), Consumer Electronic Publishing in the Competitive Environment, in: *Journal of Communication*, vol. 37, 1, Winter, 49-63.

BRUCE, Margaret (1986), *British Telecom's Prestel*. Open University Paper.

CANADIAN DEPARTMENT OF COMMUNICATIONS (1983), *1982-83 Annual Report*. Ottawa.

CHARON, Jean-Marie and VEDEL, Thiery (1988), *Videotex in France*, Unpublished Paper.

CIONI, Maria, and ASSOCIATES, Inc. (1985), *Understanding the Canadian Videotex Marketplace: Report on the Videotex Canada Meeting*. Toronto, March.

FEDIDA, Sam, and MALIK, Rex (1979), *Viewdata Revolution*. London: Associated Business Press.

FORESTER, Tom (1987), *High Tech Society: The Story of the Information Technology Revolution*. Oxford: Blackwell.

MADDEN, John (1979), *Videotex in Canada*. Ottawa: Supply and Services.

MARCHAND, Marie (1987), *La grande aventure du minitel*. Paris: Larousse.

MAYNTZ, Renate, and SCHNEIDER, Volker (1988), The Dynamics of Systems Development in a Comparative Perspective: Interactive Videotex in Germany, France and Britain, in: MAYNTZ, Renate, and HUGHES, Thomas P. (eds.) (1988), *The Development of Large Technical Systems*. Frankfurt: Campus, 263-298.

MOSCO, Vincent (1982), *Pushbutton Fantasies: Critical Perspectives on Videotex and Information Technology*. Norwood, NJ: Ablex.

NORA, Pierre and MINC, Alain (1978), *L'Information de la Société*. Paris: La Documentation Française.

PARKHILL, Douglas F. (1981), *The Telidon Story*. Address to the Rotary Club, Toronto (11 September).

SCHNEIDER, Volker (1989), *Technikentwicklung zwischen Politik und Markt: Der Fall Bildschirmtext*. Frankfurt: Campus.

SLOAN, Hugh J. III., and TALARZYK, W. Wayne (1988), *Videotex Project Reviews VI*. Columbus, OH: College of Business, Ohio State University.

THOMAS, Graham (1988), *Videotex in the UK: Opportunity Lost or Diversity Gained?* Unpublished Paper.

TYDEMAN, John et al. (1982), *Teletext and Videotex in the United States: Market Potential, Technology, Public Policy Issues*. New York: McGraw-Hill.

VIDEOTEX: REDISCOVERING ITS NICHE (1988), *Broadcasting*, (20 June), 72-73.

Part III

Large Internal Markets and the Role of the State: Is there a Need for Policies on Techno-Industrial Innovation?

8

Airbus Industrie
A Case Study in European High Technology Cooperation

Desmond Hickie

Airbus Industrie is an international cooperative venture whose aim is to provide the research, design, development, production, marketing, sales and after-sales services necessary to produce commercially successful airliners. Its member companies are: Aerospatiale, the French state-owned aerospace company; Messerschmitt-Bölkow-Blohm, the privately-owned German aerospace company, *via* its wholly-owned subsidiary Deutsche Airbus; British Aerospace, the privatised British aerospace company; and Construcciones Aeronautics SA(CASA), the predominantly state-owned Spanish aerospace manufacturer. In addition Airbus Industrie has two associate members: Fokker, the Dutch privately-owned aircraft manufacturer; and Belairbus, a consortium of Belgian aeronautical and other industrial interests, established specifically to play a part in Airbus projects. Presently Airbus Industrie has three aircraft in production: the A300, a twin-isle medium-range aircraft capable, typically, of carrying 267 passengers in its latest variant, the A300-600; the A310, a somewhat smaller twin-isle, medium-range aircraft capable, typically, of carrying 219 passengers; and the A320 a short-to medium-range airliner capable, typically, of carrying 150 passengers. In June 1987 two further development projects were formally launched: the A330, a twin-engined, medium-range aircraft, to be capable of carrying 328 passengers; and the A340, a four-engined, very long-range aircraft to be capable of carrying 262 to 295 passengers.

1. The World Market for Airliners

The world's three major manufacturers of airliners, Airbus Industrie, McDonnell Douglas and Boeing, all estimate that demand will be buoyant over the next two decades. Airbus Industrie itself estimates that between 1986 and 2005 the market for airliners with over 100 seats will be worth $403 billion (Airbus Industrie). Boeing and McDonnell Douglas make estimates of $220 billion and $280 billion, respectively, for world airliner sales in the period up to the year 2000. Yet even their more conservative views represent a major increase in demand, due both to traffic growth and to airline fleet replacement. Airbus Industrie's aim is a 30% market share (Financial Times, 6 September 1987). This target is a most ambitious one, given the post-war history of the European civil aircraft industry. It is also risk-laden, given the very nature of aircraft design and of the civil market it serves. Richard Welch of Boeing was not exaggerating when he claimed that,

> the risks are greater in this business than in any other compared to the returns. (Quoted in Newhouse 1982)

The aircraft industry is one in which costly outlay on very expensive, advanced, R&D is essential to a manufacturer's success in producing any but the most basic products. A large modern aircraft must incorporate the fruits of R&D work in a wide range of technologies, notably aerodynamics, materials science, jet engines and avionics. New product development and the exacting safety standards demanded of modern aircraft both necessitate it. To sell, an aircraft must not only be offered at a sufficiently low price. It must also be attractive to passengers and economical to operate. Such advantages are derived primarily from the aircraft's technical features, in particular its structure weight, payload, range, cruising speed, fuel economy, potential utilisation rate and likely maintenance costs. They are the product of advanced R&D.

This R&D imposes enormous technical and financial burdens upon the firms concerned. Vast amounts of capital have to be invested and large technical staffs maintained in order to develop a sizeable airliner. It has been estimated that $2,000 million was spent developing the A320 between 1983 and 1988. Where practicable, firms seek to reduce such costs by developing new variants of existing models to meet new market needs, or by using structural elements of an existing model in a new aircraft. Such approaches can significantly reduce R&D costs and the risks of technical failure as in the case of the A310, which cost about $1,000 million to develop and which had elements in common with the A300.

Yet it is not the supply of the high level of investment that causes a major financial problem for aircraft manufacturers. As aircraft have grown larger and more complex, so the lead times taken to develop them have tended to lengthen. Airbus projects have generally taken about five years to develop, fast by European standards. To heavy R&D expenditure during this period must be added the high cost of tooling up with advanced production equipment to build the aircraft concerned. Thus the aircraft manufacturer is expected to invest very heavily over a period of five or more years in non-recurring costs before a new aircraft comes into production. It may take a further five to ten years before the cash flow produced by that aircraft becomes positive, even if the aeroplane proves to be a reasonable commercial success. So, when undertaking the development of a new aircraft, the manufacturer embarks upon a project of great technical complexity the non-recurring costs of which are quite likely to be greater than the capitalisation of the whole company, and which may take a decade or more to begin to produce a return on the investment.

As if these essentially supply side problems were not enough the demand for airliners has shown itself to be unstable and unpredictable over a number of decades. This is in part because the airlines face instability and unpredictability in the demand for their services. Air traffic is highly cyclical, fluctuating with levels of activity both in national economies and the international economy. Furthermore it can be affected by unanticipated political events such as outbreaks of war or terrorism. Since the late 1970s the airlines, especially the American domestic airlines which are operating in a climate of deregulation and cost-cutting, have come to take a somewhat more cautious view of their aircraft purchases. Hard bargains have been driven on price, and aircraft manufacturers have had to time the entry of their new products into the market-place very precisely to match fleet replacement decisions.

From a specifically European viewpoint the world civil aircraft market since the 1950s has come to look even more difficult, because it has been dominated by a handful of American manufacturers. In 1970, when Airbus Industrie was created, the American share of the world commercial aircraft market was 94% (Airbus Industrie 1986) and that share was dominated by Boeing, McDonnell Douglas and Lockheed. Even since Airbus Industrie's entry into the market (and Lockheed's decision to leave it) American manufacturers remain paramount. As James Worsham of McDonnell Douglas commented recently.

> Over the past five years Boeing has averaged 56%, Douglas 25% and Airbus 15% of total world orders. (Quoted in Airbus Industrie)

The American aircraft industry came to this happy position primarily because of the vast size of its domestic air traffic, which by 1960 amounted to about 60% of all the world's air traffic. By contrast the EEC market into which Airbus Industrie sells, not all of which can be regarded as domestic because some EEC manufacturers are involved in rival projects, amounts presently to about 18% of world demand for civil transport aircraft (EEC 1975). The consequence of the huge American market has been that American aircraft manufacturers have had a large and loyal domestic market into which to sell their airliners. Their position has been further aided by government military expenditure which has been used directly or indirectly to cross-subsidise civil projects at strategic junctures in the industry's development. In addition until 1980 imports of foreign airliners were inhibited by tariff barriers. As a consequence leading American aircraft manufacturers have been able to use their huge domestic market as a secure base from which to dominate the world market. They have used large early orders from domestic airlines to cover non-recurring R&D tooling costs and to learn how to build the aircraft more economically. This has enabled them to produce and sell further aircraft more cheaply in export markets ("off the thin end of the learning curve").

Why then do European aircraft manufacturers not concentrate solely on military work? The answer lies partly in the growing financial stringency that has come to affect military aviation as well as civil aviation. Governments have sought increasingly to upgrade their air forces by improving the armament and avionics of existing aircraft rather than embark on the huge expenditures necessary to develop new aircraft. It also lies in the manufacturers' belief in the buoyancy of the civil market in the next twenty years. Though the industry has shown a repeated tendency to over-optimism, there are some good grounds for the manufacturers' confidence in future demand. Ageing fleets must be replaced and air traffic continues to grow, notably in markets, such as the Middle East, outside the American home market. Major aerospace companies also wish to produce a varied range of products. Financially it enables a company to use the funds generated by mature projects delivering positive cash flow to provide some of the funds necessary to pay for the non-recurring costs on new projects that will go into production several years hence. Having a wide variety of projects in varying stages of maturity also enables companies to move staff from project to project as work ebbs and flows, so that experienced teams can be kept together and a cross-fertilisation of ideas can occur between projects (interviews). Finally, aerospace companies have continued to participate in civil work because they have been encouraged to do so by their parent governments.

2. Airliner Development and the State

Since 1945, as non-recurring costs have risen, government funding of airliner developments has come to assume greater significance. Financial support takes a number of forms, in particular subsidies for research and development to be refunded by a levy on sales (e.g. launch aid in Britain, *advances reimbursables* in France), loan guarantees and export credits. Aerospatiale has all its non-Airbus R&D state funded as well as 95% of its development work for Airbus Industrie. CASA is similarly supported in Spain (Pearce 1985). In Germany the aircraft industry receives considerable support by way of risk capital and loan guarantees from both the federal and *Länder* governments (Hayward 1986). The Thatcher Government has effectively revived the practice of paying launch aid to assist civil projects in Britain after a decade or so when the policy had fallen into disuse. Despite this, however, the British Government, among the Airbus partners, has generally been the least willing to support civil aircraft developments, for example being prepared to fund only 250 million pounds of British Aerospace's share of the A320 launch, expecting that the other 600 million pounds would be provided by the City (Hayward 1986). This compares, for example, with 80% state funding of Deutsche Airbus share. However all the Airbus partner governments are concerned about the vast sums involved and about the likelihood of their ever seeing a reasonable financial return on the investment.

Aircraft manufacturers' airliner work in Europe, as in the United States, also benefits from the far greater volumes of money spent with these companies on military R&D which can have direct spin-offs for their civil work and provide capital equipment for the companies concerned. For example, Lockheed's work on the C5A Galaxy assisted its work on the Tri-Star (Hayward 1986). Civil aircraft manufacturers benefit from the military research work done by the various aeronautical research establishments maintained by their governments (e.g. the Royal Aircraft Establishment in Britain or ONERA in France), which sometimes has civil uses. In any event these establishments will also undertake specifically civil work, though in Britain this may sometimes have to be paid for by the manufacturer.

Governments provide tax benefits, such as favourable depreciation terms, to encourage national airlines to re-equip regularly with home-produced aircraft. Political pressures are also sometimes applied to such airlines, and even to the airlines of client states, in order to make them buy particular aircraft. More positive inducements can be provided to assist overseas sales, such as export credits and loan guarantees from government agencies such as the US Export-Import Bank or the British Export Credit and Guarantee Department. Such subsidies have risen to prominence in the mid-1980s with charges from Boeing and the US government that Airbus Industrie subsidies are in defiance of GATT agreements and counter charges that Boeing engages in predatory pricing (interviews).

Why have governments been willing to play so active and expensive a role in the civil aircraft industry? Partly because strategic purposes are served by the maintenance of a sizeable aviation industry with varied capacities, but also because it is seen as,

> ... an industry built around the technologies upon which much economic growth and strength is judged to depend. (Newhouse 1982)

Governments perceive the industry as a "technological spear-head" which will foster the development of allied high technology industries in fields such as electronics, metallurgy, composite materials, and advanced manufacturing systems (Airbus Industrie 1987). To a lesser extent it may lead to the direct spin-off of particular products. The aircraft industry is also a major employer. It employs 200,000 in Britain, 128,000 in France and 71,000 in West Germany. Furthermore it trains and employs a highly skilled and generally well-paid labour force. The industry also yields high added value to any imported raw materials it uses and potentially can export a high proportion of its production, giving it a particular significance to the balance of payments. Thus by the end of June 1987 Airbus Industrie had exported 76% of its A300s and A310s to airlines outside its six "domestic" markets (Airbus Industrie 1987). For the United States government and for Western European governments civil aircraft are also one of the few engineering products in which their domestic industries can compete on more than equal terms against Far Eastern producers. For the European governments supporting Airbus Industrie it also provides a means of avoiding dependence upon an American duopoly, Boeing and McDonnell Douglas.

There are also a number of more purely political reasons why aviation has constantly managed to attract government attention and support. Notably, in both Britain and France the aircraft industry is one of the most powerful industrial lobbies in the country, perhaps second only to agriculture in its effectiveness. Part of that effectiveness lies in its close working relations with government over a period of seventy or more years. Structures have developed both in the industry and in government to foster this relationship and a strong aviation community has developed, spanning government and industry, in both countries. Presently the Air Division of Britain's Department of Trade and Industry is the only industry specific division within the department dedicated to a particular industry. Furthermore the aircraft industry over a period of decades has fostered good public relations to enhance the visibility of its products which have often been seen as symbols of national ingenuity, and prestige. As a consequence the industry has managed to generate a good deal of public and political support. In Britain this "air-mindedness" remains but has ebbed markedly since the 1950s. Indeed most Britons probably do not realise that Airbus aircraft are part-British. In France it remains much stronger not least, perhaps, because it is tinged with an element of anti-Americanism. It should be stressed, however, that governmental willingness to aid the aircraft industry does not necessarily imply exclusive loyalty to a particular project. Governments have shown themselves quite willing to support rival projects, the most notorious case being the British government's support of both British Aerospace participation in the A310 and Rolls Royce's building of the launch engine for the Boeing 757.

3. National Concentration and International Collaboration in the European Civil Aircraft Industry

The major European aerospace companies have felt it necessary to their survival as major participants in the aviation industry world-wide that they continue to design and build major airliners. Their government sponsors have been willing to accept this judgement and to support them. However, since the introduction of jet airliners into service in the 1950s, the rising costs of developing new airliners, the risks involved, and the threat of severe American competition have led both firms and governments to participate in the creation of larger industrial formations. It is intended that such formations should have the financial, human and physical capital necessary to undertake large, technically complex projects; should be able to spread the risks inherent in such undertakings over a range of projects, amongst a number of collaborators, or both; and should be able to withstand American competition. Their creation has also been necessitated by rising costs in military aviation. For governments industrial concentration allows financial support to be concentrated on a smaller number of firms and projects, which is essential given the steep rises in developmental costs. The consequence of these pressures has been a tendency for national concentration and international collaboration amongst the major European aircraft manufacturers.

It should not be thought, however, that cooperation with other firms is a recent phenomenon for aircraft manufacturers. It has been part of the industry since its inception. Aircraft manufacturing is in large part an assembly-based industry. The manufacturer traditionally has designed and built the airframe but has usually bought in the greater part of the equipment that makes the aircraft a functioning entity. It was less common to find an aircraft manufacturer subcontracting design work on an airframe to a rival company, but it did occur, even internationally. For example, Sud Aviation and De Havilland cooperated on the design of the Caravelle nose and flight-deck. More common was building under licence, as when Sud Aviation built the De Havilland Vampire as the Aquilon in the 1950s. Clearly such cooperation has its advantages. Buying in specialist equipment allows the aircraft manufacturer to draw upon the expertise and production facilities of its suppliers. The subcontracting of airframe design work allows a firm to draw on the specialist expertise of other design teams, or to delegate detailed design work when its own design resources are fully occupied. Similarly building under licence allows a manufacturer to expand the production of an aircraft without the costs and risks entailed in expanding its own production facilities.

Although the various, rather loose and *ad hoc* forms of cooperation that existed amongst Europe's aircraft manufacturers did yield tangible benefits, it was becoming clear by the mid-1950s that in Britain and France a major process of industrial concentration was needed to reap the benefits outlined above. In 1959 Britain had almost twenty design teams. The government was prepared to assist only two of them. "Shot-gun marriages" were arranged to form two major airframe manufacturers,

cal security that purely domestic projects may not do. Once agreed upon they are more secure because they tend to be seen not simply as commercial matters but as expressions of international harmony. Thus it becomes very difficult for a single government to withdraw from a collaborative project without incurring the wrath of its partner governments.

International collaboration, then, offers a range of potential financial, commercial, technical and political advantages. To understand its growing popularity with European governments over the past quarter of a century or so one needs also to appreciate that it does not require firms to merge and sacrifice their organisational independence. Major aircraft manufacturers will strive where possible to retain a capacity for design leadership wherever they can. Thus British Aerospace are design leaders on the small BAe 146 airliner despite extensive subcontracting at home and overseas. Even Boeing requires extensive international subcontractor support. But Boeing is large and powerful enough to retain design leadership even on major projects. Despite the belief of M. Chanut, a former Vice President of Airbus Industrie, that

> ... the old concept of a dominant manufacturer, who retains full initiative, can be exceeded in efficiency by real "cooperative ventures". (Chanut 1985)

shared control over design becomes desirable only when individual control becomes untenable. Similarly the desire of firms to maximise their input into and control over the design process influences their choice of partners when choosing collaboration. Thus British Aerospace preferred to join the A310 project as a partner, than to join the Boeing 757 project as a risk-bearing subcontractor. For smaller manufacturers, such as CASA or MBB, with little or no experience of independent design or production, full collaboration rather than subcontracting offers an obvious opportunity to broaden the company's technical base and to learn from the experience of larger partners (interview).

International collaboration, whilst retaining firms' independence, enables governments to ensure that the ownership and control of these economically and strategically vital companies remains in domestic hands. Governments support their aircraft industries in pursuit of national goals. Therefore, like the firms, they wish to see national capacities to design and build aircraft maximised so that *ceteris paribus* they are likely to prefer collaboration with equals, rather than subcontracting. In these circumstances international joint ventures offer a further major advantage over international mergers to form transnational companies. Governments may support a range of collaborative projects in order to benefit different parts of their aviation industries, as the British government supports British Aerospace's commitment to the A320 and Rolls Royce's to the 757. Each enables its participant company to maximise its own design and production skills. International collaboration, then, is a means of pursuing national goals when more independent means of so doing are unavailable.

The creation and development of Airbus Industrie must be seen in this light. In October 1966 Hawker Siddeley, a German consortium (of MBB, VFW and Dornier) and Sud Aviation made a joint application for government financial support to build a medium-range airliner (Newhouse 1982). On the basis of a 267-seater outline design, the A300B, a memorandum of understanding was signed by the three governments in September 1967 which stated that the aircraft would use Rolls Royce RB207 engines. However, in the months that followed the design concept changed to the extent that the British government became disenchanted with it, in particular because it was not suited to the RB207 and because there was the prospect of a not dissimilar, wholly British, airliner project, the BAC 3-11 (Newhouse 1982). As a consequence it withdrew from the Airbus project in April 1969, leaving the French and German governments formally to launch the A300B with a new memorandum of understanding the following month. Hawker Siddeley remained associated with the A300B project in its private capacity, being contracted to design and build the wings. The joint German-Dutch aircraft manufacturer VFW-Fokker joined the project in November 1969 with the support of the Netherlands government. The German companies formed themselves into a jointly owned company, Deutsche Airbus, to channel and manage their participation in it, though Dornier withdrew in the autumn of 1970. In 1970 the Spanish aircraft manufacturer CASA joined Airbus industries as a full member.

The A300B project developed quickly, certainly by European standards. It flew in October 1972 and entered service with Air France in May 1974. Sales of the aircraft were sluggish at first but began to rise rapidly in 1978. At this time potential purchasers indicated that there would be a demand for a slightly smaller aircraft, generally compatible with the A300 (Airbus had by now reverted to their original name for the aircraft), but more economical to run and incoroporating the latest technical advances. This project, called the A310, was launched by the German and French governments in July 1978. Meanwhile British Aerospace, into which Hawker Siddeley had been absorbed, was keen to participate in the A310 project, despite blandishments from Boeing to become a major subcontractor on their 757 airliner project. The British Labour government was keen to support British Aerospace, which was its own recent creation, and so agreed to provide 100 million pounds loan capital and a 25 million pound payment to Airbus Industrie for work in progress, that enabled British Aerospace to join Airbus Industrie as a full member in September 1978 (Hayward 1986).

4. Airbus Industrie Organisation

Airbus Industrie, then, was a commercial and political response to a range of economic and technological pressures that would have driven Europe's aircraft manufacturers from the world civil market had they not been prepared to enter into some form of close international collaboration. Yet international collaboration in aircraft projects is not an unalloyed good. It raises its own problems which, it has been estimated, can increase the development costs of a project by 50% compared to those of a similar project conducted by a single company (Farrer and Balthazor 1981). It has been estimated that Boeing's costs are 30% lower than Airbus Industrie's (Sunday Times, 2 March 1986) though, if this is true, it may be as much the product of Boeing's great economies of scale as Airbus diseconomies of collaboration. Some of these cost-raising problems are largely unavoidable, being intrinsic to the collaborative process. In particular a high level of agreement is necessary amongst partners, firms and governments. A clear and mutually satisfactory project definition must be arrived at, so that all parties are clear what kind of aircraft they are designing. Any such definition must be a compromise that meets both the essential requirements of the partners and be attractive to potential airline purchasers. Equally the partners must agree to a division of labour between themselves so that each is responsible for discrete elements of the project. This can be a highly contentious matter as the different parts of an aircraft offer different potential levels of profitability and imply different degrees and facets of design leadership for the partners that undertake them.

Agreement upon these complex and potentially contentious matters can delay the start of a new project and involve compromises to the detriment of economy and good design. Currency fluctuations can also do great damage to collaborative projects. Such projects almost inevitably use US dollars for inter-company payments. Serious problems arise where domestic currencies, in which partners pay most of their bills, fluctuate against the dollar. More prosaic factors, such as travel costs and administrative costs, also edge up the price of collaborative work. Other potential costs of collaboration may be more avoidable. In particular partners need to hold in check the ever-presentHtendency to duplicate activities. It can be a clear advantage of collaboration that partners undertake their own design studies and marketing feasibility studies. Different approaches can be tested against one another. At the same time partner companies must be aware that this greater certainty is bought at a price. Of even greater significance is the avoidance of duplication at the point of production. If collaborating companies can agree to produce a standardised aircraft (rather than a range of variants) and to use a single assembly line, then economies of scale can be achieved that would not be possible otherwise.

Obviously collaboration must be organised so as to minimise its likely problems and to maximise its potential benefits. How successful has Airbus Industrie been in this regard? It was not possible for the Airbus partners to use a jointly-owned public limited company, to create an authoritative management structure for the projects. In inter-firm international collaboration such companies are primarily management organisations having a relatively small, purely nominal capital base, provided by the project partners. Given their limited liability this would mean that an airline buying aircraft from such a company would have no effective legal recourse should it fail to deliver an aircraft built to specification and on time. To avoid this problem a structure without limited liability is necessary (Betaille 1976).

As an alternative the partners looked to a legal and organisational device created in French law in 1967, the *Groupement d'Interet Economique* (GIE). This form of organisation is a body corporate set up by a number of members, usually companies, who wish to work together to achieve a limited number of agreed commercial objectives whilst the remainder of their activities remain independent. The members do not need to provide large amounts of capital to set up the GIE and are only committed to it within the agreed objectives, but within those objectives each member is responsible to the entire extent of its assets for any contractual default by the GIE or its members. For airlines purchasing aircraft from Airbus Industrie this means that their contracts are guaranteed by the assets of all of the partner companies. Providing that its objectives and functions are sufficiently clear, the GIE can give a project a central management organisation capable of acting as an arbiter and as a decision-maker if the partner companies are unable to agree about aspects of the implementation of the project. Of particular importance so far as Airbus Industrie is concerned, the GIE enables the partner companies to present the customer with a single point of contact for marketing, sales and after-sales services. This is very important because airliners have to be marketed and sold vigorously to potential purchasers, who much prefer dealing with a single point of contact than with a number of partner companies individually. Similarly, any prospective purchaser will want there to be a single, efficient spares organisation and not have to deal with each partner separately for particular spares. For all these reasons Airbus Industrie was incorporated as a GIE in December 1970 (Airbus Industrie Briefing 1986).

Formal control of Airbus Industrie is vested in a General Meeting of Members whose decisions require an 81% majority, giving all the full members except CASA a veto over its decisions. More regular accountability is exercised by a Supervisory Board of 17 very senior executives from the partner companies (6 from Aerospatiale, 6 from Deutsche Airbus, 4 from British Aerospace, and 1 from CASA) whose chairman was, until his death in October 1988, the former Federal German Minister Franz-Josef Strauss. This board meets twice a year to receive reports on Airbus Industrie activities from its President and Chief Executive, Jean Pierson, who manages the organisation on a day-to-day basis. The Supervisory Board's role is, by and large, a rather formal one. It has to agree to major shifts in Airbus Industrie policy, to changes in its internal organisation, to the commencement of new projects and to the appointment of senior executives. More regular scrutiny of Airbus is maintained by an Executive Commitee consisting of seven senior managers from the partner companies who meet monthly to consider important matters concerning the management of Airbus Industrie's programme of work (Airbus Industrie Briefing 1986; Hayward 1986). The functions of the Executive Committee, essentially, are threefold. Most importantly it has to prepare the ground for the major decisions for which final approval must be given by the Supervisory Board. It must develop policy proposals that represent a view acceptable to each of their companies and which, therefore, will receive unanimous support at the Supervisory Board. Secondly, in pursuit of the programmes agreed by the Supervisory Board, the Executive Committee takes a range of important policy decisions of its own, notably agreeing the precise shares of work amongst the partners. Finally the Executive Committee itself acts as a formal authority approving decisions already agreed below by two more junior committees, the Programme Directors Committee and the Finance Committee. Each Airbus partner has a manager appointed in the role of a programme director to maintain day-to-day control over its participation in the Airbus projects. These managers meet at Toulouse as frequently as is necessary to ensure that the partners' production and development work is fully coordinated. The Finance Committee meets somewhat less frequently, dealing with matters such as Airbus/partner financial transactions.

The role of Airbus Industrie's partners as owners of the GIE, to whom it is responsible, only explains one-half of their relationship with the organisation. In terms of the design and production work they carry out on Airbus Industrie's behalf they are like subcontractors, carrying out work according to Airbus Industrie's specifications and under its managerial supervision. Thus the partners are responsible to Airbus Industrie management for the work that they do on its behalf. Once the Supervisory Board has determined Airbus Industrie's policy on a particular matter the organisation's managers have the authority to take the decisions necessary to execute that policy. This helps to expedite decision-making and gives Airbus managers a degree of influence over the work done by partner companies on behalf of Airbus.

As might be expected with so large an international project which makes major demands upon public funds, an intergovernmental structure has been established to monitor the work of Airbus Industrie. FormalHapproval for changes in the intergovernmental agreements concerning Airbus Industrie are made at Ministerial Meetings. This ministerial level of meetings has, in the past, been largely about formalities, but over recent years ministers have begun to meet more frequently and to conduct their meetings in a more business-like way. This reflects increasing government concern about the Airbus programme as it has grown and required larger injections of public funds. It has also reflected growing concern about the adverse effect of American aircraft manufacturers' complaints about Airbus subsidies on EEC/US trading relations. Nevertheless, despite this growth in ministerial activity, more regular monitoring activities and negotiations occur at three official levels which run in parallel with Airbus Industrie's own structure, monitoring its activities with a particular eye upon their significance for intergovernmental issues. The most senior official level of scrutiny is the Airbus Intergovernmental Committee, which is made up of the senior civil servants who are the heads of the Air Divisions of their respective ministries. Formally the committee meets twice a year to review the progress of the Airbus programme but in practice (like the Ministerial Committee) it has come to meet much more often. The Intergovernmental Committee formally acts in an advisory capacity to ministers, giving its views on matters such as the desirability of launching new projects and the line to be taken regarding Airbus in EEC/US discussions about trade policy. In practice, however, policy-making is the concern of only a handful of ministers and senior officials in each member government who are in daily contact with one another, so that it becomes difficult to discern precisely where decisions are taken. Below this is an Airbus Executive Committee of somewhat more junior officials from the same departments which meets on a monthly basis to monitor the more detailed implementation of the Airbus programme as it relates to member governments. For example it deals with the matters arising from government involvement in Airbus sales campaigns, such as agreements about the levels of export credits to be paid by the various member governments. Finally there is the Airbus Executive Agency, located in Paris, which conducts the day-to-day technical monitoring of the programme and so services the three intergovernmental monitoring committees. It is small, consisting of one civil servant from each government (interviews; Hayward 1986).

There is a feeling that the French government is more closely involved with Airbus than the other member governments. Certainly, French civil servants and politicians, even the President, have been much more closely involved in Airbus sales campaigns than have their British, German or Spanish counterparts. In part this no doubt reflects the stronger French feeling of national ownership of Airbus projects than is felt elsewhere. The Airbus is assembled at Toulouse. It reflects, too, the French government's highly supportive attitude towards aerospace in general. At one point the Thatcher government came close to regarding itself merely as a banker who, having ensured that its launch aid was invested on secure terms, had no particular need to monitor progress on the projects.

Such an attitude would have been unthinkable in France. To appreciate fully French attitudes towards Airbus one needs also to appreciate the structure of the French aircraft industry, the nature of industrial policy in France and the relationship between governmental and industrial elites in France. Aerospatiale is a nationalised company and the French government over four decades has been committed to a system of sectoral planning for industry. As a consequence there has been a series of national plans for the development of French aviation. For both these reasons French ministers and officials have been committed to playing an active role in the industry's development. ONERA has a duty to work closely with Aerospatiale, rather more closely than British Aerospace works with the Royal Aircraft Establishment. Finally one needs to understand that many of the senior French figures involved in Airbus have been *poly-*

technicians familiar with the upper reaches of French government. They are rather more than simply businessmen or engineers by training (interviews).

To understand adequately how the Airbus Industrie management system works one needs to understand not only its formal structure, but also how Airbus collaboration functions at certain key stages in the design and production process. The decision to launch a new Airbus requires judgements to be made about market conditions, the outline design of the aircraft, and the availability of finance. The Airbus marketing approach has been to look for opportunities world-wide, not just in Europe, and to seek market niches that are not adequately filled. To discover such niches Airbus Industrie does its own market surveys, but so also do its partner companies. The British, French and German governments each supplement this research with in-house expertise of their own. The outline design of an aircraft to meet a perceived market opportunity is also a shared process. Airbus Industrie has its own conceptual capability to draw up in outline what an aircraft might look like to meet a particular requirement. This can be augmented by design staff from member companies, who additionally undertake their own design studies. At this pre-project phase design ideas can compete against one another and influence one another, until a point is reached when the members of the Executive Committee feel that they, and the companies they represent, have confidence both in their market forecasts and their outline design. At this point they then go to the Supervisory Board to seek formal approval (interview). The result of this process of project definition has been generally successful in that the A300, A310 and A320 have managed to establish themselves in the market-place. However, it has sometimes taken rather too long to reach agreement amongst the partners (interview).

A project approved by the Supervisory Board requires financial support necessary to cover its non-recurring costs. This is most significantly a matter for governments, for though the partner companies may raise capital from profits and from banks, no project can proceed without public funding. Such funding is not paid by national governments to Airbus Industrie. It is paid by them to their domestic partner company to participate in a particular Airbus project. The member companies do not wait until they have reached an agreement before approaching their governments. Rather they begin the process of negotiation in a tentative way several years ahead of the formal agreement to proceed. The size and the repayment terms of the financial support given to the companies varies according to national policies. The decision to provide governmental support for a project comes after time-consuming discussions at the Airbus Intergovernmental Committee and often after discussions not only in the Ministerial Meeting, but at Head of Government level. Finally each national government must make its own decision to commit its funds and this requires Cabinet-level approval.

The division of work on a project amongst the partner companies is clearly a matter of great significance, both in terms of its financial consequences and for the development of design skills. Broadly the design of an aircraft consists of two elements: the specific design of particular parts of the airframe; and the non-specific design of various aspects of the structure of the whole airframe (e.g. its aerodynamics, its structural loading). As Airbus Industrie has matured there has been a tendency for particular partners to specialise in particular areas of specific design and in associated areas of non-specific design. Thus British Aerospace has specialised in wing design and aerodynamics, whilst Aerospatiale is, *inter alia*, responsible for the cockpit, electronics and flying controls and of the aircraft. Other partners and associate companies can put forward their ideas about areas of design for which they are not specifically responsible, but there is now a very strong tendency for major parts of the airframes of successive Airbuses to be designed by the same partner. The total work on a project must be divided up between the partners and associates in accordance with the intergovernmental agreement covering that particular aircraft. However it is not only the value of the design work that is important to governments concerned with the health of their aircraft industries. It is also important to assess the extent to which that work will extend the company's design capability. Thus it may be argued that, although British Aerospace has a smaller share of the A320, they may well gain more in terms of developing the company's design capability than does MBB with a significantly larger share. British Aerospace has responsibility for the wings and thus for the aircraft's aerodynamics. MBB has responsibility for the fuselage and thus for cabin interiors and passenger comfort. The tendency to specialisation amongst the Airbus partners is, therefore, something of a two-edged sword. It builds on the proven expertise and experience of British Aerospace and Aerospatiale, but that does not necessarily broaden the design expertise of MBB or CASA very greatly. Equally it may be that specialisation will, over a period, gradually lead to a decrease in the pooling of ideas early on in the design process, so that mutual learning declines. So far as the aircraft as a whole is concerned, Airbus Industrie remains responsible for the design concept of the aircraft and is empowered in theory to take decisions as to what design will be followed when there is disagreement among the partners (Airbus Industrie Briefing 1986; Chanut 1985). Final assembly takes place in Toulouse but is worth only about 4% of the total value of production work, as subassemblies are completed so far as possible by the partner companies. British Aerospace would have liked to acquire the final assembly work for the A320 but its fellow partners resisted, regarding this as the thin end of a wedge which would result in a loss of specialisation and a good deal more in-fighting as each new project was embarked upon (Hayward 1986).

All aspects of customer relations in a cooperative civil aircraft project like the Airbus must be handled by a single organisation in order to give the customer a single point of contact. Thus Airbus Industrie handles all aspects of marketing, sales, contracting, spares services and crew training, itself. As has been indicated above the governmental role in marketing Airbus projects varies somewhat from government to government. Whilst all the member governments contribute financially by way of export credits, the British government tends to leave customer relations to Airbus Industrie and to British Aerospace, on the grounds that they know best. However the French government has been far more interventionist using diplomatic contacts, even at Presidential level, to assist the sales process. After-sales services are left entirely to Airbus Industrie.

The Airbus Industrie system of management has been an effective one in that it has enabled the partner companies to work together in relative harmony over a period of about two decades and to develop and build what will become a family of Airbus aircraft when the A330 and A340 are in production. Yet in recent times serious dissatisfaction can be discerned both amongst partner companies, notably British Aerospace, and sponsor governments regarding the efficiency of Airbus Industrie. The search for economy is bringing the organisation's management system under closer scrutiny. In particular the Airbus structure provides for a certain ambiguity. A great deal of control is vested in committees whose members are both shareholders and subcontractors. Whilst this has allowed the intercompany collaboration to develop and grow in an atmosphere of trust, because member companies can exercise an effective veto over major decisions that they do not like, it also implies a duality of interests amongst company representatives that may sit uneasily together. Equally, under current Airbus Industrie practice, the consortium's accounts are restricted to sales and servicing matters. Partners do not have access to the data necessary to inform themselves about the costs incurred by their fellow partners on Airbus work. In 1987 a group of "four wise men", industrialists and bankers, was appointed by the partner governments to review the whole structure of Airbus Industrie. The "wise men" reported in Spring 1988 that Airbus decision-making was cumbersome, in particular because of the need for unanimity, and that the financial information necessary for clear decision-making and firm cost control was lacking. To improve matters it was recommended: that the Supervisory Board be reduced from seventeen to five and that it take a more active role in the consortium's decision-making; and that the Executive Committee be replaced by an Executive Board of seven senior executives from Airbus Industrie and the partner companies, that would act like a board of directors, taking over day-to-day control of the programme agreed by the Supervisory Board. Among the members of the new Executive Board should be two particularly important new appointees: its chairman should be the Managing Director, a function seen as carrying more authority than that of the current President and Chief Executive; and there should be a Finance Director, with the authority to prepare accounts that would more adequately elucidate the extent of partner companies' commitments to Airbus work. It was suggested that under such a structure Airbus Industrie's management would be better placed to control the development of projects but that the partners, who took the ultimate risks, would be in effective control of strategic decision-making. Ministers agreed to the broad-lines of these developments in May 1988, but throughout the remainder of the year the partner companies were unable to agree the precise character of these major organisational changes.

5. Conclusion

The creation and growth of Airbus Industrie has been a response to international economic pressures and technological changes that would have driven Europe's aircraft manufacturers from any significant participation in the world airliner market without some close and permanent form of collaboration. Close collaboration was vital because Europe's aircraft manufacturers lacked the financial strength and probably the technical strength to provide leadership on a major airliner development. Permanency was vital in order to build a "family" of aircraft that would be more attractive to airlines than *ad hoc* purchases from a range of producers, and in order to develop the after-sales services so vital to successful airliner marketing.

Although the response of the Airbus partner companies to the pressures they have faced since the 1960s has been collective, their motivations have essentially been individual. Airbus does engender loyalty from the staff of the partner companies who work on its projects, especially those who have been involved with it for perhaps twenty years. Nevertheless the key companies involved would almost certainly prefer to engage in such projects as design leaders, with a range of subcontractors to support them, as Boeing and McDonnell Douglas are still able to do. Collaboration, with shared design leadership, is a second best solution in which individual companies engage in order to preserve and enhance their own design and production capacities, and to provide themselves with greater financial security by spreading their resources over a range of projects.

It is also necessary to stress that the creation and continued existence of Airbus Industrie is not simply a commercial matter. It also represents a continuing international political commitment of considerable moment. Without government approval and regular injections of financial support Airbus Industrie would have ceased to exist. The aircraft industries of Western Europe are largely in public ownership and even where they are not they are heavily dependent upon government both for military contracts and for civil launch aid. Once again, however, intergovernmental support for Airbus Industrie, like partner company participation, is motivated primarily by national concerns. Politicians may occasionally wax lyrical about the value of international economic and technological cooperation and sometimes in particular about the need for European cooperation. Governmental support for Airbus Industrie, however, is motivated primarily by the need to preserve and enhance national aircraft industries. Strategic interests dictate the desirability of maintaining a large aircraft industry with varied capacities and a range of projects capable of keeping design teams fully employed and developing their talents. Equally the aircraft industry is seen as one arm of technology policy: encouraging advanced technologies; providing some direct product spin-offs; and fostering the growth of a highly-skilled labour force. Broader economic goals are aided by import saving and through airliner exports. Finally governments support Airbus Industrie for more straightforwardly political reasons: the pursuit of foreign policy goals, in particular European collaboration; responding to well-organised industrial pressure group activity; and, especially in France, responding to national sentiment.

Given the practical difficulties likely to arise in major international collaborative aerospace projects, good organisation is as important to the success of such projects as both good design and efficient production. Indeed, they are both largely contingent upon the effective organisation of a project. If any international collaborative project is to work there must be unambiguous agreement about its purposes. In aircraft development this means that there must be an agreed operational requirement for the aircraft that is to be built so that all the parties concerned know what the aircraft will be like and to what sorts of use it will be put. The early disagreements between Britain and the oher Airbus partners about the size of A300B illustrate this point. The GIE structure used for the Airbus would appear to have a number of clear advantages as an organisational framework within which to undertake international civil aircraft projects. In particular, its flexibility, its capacity to give financial reassurance to potential purchasers, and its capacity to provide for a centralised control of certain key functions (e.g. marketing). Nevertheless to take full and efficient advantage of the boom in airliner demand they believe is forthcoming the partner companies must restructure Airbus Industrie. To prosper, collaboration will have to grow deeper.

Bibliography

AIRBUS INDUSTRIE (1986), *Airbus Industrie Briefing*.

AIRBUS INDUSTRIE (1987), *Airbus Industrie Briefing*.

ARGIROPOULOS, K.O. (1982), The Airline Fuel Crisis of the 1970s, in: G.W. JAMES (ed.), *Airline Economics*, Lexington Books.

BETAILLE, R. (1976), Organisation of the Collaborative Programme for the A300 Airbus, in: *Aerospace*, November.

BOEING COMMERCIAL AIRPLANE COMPANY, *Setting the Record Straight*.

CHANUT, R. (1985), A European Joint Venture in Aerospace, in: *European Management Journal*, Vol.3, No.2.

EEC (Action Programme for European Aerospace) (1975), *The Spinelli Report*, October.

FARRER, D., and BALTHAZOR, L. (1981), Analysis of High Technology Collaboration, in: *Royal Aeronautical Society Spring Convention*, May.

HARTLEY, K. (1974), *A Market for Aerospace* (Institute for Economic Affairs), London.

HAYWARD, K. (1983), *Government and British Civil Aerospace*, Manchester University Press, Manchester.

HAYWARD, K. (1986), *International Collaboration in Civil Aerospace*, Frances Pinter, London.

HOWARD, L. et al. (1982), The Challenge of Capital Acquisition in the 1980s, in: G.W. JAMES. (ed.) *Airline Economics*, Lexington Books.

LERONOWITZ, J.M. (1988), Aerospatiale Supports Management Changes in Airbus Consortium, in: *Aviation Week and Space Technology*, May 2.

MILLER, R., and SAWERS, D. (1968), *The Technical Development of Modern Aircraft*, Routledge and Kegan Paul, London.

NEWHOUSE, R. (1982), *The Sporty Game*, Alfred Knopf, New York.

PEARCE, A. (1985), The Business of Meeting Aerospace Needs, in: *Aerospace*, October.

VAN RHIJN (1973), Opening Address, in: *Royal Aeronautical Society*, Macmillan, London.

SALVY, R. (1974), The A300B Airbus Enters Service, in: *Interavia*, April.

STRATFORD, A. (1973), *Air Transport Economies in the Supersonic Era*, Macmillan, London.

TAYLOR, J. (ed.) (1985), *Jane's All the World's Aircraft 1984-85*, Jane's Yearbooks, London.

9

Techno-Industrial Innovation and State Policies in the United States and Japan

Jill Hills[1]

The telecommunications sector and telecommunications policy have become salient political issues in the past five years. All governments in the industrialised countries have seen telecommunications as a channel for the improvement of innovation. Yet with its origins in the telegraph, by the late 1970s domestic telecommunications had become a mature, primarily voice oriented, sector. Slow depreciation of network equipment, often over twenty or more years, necessary to keep prices down for individual consumers, held back the introduction of expensive new technology.

---

[1] This chapter was prepared with the support of the British Economic and Social Research Council, Grant E0023 2196. The author would like to thank Professor Hideyoshi Tominga and the Electrical Engineering Department, Waseda University, Tokyo for their hospitality in 1987, and all the Japanese people who agreed to be interviewed.

advance. The changes in the Japanese domestic market evident before privatisation have speeded up, with a greater proportion of the market now taken by the private sector. Competition has been introduced to both domestic and international telecommunications carriers. Tariff policy provides a greater threat to NTT than to AT&T, and it is NTT's R&D expenditure which has been redirected away from basic research to development work.

1. Global Concentration of Business and Telecommunications

Liberalisation in the United States involved the imposition of large business' priorities on to AT&T. The concepts of liberalisation and privatisation of telecommunications markets have spread out from the United States and owe much of their popularity to the globalisation of manufacturing, financial and retail markets. They have found favour in other countries, partly because they coincide with the political and economic ideology of conservative governments, and partly because multinational and large-scale businesses want similar costs in whatever country they operate in. It can be argued that regulation and public ownership impede business by offering long-distance and international call tariffs at higher than marginal cost in order that the use of the basic telephone service for domestic consumers should be subsidised. Liberalisation in both the USA and Britain has been characterised by a "rebalancing" of costs and charges. Decreases in long-distance and international tariffs have gone together with increases in local call rates and charges for access to the network. To the extent that business has reaped reduced costs so its competitiveHadvantage has been increased.

New actors have entered into the traditional telecommunications market - actors such as computer equipment manufacturers and large users, such as banks. The process of digitalisation of transmission and advances in the amount of data which can be passed over long distances via satellite and optic fibre have provided the opportunity for private global networks. In general these networks have relied on leased lines from PTTs and have been data oriented, but in 1987 a Japanese company announced its own private international ISDN, integrating telephones, telexes, facsimile and data communications and linking

Tokyo, Osaka, New York and London (Japan Economic Journal, 17 October 1987).

In the USA large companies are utilising leased lines to bypass the local network. General Motors, for instance, has a private network linking 250,000 telephone sets and the same number of computers (The Economist, 17 October 1987). Companies are increasingly driven to cut costs where they can. Hence governments are under pressure to liberalise and privatise, or to so organise international telecommunications for large companies via such initiatives as Teleports, that the companies do not have to contribute to the costs of the domestic network.

Yet although liberalisation may produce decreased costs for certain large-scale businesses there may well be a negative trade off for governments where there is a domestic telecommunications manufacturing industry. Under a regulated monopoly the telecommunications network provides a controlled market for domestic industry. In an industrialised or industrialising country R&D costs for switching equipment sold to the network may be higher than they would be under competitive conditions, but a domestic industry with its employment, technological and export potential is retained. The introduction of competition in the network and the sale or fragmentation of publicly owned PTTs may alter that established relationship, to the detriment of innovation. In particular the demand pull of stable, protected domestic procurement is of importance in the first stage of the innovation cycle.

This alteration in switching markets comes just as the amount of money required for R&D for new large-scale switching systems has become more than many of the established players can finance. Although the Italian, Indian and Korean switches have been developed at considerably less cost, estimates suggest a figure of $1 billion, 80% of which is for software development. It is thought necessary for a company to have 10% of the world market in order to recoup those costs. In response to these R&D costs and to the need for expertise in the several newly related technologies of data, voice and image transmission, the industry has begun a process of cross-national collaborations and of concentration. Following divestiture AT&T is at the forefront of this international collaboration, joining with Philips of Holland in order to penetrate Europe. It has been relatively unsuccessful despite AmericanHgovernmental pressure on France and West Germany. Over-capacity in the world switching market has led to extreme competition so that the strategy of divestiture has resulted in some foreign penetration of the American market.

2. Domestic and International Markets

Japan's dependence on exports to the USA for a high proportion of GNP is of crucial importance in considering how its domestic policy is currently being defined. The liberalisation of the American market began in 1968, when the Federal Communications Commission ruled that equipment which would not harm the network could be connected to it, regardless of source. But at that time the Japanese telecommunications network was also growing last. From about 1980, growth in Japan slowed, particularly in the telephone market, so exports increased. On average production increased by 15% per annum from 1980 to 1985 with the proportion taken by exports increasing to 30% in 1983 and 35% in 1984. It was primarily the increase in exports to the USA which fuelled expansion of Japanese production in 1983 and 1984. In 1984 the USA was taking almost 20% of Japanese telecommunications production.

The divestiture of AT&T took place in 1984. The domestic regulated network market subsequently consisted of AT&T, responsible for long-line provision, seven Regional Bell Operating Companies (RBOCs) responsible for the provision of local telephone services and numerous small independent rural telephone companies. The non-regulated market consisted of competitors to AT&T long-lines, the seven RBOCs which could provide enhanced services in separate subsidiaries and numbers of resellers. Instead of one major purchasing entity the new market contained ten or more, each competing to lay new lines, to introduce new switching technology and to market associated customer premises equipment.

Despite the fact that in 1981 Fujitsu was denied a contract for optic fibre with AT&T on the grounds of national security, AT&T's divestiture has produced enormous demand (Hills 1983). Some 45,000 miles of optic fibre were laid in the USA in 1986. As a result of Japanese penetration of the optoelectronics market and that of the customer equipment market, particularly in key telephones and facsimile machines, the American overall trade deficit in telecommunications equipment in 1986 reached $1.9 billion.

Whereas Japanese manufacturers are particularly strong in consumer equipment, the Americans are particularly strong in switching equipment and in satellite production. Japan's communications satellite industry is still underdeveloped, although KDD (the previous international monopoly carrier) has recently produced a data packet switching technology for use with satellites and the Japanese have 50% of the world market in small satellite terminals (Jussawalla 1987). At one stage NTT attempted to buy the necessary know-how from the Americans, but subsequently Japan has concentrated on developing its own. In February 1983, Japan's first operative communications satellite was launched to provide direct dialling between the mainland and the southern islands of Ogasawara. In 1984 another satellite was launched to carry direct broadcast television, and the Japanese are the only country to have a proper DBS.

One probable reason for the lag in development of satellite technology is the lack of Japanese military R&D and therefore of a domestic customer base. However Japan is the major competitor to America in optic fibre and American Corning Glass has alleged patent infringement. NTT and KDD have been at the forefront of optic fibre research. NTT has laid optic fibre the length of Japan. Latest plans include a stretch of 120 km undersea cable without repeaters. In 1986-87 the value of the optic-fibre industry in Japan reached ¥63 billion and is expected to reach ¥230 billion by 1991. NTT has been a major customer and has also been responsible for devising a method of manufacturing the fibre which is more economical than that previously used (Japan Economic Journal, 19 December 1987). Increasingly the long-line competitors to NTT are laying optic-fibre cable and Japanese companies have benefited from plans for two Pacific Ocean cables. In satellite technology the Japanese have been concentrating on developing satellites to broadcast in the Ka band - the highest available band. The Ka band will be utilised to link up with high definition television and computerised compact disc players. The failure of the Space Shuttle compounded existing problems of over-capacity in the American industry caused by the rising competitiveness of the European consortia and the Ariane launcher. Intelsat which has been the financier of much American satellite R&D is primarily now a replacement market. Because of these problems the American industry is looking for market opportunities outside its traditional outlets. This search has led to the decision to allow private satellites to compete against Intelsat satellites over the Atlantic, and led to pressure on Japan to buy satellites for use by NTT's new long-line competitors. These purchases for two competitors have been funded by the Japanese government.

American pressure exerted on NTT over a number of years has not been overly successful. Although in 1981 NTT introduced a more open procurement procedure and began to make specifications in English, in 1984 NTT purchased only about 6% of its total budget from the USA. And in 1987 less than 3% of NTT's capital expenditure was spent on equipment from overseas.

In fact, only a year after privatisation NTT began to cut back on increases in capital expenditure. In real terms the value of orders in 1986 stood still. Only after a government request to increase its capital expenditure in 1987 in line with government attempts to expand the domestic economy did it do so by 11%. The Ministry of Posts and Telecommunications has instructed NTT to hasten digitisation so that its competitors may reach a larger proportion of the population with their service. Therefore, as the network is progressively digitised, expansion at about the same annual level is expected for several more years.

For the Americans there have been some successes in the Japanese market. One of the competitors to NTT has bought switches from the USA. Two of the long-distance competitors will use American satellites. Motorola is providing a form of mobile telephone in the south of the country and has become the first American manufacturer to start production in Japan. NTT has ordered optic fibre from an American manufacturer, has ordered multi-purpose telephones from Crest of the US, switches from Northern Telecom and has bought a supercomputer from Cray. But overall penetration is disappointing.

In fact in 1985 and 1986 Japanese exports to the USA fell by 5% and 25% but the proportion of US exports to imports did not rise. In 1985 only 10% and in 1986 12% of Japanese exports to

America were balanced by imports. In 1986 the USA still took 42% of Japanese telecommunications exports - almost the same proportion as in 1983. It is against this background that the Americans have argued for liberalisation of the Japanese market and for increased American equipment purchasing by NTT and its competitors. There has been a backlash against Japan in the United States and threats of reciprocal trade legislation.

To reduce such problems and to combat the appreciation of the yen to the dollar Japanese manufacturers have increased their manufacture within the USA. For instance Fujitsu by 1988 will produce half the value of its sales of $2 billion to the USA in that country. Hitachi has expanded American production of private exchanges and Mitsubishi is importing cordless telephones into Japan from its subsidiary in Florida.

One reason for American lack of success in penetrating the market in Japan has been the changing nature of that market. Whereas in the 1970s 50% of the equipment market was accounted for by government, by 1983 only 36% of production was taken by the public sector. NTT's share of national production fell from 38% in 1980 to 27% in 1986 compared to the 36% of the domestic market accounted for by private consumption. In turn switching equipment has seen relative low growth rates in production compared to other equipment. Since 1983 the Japanese switching market has grown by an average 8% per annum but from accounting for 28% of the domestic market in 1979 it accounted for 19% in 1986.

These changes have impacted on the attitude of Japanese manufacturers. Although NTT is still the largest, most important customer of companies such as Fujitsu and NEC, NTT took only 10% or less of their production in 1984. They were therefore not dependent on NTT. These trends have been furthered by NTT's diffusion of procurement. Yet NTT remains an important influence on the market. Because of its renewed capital investment in 1987, the Japanese industry's growth, which almost halted at 2.2% in 1986, resumed an upward trend of 10%.

Changes in the type of equipment sold have also produced changes in manufacturers. Hence the explosion in production of telephones which greeted the withdrawal of NTT's monopoly on the first telephone (up by 35% per annum between 1983 and 1986) brought in companies such as Sony. And the increase in

domestic and export markets for facsimile machines has favoured companies such as Matsushita. Toshiba and Mitsubishi are
also new entrants to a market which previously held only twenty
companies. NTT itself buys from the manufacturers and at one
point relations between the two reached crisis point when NTT
demanded facsimile machines at below cost. Although output
has increased manufacturers' profits have been cut in the new
competitive environment and some of the traditional telecommunications manufacturers have moved into the red. It seems
likely that concentration will result, with the large diversified
electronics companies taking larger shares of the market.

These changes in the Japanese domestic market are similar
to those which have taken place in the American market following liberalisation of equipment. The difference is that being
so strong in the major growth area of customer premises equipment the Japanese manufacturers have kept hold of that domestic market. Nevertheless it is these trade concerns which form
the backdrop to current policy-making in Japan and the USA
and which fuel American worries on competitiveness and R&D.

3. Japanese Policy-Making

Various models of Japanese policy-making have been put forward in the last twenty years. Among the most popular have
been those which describe it in a corporatist manner and ascribe
to Japanese bureaucracy a far-sighted vision which guides
Japanese industry. For some American writers an assessment of
the influence of the Ministry for International Trade and
Industry (MITI) has been linked to the desire to see an American industrial policy constructed on Japanese lines so as to combat declining competitiveness (Borrus and Zysman 1984; Hugh
1986; Zysman and Tyson 1983).

My own interpretation has tended to emphasise the conflict
between Japanese bureaucracies as a salient factor in policy-
making, particularly in telecommunications. For the past five
years, MITI (Ministry of International Trade and Industry) and
the MPT (Ministry of Posts and Telecommunications) have been
engaged in a turf war over their proper spheres of influence.
This turf war was brought on by the technical convergence of
computing (MITI's province) and telecommunications (MPT's

province). Committees containing outsiders are duplicated in each of the Ministries and the forays of one Ministry are matched by the other.

There seems little doubt that MITI's influence over industry has been eroded over the past twenty years as markets have been opened to competition and Japanese industry has internationalised. MITI's current determination to build model cities can be interpreted not simply as a means of decentralisation of R&D and technology transfer (Imai 1986) but also, as Sheridan Tatsuno points out, can be construed as "castle building" to subdue industry and bring it back under its influence (Tatsuno 1986). Not to be outdone the MPT has pushed forward with a programme of "teletopia model cities" in competition to those designated by MITI.

Ironically the American determination to punish Japan for breaking the export embargo to the USSR on advanced machinery and its agreement on the global pricing of microchips has had the effect of strengthening MITI's waning control over industry. It polices the semiconductor agreement, distributes quotas and controls export licences of information and communications technology. However in 1987 it unsuccessfully attempted to extend this newfound authority with a proposal to "co-ordinate" supply and demand in the exports of the machine tool and information equipment industries, so as to further "harmonious relations" with foreign nations. Industry was sceptical about its motives and unwilling to allow further government intervention in its affairs (Japan Economic Journal, 5 September 1987).

It was always unlikely, in view of its historic role as the guider of Japanese industry, that MITI would be prepared to sit down under a revamped MPT traditionally stocked with less talented bureaucrats than itself. The story of the liberalisation of Japanese telecommunications inevitably contains elements of bureaucratic conflict between Ministries (Hills 1986). This fighting reaches right down into the organisation of NTT with some research groups responsible primarily to MITI and others to the MPT. The issue of standards has been particularly fraught with bureaucratic conflict. But there has also been industry dissatisfaction with MPT over the handling of the introduction of competition into international communications. Its control of NTT also continues to be an important arena of tension.

4. Liberalisation and Privatisation of NTT

The legislation which "privatised" NTT was passed at the end of 1984. However, the term "privatisation" which is generally assumed to mean that control of an economic entity has passed out of government hands into the hands of shareholders does not describe the reality in Japan. Prior to privatisation telecommunications came under the official aegis of the MPT. However when NTT was created in the 1950s it was created partially from the then Ministry of Communications and partially from that Ministry's research labs. In effect the Ministry became NTT or NTT became the unofficial Ministry. The MPT's officials concentrated on and were trained in posts rather than telecommunications, and NTT ran telecommunications responsible officially to the Diet for its annual allocation and not to the Ministry.

The privatisation of NTT removed its unofficial status as a Ministry for Telecommunications while at the same time placing a Ministry whose personnel had relatively little expertise in telecommunications in control of not only NTT but the whole range of telecommunications network operators brought into the market by the liberalisation of NTT's monopoly.

In the same period the telecommunications sector gained in political saliency in relations between America and Japan. The items of dispute centred mainly on equipment sales and the imbalance of trade between the two countries, but also ranged over the question of how much foreign ownership would be allowed in network operations, equipment standards and entry into NTT's research and development programme.

Japan allows two types of competitors to NTT. Type I provides its own facilities. Type II leases lines. Foreign ownership is controlled amongst Type I carriers. Type II carriers are divided between Special and General Type II. Special Type II carriers are those which provide a service to third parties, are nationwide and may become international carriers. They can provide basic voice and data communications as well as enhanced services. General Type II carriers are those which provide mainly data communications between their own companies, but again on leased lines. Only Type I regulated entities may construct their own networks.

NTT faces competition from both Type I and Type II carriers. Of the Type I carriers three companies which began with the provision of leased lines between Tokyo and Osaka introduced public switched services in September 1987. In addition two "local" competitors will join up with the new carriers to provide an end to end service on an alternative network to that of NTT. The competitors' leased line prices began 20% below NTT's but NTT then reduced its prices by 10%. Tariffs on the public switched longdistance service also undercut NTT by about 10%. NTT has not been allowed to deaverage its tariffs for long distance in order to compete with the newcomers. Hence it must expect its income to decline rapidly as its market share on its busiest route is eroded. The newcomers meanwhile may not compete among themselves on price - each must charge the same, thereby protecting all, despite the fact that different technologies (microwave and optic fibre) have different cost structures.

Each of the three competitors is aiming for 10% of the domestic market within three years in order to break even on investment. As mentioned earlier two further competitors will provide leased lines on the same Tokyo-Osaka route by satellite, but are delayed by launching problems. NTT will lease capacity on at least one of them - whether voluntarily is unknown. Given recent increases in satellite insurance costs it seems unlikely that these competitors will be able to meet the prices of the land-based.

Until recently there was no machinery for measuring local traffic and ironically the relevant equipment has had to be bought from AT&T. No one is clear yet as to how much cross-subsidy is taking place although it is recognised that average pricing has to be replaced by something nearer cost-based pricing. However although the Ministry will allow NTT to reduce its long-distance call charges universally it will not allow it to raise its local call tariffs. Because it may not rebalance its tariffs NTT is not yet reducing its long-distance charges on the grounds that it will wait and see what inroads its competitors make into its market. NTT argues that the effect of the interconnection agreement is that the newcomers do not contribute to the local network costs. Nor has it been allowed to charge them for access to its network. For that reason NTT has been cutting costs, reducing staff through natural wastage, reducing the pace of investment, and hiving off staff into subsidiary companies where possible. These subsidiaries continue to provide the same services as they previously supplied internally to NTT but are also expected to use spare capacity to make a profit.

In Japan privatisation went hand in hand with further liberalisation of the equipment market and of the network. Yet to date there has actually been very little competition for NTT which has temporarily had the status of a private monopoly. As a result NTT's profits have risen and its share prices have become so high that many commentators consider them overvalued. This situation seems unlikely to last.

In Japan the prime beneficiaries of privatisation and liberalisation have been the Ministry of Posts and Telecommunications, which has extended its power, together with NTT's shareholders and NTT's competitors. At the present time these competitors are being helped technically and are being subsidised by NTT, in the same way as AT&T subsidised MCI and GTE before access charges to the local network were equalised. The Ministry favours NTT's competitors - cynics argue because it will then have more companies in which to place its bureaucrats when they retire. Further uncertainty has been introduced by the proposal to split NTT into regional entities which MPT is also expected to favour on bureaucratic grounds. Because NTT has made profits considerably over expectation in 1986 and its share price has risen again after the December 1987 crash, it seems that the possibility of it losing money is considered likely only by the Trade Union. The Ministry seems to have no long-term strategy to cope with this eventuality or a run-down in R&D. The privatisation of NTT came about partly as a result of the battles for control of telecommunications between the MPT and MITI and current strategy continues to reflect short-term aims.

Because of the plentiful supply of capital waiting to be invested NTT's competitors are primarily funded by Japanese capital. American companies such as AT&T, IBM, Motorola, Telenet, Tymnet and GEISCO take part in the network market but in co-operation with Japanese partners. Japanese money is being sunk into telecommunications, particularly value added networks, for long-term rather than short-term returns. There is no indication that the Type II carriers are making much money and some Japanese suggest that many of those registered are not active.

In this scenario of a plethora of value added networks, NTT's INS has become yet another VAN albeit on a larger scale. The decrease in costs which it was anticipated that INS would bring are not yet evident and just as PTTs in other countries have cut back on supply-led plans so have the Japanese. Privatisation seems to have induced caution and a focus on large business customers rather than individual households. NTT is not allowed to extend INS to the international arena and has therefore joined with IBM to exploit the 1987 liberalisation of that market.

Whereas NTT's procurement, at least in the 1970s, produced a close relationship between some manufacturers and itself nothing of the kind exists in 1988. The "family" concept conceived by the Americans to explain the development work which went on between NTT and the major manufacturers began to disintegrate with the appointment of the current president of NTT, Hisashi Shinto. Appointed by Prime Minister Nakasone Mr Shinto had worked at one time for Toshiba, which, after the second world war, was excluded from the telecommunications market by Fujitsu and NEC. Historically therefore there has been competition between these manufacturers and the new President of NTT, who has followed a policy of diversification in equipment supply.

5. Research and Development

Although from late 1986 NEC and Fujitsu benefited from NTT's increased demand for digital switches, it is evident that NTT is now working on the development of products with many other manufacturers. It is Matsushita which together with American OEC will develop the central processors for the testing system of NTT's digital exchange - a means of transferring American technology to the Japanese company (Japan Economic Journal, 21 November 1987). It is with six manufacturers, including Oki, Toshiha and Mitsubishi, that NTT has finalised the standard operating systems interface for communications equipment in line with a new Japanese standard TRON. It is with Northern Telecom that NTT has developed a digital switch.

There are some problems brought about by this increased pluralism. It was with Sony that NTT developed a still-picture telephone and provided the design to Fujitsu, Hitachi, Sanyo and Sharp. Mitsubishi, Matsushita and NEC which had developed a video-telephone to another standard looked as though they would be excluded from the market. Finally a new standard for all has been agreed, but it is incompatible with existing equipment.

Under the terms of the Telecommunications Business Law NTT is obliged to retain its R&D facilities in the national interest. There was considerable concern at the time of privatisation that these might be cut back for short-term gains. The problem is more important in Japan than in the USA because there is little or no university-based research to compete with or replace that of NTT.

Also Japan has relied heavily in the electronics industry on imported technology from the United States. Although the Japanese imports and exports of technology seem to be roughly in balance Japan continues to import software and electronics know-how from the USA and exports plant and machines to the Newly Industrialising Countries in Asia (Japan Economic Journal, 17 October 1987). As a result of the imbalance in technology trade the United States Congress is considering measures to tighten further access to American research results. Because of international problems with copyright and patent infringements relating to American technology, MITI has pinpointed basic research as being an area needing expansion.

For these various reasons NTT's research facilities are of national importance. At one point during the privatisation debate some form of government subsidy towards them was considered with the objective of protecting basic research in the national interest. In 1986 NTT spent $757 million on research and development or 2.7% of operating revenues. It employed 3,900 researchers and support personnel in nine laboratories structured on market lines. In 1987 these figures had increased to 2.8% of operating revenues and 5,000 workers respectively. The most recent figure compares favourably to the 2.1% of operating revenues spent on research and development in

1983-84, immediately prior to privatisation. Hence privatisation has not yet curtailed funds for research.

Yet NTT has been faced with the need to reduce expenditure, increase product innovation and upgrade services in response to competition. Research and development have been affected, the emphasis, passing towards development and away from basic research. In 1986 the R&D facilities were organised into nine laboratories on market rather than geographical lines. Then in 1987 a major reorganisation took place in the R&D laboratories, reflecting the previous reorganisation within NTT itself. Development work, now given increased emphasis, is separated from research and located with product specific sections responsible for marketing. The four goals of R&D are said to be first integration of digital telecommunications technologies in the network, second the provision of more sophisticated and diverse services, third improving operating efficiency and reliability and fourth advancing basic research (NTT Annual Report 1987). Following management consultant's advice, the intention is to respond to market demand and to produce specialised market-led equipment and software quickly. The effect from the engineers' point of view is to break up research teams into separate locations, and to place less emphasis on basic research.

One obvious way out of the impasse of reliance upon private companies to fund basic long-term research at a time when profits are under pressure from competition would be for the Ministries to restructure post-graduate education and university research. In fact government spending on R&D totalled only 20% of total R&D spending in 1985 and government research laboratories were said in 1987 to be suffering from a lack of resources and equipment. Unless education is reformed it seems unlikely that the desire of MITI to upgrade Japan's basic research capability can be much more than words on paper.

To some extent the United States is now suffering the same problems as the Japanese. Before divestiture AT&T's Bell Labs were responsible for many of the technological breakthroughs of the post-war world. Because AT&T was a regulated entity and could not compete abroad its technology was made freely available. It served as a national resource. However following divestiture Bell Labs became linked to the market strategy of AT&T. Michael Noll estimates that the number of research workers at

AT&T Bell Labs has remained fairly stable since 1982, but that the numbers involved in development work has increased giving a total of about 24,000 workers in R&D in 1985. That number is almost five times the number in NTT. He also estimates that AT&T spent 6.8% of total revenues on R&D in 1985, or twice the proportion spent by NTT. Of the three sources of revenue, sales of services, rentals and products, the highest proportion of R&D to revenues was in the product sector where he estimates AT&T to have spent almost 18% of revenues. He points out that this large expenditure can be viewed as either a good or bad thing depending on the reasons for it, but that so far output of patents from Bell Labs has not been affected by divestiture.

In addition to AT&T Bell Labs, the RBOCs also have a joint research lab, Bell Core, focused on local telephone exchange and exchange-access services. A little less than 1.4% of revenues is being spent on this R&D and Noll suggests that this figure probably demonstrates underinvestment in R&D. None of the seven regional companies yet has its own R&D facility, although each has its non-regulated business in competition with the others (Noll 1987). Although in total research spending seems to have increased since divestiture, given the fact that AT&T has not yet been oversuccessful on its consumer equipment side, and that the regional company expenditure is subject to state public utility commissioners, the future pattern of R&D is not clear or certain. If the RBOCs were to be allowed into manufacture then it seems obvious that they would immediately up their research expenditure. Some commentators have urged their release from regulatory control, so that they can compete in R&D and products with the Japanese equipment manufacturers (Geller 1986).

These concerns surrounding technology and the possible failure of American industry, fuelled by the burgeoning trade deficit, came to a head in 1987 when the Japan-US Technology Agreement first signed in 1980 came up for renewal. Under this agreement the American government had demanded that the Japanese should hand over civilian technology which could be utilised for military purposes. Eventually the Japanese had agreed (Hills 1983). Later, in 1985, IBM was allowed entry to technology developed in research projects partially financed by the Japanese government.

In 1987 the American government cited as a problem the imbalance of US technology exports to imports - the balance of trade being in America's favour. It demanded not "equal access" but "symmetrical access" to Japanese public and private R&D; that the Japanese should open up to American companies the technology which resulted from American original research; that Japanese government sponsored R&D projects should be opened to American researchers, and that the number of American researchers in Japan should be increased. The Japanese agreed to the latter three demands and also agreed to joint research in nine areas including information technology, superconductors, and the development of databases. In fact the US negotiators wanted more access to private sector technology. The President of NEC is quoted as saying, "We will not escape, but we have to make it clear what we can do and what we can not" (Japan Economic Journal, 16 January 1988).

One reason for the pessimism of the Japanese is the number of bills concerned with intellectual property rights which are before the American Congress in 1988. These include a proposed amendment to the Tariff Act's Section 337 which would allow American companies to ask for imports to be stopped from any company which is alleged to be infringing its patent (no evidence of damage would be necessary). It is reported that an increasing number of American conferences also exclude Japanese personnel (Japan Economic Journal, 12 December 1987). Hence the research currently adopted by a number of disparate elements in American government ignores alleged weaknesses in American R&D - its overemphasis on defence, its underfunding of civilian R&D and basic research, its poor production of scientific graduates and declining research facilities - and concentrates on protection against Japan's rising technological capability (Bloch 1986).

6. Conclusion

The purpose of this chapter has been to demonstrate that those perceptions of the liberalisation of American telecommunications which see it as damaging to American long-term innovation can be replicated in relation to Japan. As markets become more competitive so it is likely to be more difficult to finance R&D

privately. AT&T has not yet been affected - partly because it is making money from long-distance services, whereas its competitors are not. Subject as it is to oscillating bureaucratic control NTT may have a harder time. Its new emphasis on short-term development reflects its fears and echoes similar trends in Britain.

Current conflict concerning trade in technology between the USA and Japan is part of the wider dispute on the trade imbalance. In the telecommunications sector the impact of liberalisation has been first to increase the private consumer market and second to increase facilities investment. The Japanese manufacturers have benefited from both markets in both countries, whereas the American manufacturers have benefited primarily from facilities investment in the USA alone. Hence it seems likely that the present pressure on Japan in the field of technology will increase. However without a restructuring of the educational field and more university-based research it seems unlikely that the Japanese will be able to retaliate by conducting their own basic research. One may therefore expect less competition and a growing cooperation between the USA and Japan in telecommunications and information technology. And this cooperation will be built on the very government control of private industry which the American government so dislikes.

Bibliography

BLOCH, Erich (1986), Managing for Challenging Times: A National Research Strategy, in: *Issues in Science and Technology*, Winter, 20-9.

BORRUS, Michael, and ZYSMAN, John (1984), *The New Media, Telecommunications and Development. The Choices for the United States and Japan*, BRIE Working Paper 7.

GELLER, Henry (1986), Telecommunications Policy Today: Against Technology, in: *Issues in Science and Technology*, Winter, 30-7.

HILLS, Jill (1983), Foreign Policy and Technology: The Japan-US, Japan-Britain, and Japan-EEC Technology Agreements, in: *Political Studies*, XXXI, 205-23.

HILLS, Jill (1986), *Deregulating Telecoms. Competition and Control in the USA, Japan and Britain*, Frances Pinter, London.

HILLS, Jill (1988), *Issues in Telecommunication Policy: A Review*, Oxford Surveys of Information Technology, Oxford University Press.

HUGH, Patrick (ed.), with MEISSNER, Larry (1986), *Japan's High Technology Industries. Lessons and Limitations of Industrial Policy*, University of Washington Press, Seattle & London.

IMAI, Ken-ichi (1986), Japan's Industrial Policy for High Technology Industry, in: HUGH, Patrick (ed.) with MEISSNER, Larry, 137-70.

JUSSAWALLA, Meheroo (1987), The Race for Telecommunication Technology, in: *Telecommunication Policy*, September, 297-307.

MCDONALD, John (1987), Deregulation's Impact on Technology, in: *IEEE Communications Magazine*, Vol. 25, 1, 63-5.

NOLL, A. Michael (1987), The Effects of Divestiture on Telecommunications Research, in: *Journal of Communication*, Winter, 73-80.

NTT (1984), *Annual Report*.

NTT (1985), *Annual Report*.

NTT (1986), *Annual Report*.

NTT (1987), *Annual Report*.

TATSUNO, Sheridan (1986), *The Technopolis Strategy. Japan, High Technology and the Twenty-first Century*, Prentice Hall Press, New York City.

ZYSMAN, John, and TYSON, Laura (1983), *American Industry in International Competition. Government Policies and Corporate Strategies*, Cornell University Press, Ithaca and London.

10

Japanese R&D Policy for Techno-Industrial Innovation

Takayuki Matsuo

Today the prosperity of nations, their economy, national security, and social harmony are linked intimately with technological development. Technology has become a source of wealth in the same way as the possession of natural resources was in the past. A nation which manages to promote innovation, to produce new products and processes at an earlier date, can increase its productivity, lower its costs, conquer new markets and acquire a comparative advantage.

In the field of technology , we are faced with a radically new situation. Information and telecommunications, life sciences, new materials, robotics, space, new energy, etc. have caused rapid and profound changes in our society. Not only is each sector of technology dynamic in itself, but each technology interacts with others. Technology has become more interactive and complicated. Each technology also comprises a vast network of interaction, operating not only in domestic markets but also at inernational levels. This makes interdependence between each sector of a nation, and with foreign countries, stronger, and the network of technology interaction is becoming internationalized.

Under these circumstances in the technology field, it is noted that new and epoch-making changes are emerging in Japanese industrial society. While these technological changes are now creating a new industrial system, Japan is also facing structural economic and social changes. With a higher degree of mutual interdependence between Japan and other countries, and with Japan's expanding role in the world economy, Japan aims at international cooperation, innovative growth of the world economy, industrial adjustment towards the enhancement of international harmony and cooperation, a relatively high economic growth rate based on domestic demand, and at responding to social needs for a new cultural life style resulting from the pluralization of value concepts, spiritual and cultural richness and aging of society.

Thus Japan is now at a turning point with regard to technology development. Faced with many constraints, such as the lack of resources and land, it is essential actively to promote technology development in order to assure the basis for continued economic development and to contribute to the international community. After achieving brilliant results in improving and applying imported technologies in the catching-up stage after World War II, Japan now needs to develop a more original and creative basic technology as the seed for future new development and production. That is one reason why the Japanese R&D system and governmental R&D policies have also been changing at the current turning point.

The purpose of this chapter is to characterize and analyse Japanese techno-industrial development and the change in governmental R&D policies at this turning point.[1]

1. The Technology Level and the Current Trend

Of all the industrial countries, Japan spent the least on R&D up to the mid-1960s. Japan's R&D expenditure rose sharply from the latter half of the 1960s to the early 1970s. Today, Japan is

---

[1] Especially R&D policies taken by the Ministry of International Trade and Industry which is in charge of policies for techno-industrial innovation.

showing rapid growth in R&D expenditure and the total R&D expenditure in Japan for fiscal year 1985 amounted to about 8.9 trillion yen, about one-third of that of the U.S. which ranks top. Japan ranks second, following the U.S., and has surpassed the Soviet Union. The total R&D expenditure (natural science) in Japan for fiscal year 1985 is up 13% from the previous fiscal year, showing a steady rise. The private sector continued to invest in R&D in a brisk manner (recording an increase of 15%), while the governmental sector's investment in R&D registered 7%. The rate of growth, adjusted for inflation, for the ten years from 1975 to 1985, was 30%, compared with 14% for West Germany, 25% for France and 28% for the U.S. It is noted that economic difficulties caused by the oil crises were forcing most other advanced countries to reduce their R&D efforts. Japan accelerated technology development and became keenly aware that the human mind was its only resource and that Japanese survival lay in a technology-based nation.

The share of R&D spending in GNP in fiscal year 1985, which indicates the level of national R&D investment, was 2.77% for Japan, showing a steady rise, 2.84% for West Germany and 2.72% for the U.S. (fig.1).

The ratio of the budget for science and technology to the total national budget in major countries is on the gradual increase. However, that for Japan is 2.9% which is relatively low compared to those of other major countries (fig.2). The R&D expenditure per researcher in Japan for fiscal year 1984 is about 18 million yen which is also relatively low.[2]

The total number of researchers in natural science in Japan in fiscal year 1986 is about 400,000 thousand, which shows a minor rise. This places Japan second following the U.S. In terms of organizations, industry showed a continued increase, whereas the share of research institutions and universities dropped.

The total expenditure on R&D (natural science) in Japan in fiscal year 1985 was 8.2 trillion yen, with the industrial sector accounting for 77.1% (which is higher than in the U.S. and Europe), the universities sector for 13% and the governmental

---

[2]   In West Germany this accounts for 32 million (1983), in the UK for 24 million (1983), in France for 28 million (1983), and in the United States for 30 million (1984).

Figure 1:   R&D Expenditure to GNP Ratio in Selected Countries

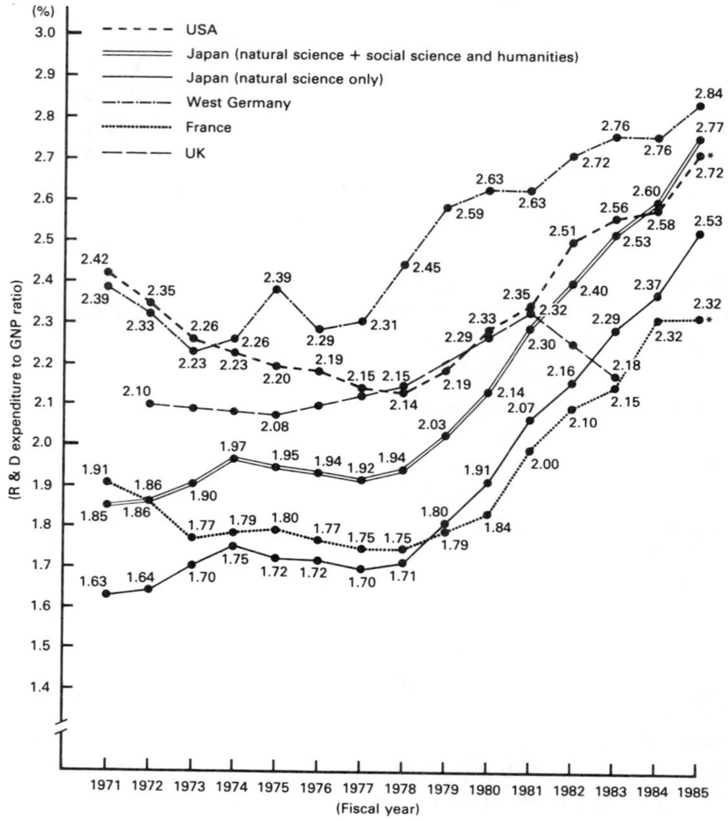

Note:
Data represents the total sum, including natural science, social science and humanities.
The asterisk '*' indicates an estimated value.

Sources:
Japan – Report on the Survey of Research and Development 1972–85, The Outline of Results on the Survey of Research and Development 1986 (Management and Coordination Agency), National Accounts (1980 Standard), National Accounts for Fiscal 1985 (Economic Planning Agency).
USA – National Patterns of Science and Technology Resources 1986 (NSF).
West Germany – Faktenbericht 1986 zum Bundesbericht Forschung (Bundesministerium für Forschung und Technologie), IMF 'International Financial Statistics' [cited from Scientific and Technological White Paper, 1986 Edition].
UK – 1986 Annual Review of Government Funded R&D, IMF 'International Financial Statistics' [cited from Scientific and Technological White Paper, 1986 Edition].
France – Projet de Loi de Finances Pour 1987.

Figure 2: Ratio of Budget for Science and Technology to Total National Budget in Selected Countries

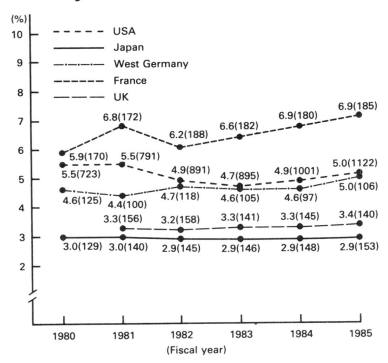

Notes:
1. For West Germany, only federal budgets are indicated.
2. For Japan, the general accounting budgets are indicated as the total budgets. The budget for science and technology includes scientific and technological promotion expenses, research and development expenses as part of the energy resource development expenditure, and research and study expenses in universities' special accounting.
3. Those parenthesized show the budgets for science and technology (in ¥ 10 billion).

Sources:
Japan – Scientific and Technological White Paper, 1986 Edition and Scientific and Technological Development Budget Fiscal 1986 (Science and Technology Agency).
USA – Budget of the US Government: Special Analyses.
West Germany – Faktenbericht 1986, Finanzbericht [cited from Scientific and Technological White Paper, 1986 Edition].
UK – Annual Review of Government Funded R&D, The Government Expenditure Plan 1985–86 to 1987–88 [cited from Scientific and Technological White Paper, 1986 Edition].
France – Projet de Loi de Finances Pour 1986 and 1987.

sector for 10% respectively. The R&D in the private secto emphasizes the development stage (about 70% of total R&D in the private sector) and is aimed at generating relatively short-term profits. On the other hand, the R&D activities undertaken by the government tend to emphasize the basic and applied stages, which are difficult for the private sector to tackle. While industry has shown an annual increase, the share by universities and the governmental sector is decreasing. The percentage of R&D financed by the government in Japan was very low, only 9.2% in fiscal year 1985, compared with 12.1% in the U.S. (fiscal year 1985), 22.7% in the United Kingdom (fiscal year 1983), and 27.5% in France (fiscal year 1984) (table 1). The ratio of R&D expenditure by the government in Japan, excluding defence R&D expenditure, in fiscal year 1985 is smaller than that of the U.S., which shows that Japan is at the lowest level among major countries. Moreover, the share of R&D financed by the Japanese government has been declining since reaching a peak of 13.5% in the fiscal year 1978. The R&D expenditure to sales ratio in Japanese industry in fiscal year 1985 continued to rise.[3] These figures show that the private sector is taking the lead in R&D in Japan.

The rate of basic research in total R&D expenditure for fiscal year 1985 is 12.9% which is significantly below the share in the past, showing a trend to decrease every year.[4] Generally speaking, the organizational structure of basic research expenditure in each country shows that the universities have a high rate of basic research while industry has a low rate. The weight of industry in applied research and development, and especially in basic research in Japan, is increasing (table 2). As for R&D expenditure in Japanese industry for fiscal year 1985, about 70% is for the development stage and only 6% is for basic research.

---

[3] From 1.42% in 1974 it remained fairly static until 1980 at a level of 1.48% and increased to 2.31% in 1985.

[4] While the share of basic research was decreasing from 17.5% in 1974 and 14.5% in 1980 to the share just mentioned, applied research remained constant at a quarter of the expenditure and development activities increased from 58% (1974) to 60% (1980) and 62.2% (1985). It is interesting that expenditures on development increased 3.6 times between 1974 and 1985, while in basic research it was only 2.5 times during this period.

Japanese R&D Policy for Techno-Industrial Innovation

Table 1: Ratio of R&D Expenditure by Performer in Selected Countries

Country Fiscal Year		Industry	Government	Non-profit-making research institutions	Universities
Japan	(1983)	63.5	9.6	3.9	23.0
	(1984)	65.1	9.2	3.9	21.8
	(1985)	66.8	9.2	3.9	20.1
U.S.A.	(1983)	72.7	12.1	3.1	12.1
	(1984)	73.1	11.9	3.1	11.9
	*(1985)	73.1	12.1	3.0	11.9
UK	(1978)	64.2	21.2	3.2	11.4
	(1981)	64.1	22.6	2.7	10.6
	(1983)	64.1	22.6	2.7	11.4
West Germany	(1983)	71.4	4.0	9.8	14.8
	(1984)	71.8	3.8	9.8	14.5
	(1985)	72.2	3.7	9.9	14.2
France	(1982)	57.9	25.2	0.9	15.9
	(1983)	56.8	26.4	0.9	15.8
	(1984)	56.8	27.5	0.9	14.7

Notes:
- The data represents the sum of expenditures for natural science, social science and humanities.
- The government sector includes research institutions that are not privately owned. The non-profit-making research institutions are regarded as privately owned research institutions.
- The asterisk indicates an estimated value.

Sources:
Japan - Report on the Survey of Research and Development 1984-1985, The Outline of Results on the Survey of Research and Development 1986 (Management and Coordination Agency).
U.S.A. - National Patterns of Science and Technology Resources 1986 (NSF).
UK - OECD Statistics (cited from Scientific and Technological White Paper, 1986 Edition).
West Germany - Faktenbericht 1986 zum Bundesbericht Forschung (Bundesministerium für Forschung und Technologie).
France - OECD Statistics (cited from Scientific and Technological White Paper, 1986 Edition).

One of the important factors for basic research is the creativity provided by human resources, whose training centre is mainly the university. Japan has more students in engineering fields than in scientific fields, i.e. mathematics, physics, chemistry

Table 2: Breakdown of R&D Expenditure in Japan by Character and by Performer (Natural Science)

		Total Expenditures (Unit: 100 million yen)	share (%) Universities	Research Institutes	Industry
Basic Research	1983	8,967	58.5	12.5	29.0
	1984	9,599	56.8	13.0	30.2
	1985	10,306	53.1	12.8	34.1
Applied Research	1983	16,301	21.6	17.0	61.4
	1984	17,808	20.4	16.2	63.4
	1985	20,018	18.9	16.0	65.1
Development	1983	38,828	2.0	13.0	85.0
	1984	43,402	1.9	12.4	85.7
	1985	49,859	1.7	12.4	85.9

Sources:
Report on the Survey of Research and Development 1984-1985, and the Outline of Results on the Survey of Research and Development 1986 (Management and Coordination Agency).

and biology, compared to universities in Europe and the U.S. The Science fields tend to search for more basic knowledge. This is one of the characteristics of Japanese universities which provide engineers to industry.

2. The Historical Development of Technology and the Current Turning Point

2.1 Catching up in R&D

Immediately after World War II, industrial facilities were almost completely destroyed and conditions for production were in terrible disarray. There was a strong need for Japan, as a trade-based nation, to revitalize the economy and to achieve a level comparable to that of Western countries by modernizing and developing its industrial society and utilizing imported technologies. The Japanese economy showed a remarkable recovery and progress after World War II.

Japanese technological capability has been one of the most important factors in helping the country to achieve economic growth. In the postwar period, Japan depended greatly on foreign countries for technological development. Foreign technology played an important role in helping Japan to catch up industrially to the level of Western countries. Therefore, the technology development in the postwar period was characterized as product-type.

From the 1960s Japan tried to move on from merely manufacturing products based on imported technology, to change her industrial structure to emphasize the heavy and chemical industries. This focused on the mass market and was symbolized by the technology development for mass-production and quality improvement of items such as steel, automobiles and electronic appliances. R&D expenditures were spent in pursuit of the development of civilian products and cost reductions. Defence and military-purpose R&D, which gave priority to performance rather than to costs, was much smaller than in the U.S. at that time. In the 1970s Japan began to make a great effort in developing new energy and energy conservation technologies to overcome the limited availability of energy after the oil crises. The following characteristics of R&D in the postwar period (1950s-1970s) contributed significantly to the high rate of economic growth and the present state of technological advancement.

The *Japanese corporative system*, characterized by strong coordinated cooperation for a certain purpose, especially for increasing corporate profit, has functioned well in helping Japan to attain the current level of technology development. The Japanese R&D system has emphasized cooperation in pursuit of a shared goal in the organization. The organizational system for the management of innovation in Japanese companies is the institutional arrangement which informs individual members and monitors their performances in order to attain the organizational goals as effectively as possible. Good relations between managers and workers in sharing information and goals within the organization contributed to the founding of mutual respect and the commitment needed to build cooperative efforts. Quality control in factories is one good example. These cooperative efforts and the consensus approach have lead to organizational efficiency.

The lifetime employment system, one of the distinctive characteristics of the Japanese management system in the catching-up stage, is also one of the essential factors in promoting organizational and functional R&D cooperation. Through this system, companies can accumulate experience effectively and continue the upgrading of human skills through company education over the full length of the professional lifetime of each member. People who are trained together tend to communicate better, not only because they share common information but also because they share common experiences and interests. The lifetime employment system has contributed toward attaining relatively high levels of technological knowledge among employees in all positions.

Recently, the lifetime employment system has been changing a little under economic and industrial structural changes, the growing pluralism of the social value system, and the internationalization of Japanese society. It is hard to say that the lifetime employment system itself is one of the native Japanese cultural characteristics. Generally speaking, however, these Japanese corporate characteristics in the management system also functioned effectively in the catching-up process in R&D. These characteristics in the management system and organizational cooperation have made it easy to set up long-term strategies toward marketing and developing technologies.

Organizational Cooperation in R&D among Large Versatile Companies. In the U.S., many companies are spontaneously taking up the challenge of risky innovative R&D projects. The success of such ventures can mean enormous profits. In Japan, however, there were few examples of this kind of innovative small venture business during the catching-up stage. Typically, large companies were willing to take technological lead in the private sector. In the catching-up stage, organizational R&D cooperation among large companies was one of the best ways to promote technology development based on imported technology. This avoided duplication of R&D investment. This R&D cooperative style could also improve the learning process and diffusion of technology very effectively.

The scale of R&D, the effects of mass-production and the capacity for quality control in large versatile companies are also very advantageous for producing sophisticated commercial products and increasing market shares effectively. Large versatile companies usually had their own markets already for various types of products such as those in the electronics fields.

Another characteristic of R&D during the postwar period was the *subcontract production system*, which played an important role in the technology diffusion process. Master companies gave intensive guidance in the improvement of production equipment, quality control, training, and in mastering foreign technology. It can be said that master companies and subcontracting companies have a network system for information and technology exchange among themselves which facilitates technology diffusion and technology development. Japanese small businesses have become more competitive at high technological levels by producing reliable parts and semi-finished products. These small businesses were key factors in the improvement of technology development during the postwar period.

Industrial R&D Efforts and Government Support. The success of Japanese industrial development based on advanced technology is mainly the result of competitive, intelligent, persistent, industrial R&D activities and management. Private companies in Japan have been trying to make long-term R&D plans to promote technology development. They have imported their production technologies by learning from customers how to improve them in the market. Thus the commercial R&D success of Japan has been driven not by the government but by industry itself.

The government is expected to play an important role in R&D in those areas where social needs are very high and yet where private firms alone cannot be expected to be motivated to engage in the development of technologies for reasons of high risk, long duration and enormous capital requirement. The government is expected to create an environment conducive to enterprise in the private sector so that private firms can engage in more autonomous and active technological efforts.

In the catching-up process in technology development in Japan, the government supported and encouraged industrial R&D activities. Government R&D projects functioned to promote technology diffusion to member companies. In the case of integrated circuits as one example, the participant companies in the government-sponsored cooperative project returned to their own laboratories to develop further the actual commercial random access memory chips that have been so successful in the market place.

Another important characteristic of R&D that contributed to Japan's economic success was deliberate and close *government-industry collaboration*. This collaboration can be compared with the close university-industry collaboration which created new innovative technologies in the U.S. In the postwar period, government-industry collaboration functioned very well. Based on imported basic technology, the government could create the vision which guided the private sector in promoting technology development and coordinating R&D projects. These R&D projects have been characterized by an efficient division of labour between firms and efficient technology diffusion to cooperating firms. Such projects also eliminated duplication of efforts in R&D. There has also been a close relationship between government and industry in Japan in setting long-term goals and establishing a consensus framework for promoting industrial and technological development. In contrast, it is often said that university-industry collaboration has been more advanced in the U.S. in terms of developing new innovative technology, while it has been lacking in Japan.

Science and Technology Education in Japan. Japan has shown a rapid increase in the number of researchers since World War II. Since the 1970s this growth rate has been even faster than that for R&D expenditure. The modern education system in Japan was established after the major reform of the traditional system (which was developed after the Meiji Restoration in 1868) and is based on the European system having been implemented after World War II. The rapid progress in middle and high school education, as well as intra-company education, is a clear indication of the special enthusiasm of the Japanese for learning.

Modern science and technology education in Japan is different from that in other countries. Historically, in contrast to the Western system which has emphasized improving the human intellect through basic studies in science and technology, the Japanese system has given more priority to the practical aspects of promoting industrialization in science and technology which has helped Japan to catch up in the development of industrial technology. Universities have the practical role of supplying highly qualified engineers to industry. The relationship between universities and industry has been close at the human level in offering numerous opportunities for individuals to exchange information and engage in personal collaboration. There was not much active cooperation in research studies in comparison to that of the U.S. and other Western countries. Rapid technological innovation and a subsequent change in the industrial structure have placed importance on company education, which has tended to emphasize practical technology, while the universities have dealt with fundamental knowledge and basic engineering training. Japan's successful progress in company education is closely related to those Japanese business characteristics which include lifetime employment, the seniority system and the job rotation system.

2.2 Turning Point in R&D

Today, these situations in technology development have been changing for a number of reasons:

(1) Japan has begun to lead the world in a growing number of fields such as electronics and has come to the stage of maturity in conventional technology fields. New technology such as information technology, telecommunications, life sciences, new materials, robotics, space and new energy technologies have caused rapid and profound changes in our society. Japan has come to the point of placing much more emphasis on basic technology than product technology to develop these promising new fields in particular; the development of information and telecommunications systems is changing our society, industrial fabric and organization, administrative systems, life style and education system.

Not only is each sector of technology development dynamic in itself, but each technology interacts with another. Technology has become more interactive and complicated. Each technology also comprises a vast network of interaction operating not only in domestic markets but also at international levels.

(2) As the second ranking nation in terms of gross national product among the Western industrialized countries, Japan has become increasingly aware that the ultimate aim of technology development should be to make a valuable contribution to international society. It is now very important for Japan to set up a "technology-based nation" by making maximum use of brain

power, which is the greatest and only resource in developing innovative technology.

Recently, Japan has faced mounting competition from newly industrialized countries (NICs) such as South Korea, Taiwan, Hong Kong and Singapore. From the standpoint of establishing a desirable form of international division of labour, Japan has been positively requested to transfer technology to developing countries.

Japan has also been faced with the increasing difficulties involved in production dependent upon imported technologies. The U.S. is said to be showing a tendency to restrict technology transfer to Japan because of national security.

Under these circumstances it is vital for Japan to develop basic technology as a kind of international public good, to promote technical tie-ups with Europe and the U.S., to supply technology to developing countries, and to cooperate positively in international research projects.

(3) Japanese industry has been faced with major structural changes since the end of the high economic growth in the 1960s. Two oil crises generated the change toward technological innovation, the key for Japan to survive. In other words, we can say that we are transferring from the age of a technological culture, which depends heavily on energy from oil, to the age of new technology which has various fields of application developed by high technology.

Another major structural change came from Japan's widening international trade imbalance with other countries which led to the yen's appreciation since 1985. Japan's growing external imbalance is not desirable for the world economy nor for Japan itself, taking into consideration the future world economic situation in which international interdependence will increase. International economic imbalance can be corrected only through a well-directed policy coordination among the principal countries. So Japan has been placing emphasis on reorganizing the industrial structure so that it harmonizes with the international economy in the medium and long term and on accommodating Japan's savings and technological capabilities to contribute to the revitalization of the world economy as well as to progress in academic and basic research.

Under the economic structural change, Japan is trying to develop new businesses and the domestic market and to secure domestic investment opportunities, especially for improving the industrial infrastructure (R&D infrastructure, information communications systems, high-speed traffic networks, life-related environmental facilities, etc.).

The rapid appreciation of the yen has also affected the subcontractors of large enterprises, in the form of a decline in orders or in the unit prices of contracts. In addition, parent companies have shifted to overseas operations and the import of machine parts is expected to accelerate given current movements in the production costs. These structural changes have significant effects on small businesses and the R&D system, in terms of changing and reorganizing their conventional subcontract production system, or the network system, between parent companies and subcontractors, and transferring business attention positively towards domestic markets.

(4) Under the circumstances mentioned above, Japan's socio-economic needs include a more advanced industrial structure that maintains and creates employment; an improved trade structure and positive industrial adjustment; overcoming restrictions on natural resource and energy supplies; and coping with diversified consumer needs, the aging of the population and a highly information-based society.

3. R&D Policy for Techno-Industrial Innovation

The industrialized nations are trying to develop innovative technology in order to upgrade their industrial and employment structures and expand international trade. As mentioned above, technological innovation is essential for Japan from the following viewpoints: (i) acceleration of the sophistication of the industrial structure and the labour structure, and promoting the structural change of the Japanese economy and industry; (ii) a contribution to revitalize the international economy and trade; (iii) a contribution to improve the quality of life; and (iv) because of the significance of technology development from the aspect of economic security as it strengthens national bargaining power.

3.1 The Need for Basic Creative Technology

While Japanese industry achieved brilliant results in improving and applying imported technologies in the catching-up process, it is essential for Japan to develop technologies of its own. Japan has now started a new stage in the development of its technology. It can also be said that the development of available or existing technology in Japan is nearing completion. Japan needs more basic creative technology as a seed for future new production, while Europe and the U.S., on the other hand, have been making much greater efforts to develop new basic and product technology.

The technology trade in Japan has almost reached a balance after the large excess of imports in fiscal year 1985. Breakdown of technology trade by region and country in fiscal year 1985 shows the great excess of imports from the U.S. and Europe and the great excess of exports to Asia and other developing countries. While these trends mean that Japan's R&D position has recently been changing from conventional dependence on foreign technology to independent innovative technology, Japanese technological levels relatively still lag behind those of the U.S. and Europe in basic creative technology.

Japan is now setting up an R&D system of the self-developing type that requires more creativity than the conventional improvement type R&D system. Japan is also trying to change from a demand-led and mass-production economy to a demand-creation and high value added, R&D-based system. For this purpose, Japanese R&D policies, including educational policy, emphasize the development of creative technology. This necessitates the training of personnel capable of achieving technology breakthroughs, the systematic promotion of technology which identifies the priority for long-term technology developments, the establishment of systems, and funding, not least for governmental national projects for large, long-term, and risky technology developments. In order to push basic and innovative technology development and move into a new, prosperous stage, Japan needs major technological efforts, such as a new application and combination of existing technologies; the flowering of new technology, resulting from a new application of science and technology; and preparation for the next generation's epoch-making technological innovations.

In the 1980s, Japanese R&D policy has focused on developing fundamental technology through establishing and promoting: the Research and Development Project of Basic Technology for Future Technology which has been devoted to the development of such frontier technologies as new materials and new function elements; the Large Project (National R&D Programmes) which has brought together government and private companies in projects important to the national economy: R&D Projects on Energy such as the Sunshine Project (the utilization of solar energy, geothermal energy and coal conversion); the Moonlight Projects (highly efficient energy conservation by MITI in 1981); and various measures to promote the university-industry-government collaboration system.

3.2 University-Industry-Government Collaboration in R&D

In order to develop creativity, it is essential not only for industry, university and government to do their best in their respective capacities, but also for them to coordinate and share the work. Technological changes now require a higher level of cooperative R&D activities and close interaction between basic science and product and process technology.

Overall, innovation includes a wide range of activities from basic research to commercial application and marketing. The creation of new technology and knowledge and the translation of those into commercial products and services should be linked to the process of innovation diffusion. Thus, the university-industry connection is essential for enhancing the basic research and innovation development linkage and is going to be much more important for promoting basic creative technology. The university is a key centre for basic research but has difficulties pushing R&D itself without sufficient funds. Industry wants to acquire new innovative technology by utilizing the human resources and facilities in universities. Cooperative R&D is one of the effective strategies for companies faced with shortages of personnel and resources.

As mentioned before, Japan is now at a turning point with regard to technology development. After achieving brilliant results in improving and applying imported foreign technologies, Japan now needs to develop more original and creative technology as a technology-based nation. On the other hand, faced with strongly growing international competition, the U.S. is also trying to develop not only creative basic technology but also applied and product technologies.

It can be said that the R&D system, particularly the university-industry-government R&D collaboration, has been quite different historically in the two countries. Generally speaking, the key collaboration in R&D in the U.S. to develop creative basic technology is ascribed to the collaboration between research universities and industries, and also to national military projects. The development of Silicon Valley is a typical example.

Technology development in the postwar period in Japan was characterized as a product and process type development based mainly on imported foreign technologies. The key collaboration in Japan is the collaboration between government and industry, and among firms. The differences arose from historical needs for technological development, business practices, governmental policies, industrial structures, cultural factors, etc. At the present turning point, it can be said that the R&D system with regard to the university-industry-government connection in both countries is changing toward setting up a new R&D collaboration.

In the U.S. many universities and companies have established many varied types of relationships to meet the different objectives of the two sectors, such as Research Parks, the Cooperative Research Center, Industrial Affiliates Programmes, the Technology Licensing Programme, consulting, personal and information changes, philanthropy, and shared equipment use. The federal and local governments have played a significant role in creating and sustaining various types of university-industry collaboration and expediting technology transfer. Cooperative R&D can mean various types of collaboration with regard to the university-industry-government connection, and each type has positive and negative aspects as regards promoting technology development. While various university-industry collaborations have many mutual benefits, several factors (restrictions in communication of research agenda priority, faculty involvement in business activities, conflicts of interest and direction of effort, etc.) pose problems. In order to achieve a more effective type of collaboration, Japan is trying to set up a new university-industry-government collaboration in R&D, especially university-industry collaboration, and needs to reduce institutional and psychological barriers and strengthen university-industry-government collaboration by alleviating the cumbersome handling of the research contracts, and improving various areas related to human and financial activities and the use of facilities and equipment.

As for industrial technology development policies, the government has a major role to play in promoting fundamental research, applied research and other related activities to create an environment which enables private firms to make full use of their vitality, in view of the fact that at present approximately 70% of the total expenditure of technology development is made by the private sector in Japan. In recent Japanese R&D policy, the Japanese government passed a bill for the facilitation of research in fundamental technologies in 1985 to enable the use of national assets so as to facilitate research in fundamental technologies by private firms and to establish the Japan Key Technology Center as an organization to promote research through the supplying of risk capital and of other needs in fundamental technologies both by private firms and by government-industry-university collaboration in R&D. Other policies such as tax incentives for R&D in fundamental technologies, conditional loans for important R&D projects, a joint R&D system between industry and national universities, the Technopolis programme and the R&D system of basic technology for the Next Generation Industry have also been set up to promote government-industry-university collaboration. There are also university-directed R&D projects. Thus, Japan is also now trying to overcome conventional institutional constraints, to change the R&D system and set up new government-industry-university R&D collaboration, and to change the function of the university so that it becomes much more important than hitherto in the development of original and creative technology.

3.3 State-Led Innovation Aiming at a New Stage of the Industrialized Country

The scale of R&D is increasing larger and innovation is becoming much more costly and difficult. To overcome these global problems, that cannot be dealt with by a single country alone, cooperation among industrialized nations in R&D is vital for advancing technological development and the progress of the world's economy. Joint research projects, in which all participating countries contribute, are most effective for technology development in solving universal problems and overcoming the difficulties of large-scale technology.

Under economic and industrial structural change, Japan is also trying *to vitalize regional economies through various R&D projects*. For instance, there are many laboratories under the Agency of Industrial Science and Technology (MITI) in Tsukuba research park and other places which take the lead in basic R&D, reinforcing tie-ups among private industries, universities and government agencies to promote joint government-private sector research. The Technopolis plan and other regional plans such as the New Media Community plan aim at revitalizing and further developing regional economies based upon high-technology industrial complexes, information networks and other high-technology facilities and industries.

Aiming at the creation of attractive towns in which industry, academia, and housing are organically united, the Technopolis plan provides for introducing technologically advanced industries into regional towns, and raising the technological level of existing industries. In an effort to build independent and vigorous regional economies, technology is used as the nucleus and regional autonomy is encouraged as is active participation by the private sector. The Japanese government, in order to provide long-range guidance on policy aims, enacted the Law for Accelerating Regional Development based upon High-Technology Industrial Complexes in 1983, along with establishing accreditation procedures, incentive measures such as in the tax system (special depreciation and loss allowances, the reduction of local taxes), finance (a special lending system provided by the Japan development Bank and other banks for the encouragement of regional technology), a subsidy system (for R&D), and other steps toward the concept's realization. Up to 1987 there have been 20 areas in 21 prefectures which have applied for approval of their technopolis development plans based upon this law.

As mentioned above, Japan is helping industries *diversify their efforts at technology development* and *create better linkages between technologies*, by identifying ways in which technologies from different fields can be organically merged to bring about new technological innovation. Economies of scope, in contrast to economies of scale, are becoming increasingly more advantageous along with moves toward fusion on technologies of different fields and toward more divided and small quantity demand. The expansion of basic research activities and promotion of technology fusion between different fields are expected to lead to increasing market opportunities for technologically innovative areas in the future, especially for small businesses in Japan to convert their businesses and develop their new fields under the conditions of economic structural change. The Japanese government is now promoting the fusion of technologies and industrial sectors in such ways as the diversification of businesses or tie-ups between firms operating in different sectors of industry. Progress is likely in the future through various policy measures such as tax changes, financial assistance, subsidies for R&D in small business, the setting up a new organization of small businesses in different fields to promote industrial restructuring after the yen's rapid appreciation in 1987.

The situation of small businesses in Japan, especially in manufacturing industry, was stagnant due to the effect of the high value of the yen in the fiscal year 1986-87. This high value of the yen caused not only short-term but also long-term problems, including changes in Japan's competitiveness against the NICs in Asia, overseas production, and an increase in the import of parts. In order to survive in such an environment, small businesses are trying to change from an export orientation to be more domestic-demand-oriented, and are trying to improve further managerial resources, new technology, information technology, skills and funding. Small businesses have contributed greatly to structural change, especially in Japanese manufacturing industry, through opening and closing of businesses, changes in industrial structure, company scale and product, and promoting frontier technology development.

granting of funds to firms. The state in Japan, consequently, aims at university-industry linkages, and uses its powers and its funding to introduce the necessary relationships. Science becomes an instrument of state policy on techno-industrial innovation; the Technopolis strategy highlights this most impressively.

The amortization of the investments, on the other hand, is not really a problem, because the domestic market is large enough to avoid this problem. International markets, in addition, are open to export sales from the enterprises that have become powerful because of the domestic sales opportunities. The fact that there is no need for the organization of markets to guarantee amortization of investments draws particular attention to the importance of techno-scientific progress. The turning point in R&D stands for a new (science-based) industrial development, but it also indicates the continuation and increase of the important role of the state in economic development.

Bibliography

AN OUTLOOK FOR JAPAN'S INDUSTRIAL SOCIETY TOWARDS THE 21ST-CENTURY (1986), *Interm Report by the Industrial Structure Council Focussing on International Perspective*, MITI.

DEVELOPMENT OF UNIVERSITY-INDUSTRY COOPERATIVE RESEARCH CENTERS (1984), *Historical Profiles*, National Science Foundation, November.

THE FEDERAL ROLE IN FOSTERING UNIVERSITY-INDUSTRY COOPERATION (1983), *General Accounting Office*, May 25.

GUIDE OF POLICY MEASURES FOR VENTURE BUSINESSES (1987), Venture Enterprise Center.

HAYASHI, Yasuo (1985), *Technology Policy of Japan - Government Policy towards Industry in the U.S. and Japan*.

INDUSTRIAL INVESTMENT IN JAPAN (1987), MITI.

THE INTERIM REPORT BY THE RESEARCH GROUP ON VENTURE BUSINESSES (1984), MITI.

JAPAN IN THE GLOBAL COMMUNITY: ITS ROLE AND CONTRIBUTION ON THE EVE OF THE 21ST CENTURY (1987), Round Table Discussion on Japan in the Global Community.

LARGE NATIONAL PROJECT (1987), *Agency of Industrial Science and Technology*, MITI.

MITI, LONG-TERM VISION OF JAPANESE INDUSTRIES, 1970s, 1980s.

OUTLINE OF THE SMALL AND MEDIUM ENTERPRISE POLICIES OF THE JAPANESE GOVERNMENT (1986), Small and Medium Enterprise Agency.

REIMERS, Nils (1984), *The Government-Industry-University Interface: Improving the Innovative Process*, Technological Innovation the 80s.

THE REPORT OF THE STRUCTURAL CHANGES OF JAPANESE SOCIETY AND THE OUTLOOK OF TECHNOLOGY INNOVATION (1987), MITI.

ROGGERS, Everett M. (1985), *Role of the Research University in the Information Society: Lessons Learned from American Universities and Technological Innovation.*

ROGGERS, Everett M., and LARSEN, Judith K. (1984), *Silicon Valley Fever: Growth of High-Technology Culture*, New York: Basic Books.

THE ROLE OF SMALL AND MEDIUM ENTERPRISES IN JAPAN'S INDUSTRIAL STRUCTURE (1986), Small and Medium Enterprise Agency.

SURVEY ON JAPANESE VENTURE BUSINESSES (1986), Venture Enterprises Center.

THE TECHNOPOLIS PLAN, THE HUMAN FRONTIER SCIENCE PROGRAM (1987), *News from MITI.*

TRENDS OF PRINCIPAL INDICATORS ON RESEARCH AND DEVELOPMENT IN JAPAN (1987), Agency of Industrial Science and Technology, MITI.

THE TWENTY-FIRST CENTURY ENERGY VISION (1987), MITI.

UNIVERSITY-INDUSTRY RESEARCH RELATIONSHIP: SELECTED STUDIES (1982), National Science Foundation, May.

WHITE PAPER ON ECONOMIC COOPERATION (1987), MITI.

WHITE PAPER ON INTERNATIONAL TRADE (1987), MITI.

WHITE PAPER ON SCIENCE AND TECHNOLOGY, SCIENCE AND TECHNOLOGY AGENCY (1986-1987), MITI.

WHITE PAPER ON SMALL AND MEDIUM ENTERPRISES (1987), MITI.

11

Manufacturing Innovation and American Industrial Competitiveness

Stephen S. Cohen and John Zysman[1]

A growing debate on American competitiveness and productivity has focused attention on manufacturing and manufacturing innovation (Cohen and Zysman 1987; Cohen et al. 1984; Krugman and Hatsopoulos 1987; Scott and Lodge (eds.) 1985). The scale and composition of the trade deficits of the past few years are the most prominent indicator that the competitive position of the American economy is weakening (Kremp and Mistral 1985). The debate is about why the deficits have developed and what they mean. Our position is that much of the problem lies in an erosion of American manufacturing skills and capacities. If our position is correct, traditional economic remedies cannot in themselves reverse the decline in America's position in the international economy.

---

[1]   This article was first published in *Science*, March 1988, Vol.239, 1110-1115.

The huge trade deficits of the 1980s were driven by sharp increases in the value of the dollar that priced American goods out of world markets and made imports a bargain. The inflow of funds to finance the budget deficits pushed the exchange rate up. Consequently, some economists argue, the problem is fundamentally one of mistaken domestic macro-economic policy. The process that created the trade deficits is reversible: reduce the budget deficit, thereby reducing demand for foreign borrowings to finance it; thereby reduce the trade deficit. To us this view is not so much wrong as it is limited and limiting.

Fifteen years ago this traditional remedy worked; devaluation rapidly reversed trade flows. This time, however, it has not, at least not as expected. Since 1985, the dollar has lost about one-half its value against the yen, but the trade deficit has stubbornly refused to follow suit. Only at the end of 1987 was a monthly decline first registered, and that to $13 billion, itself a record just a few months earlier. Certainly there is some price for the dollar at which imports would dry up and exports explode - if people had confidence that the exchange rate advantage would last. But balancing our external trade account is not the objective. All nations, even the poorest, eventually do. The trick is to do it with high and rising incomes: that is the definition of competitiveness (Cohen et al. 1984). A permanently falling dollar translates into a continually impoverishing America. Clearly something new is affecting America's position in the international economy. What is it?

First, we have new competitors. The most important are Japan and Asia's newly industrializing countries (NICs). Japan's trade pattern is quite contrary to those of other advanced economies, for which intrasectoral trade has been the key to open trade. Japan uniquely has imported almost nothing in those sectors in which it is a major exporter.[2] Second, the currencies of the Asian NICs with whom we run major trade deficits have not risen against the dollar to the extent the yen and European currencies have.

Most important, the United States once had dominant positions in product and production. We made products others

---

[2] Cohen and Zysman 1987: tables 8.1, 8.2, and 8.3.

couldn't make or couldn't begin to make competitively. Consequently, high wages and a high dollar did not displace us from markets. That situation has changed. In more technical terms, the price elasticities of American imports and exports have changed (Kremp and Mistral 1985).

In the past two years the soaring yen has confronted Japan with a currency shock similar to the one we faced in 1981. A comparable percentage rise in the dollar flattened industrial investment and created massive trade deficits. But despite a doubling of the yen against the dollar, and a set of special emergency measures aimed at increasing imports, the Japanese increased investment in production and have sustained a trade surplus. Why are the American and Japanese responses to massive currency movements so different? The contrasting behavior of the two economies in analogous situations suggests different efforts and capabilities to respond to economic challenges through innovation in manufacturing (Dosi 1984; Pavitt 1984; Rosenberg 1982).

Determined Japanese firms attempt to increase productivity and flexibility and introduce new products as a means of defending market position. Certainly many Japanese firms have absorbed yen increases, often out of exceptional profit margins that resulted from a combination of U.S. quotas on imports and Japanese production advantages. And some costs are reduced as a strengthening yen lowers import costs of raw materials and components. A year ago major firms announced that they would remain competitive from a Japanese production base even if the yen rose to 120 to the dollar, while in some segments of electronics the principal Japanese firms could remain competitive with the yen at 90 to the dollar (Japan Economic Journal, 27 December 1986).

We must not lose perspective. Not all Japanese producers are that good, and not all production activities lend themselves to such dramatic improvements. Japanese firms are also moving production off-shore, although their capacities for production innovation remain great. However, there is little belief in Japan that moving off-shore to produce in a cheaper labor environment is a viable long-term solution.

Yet another view of the trade deficit argues that the problem is not one of American firms, which know perfectly well how to produce and compete, but of America as a production location (Kravis and Lipsey 1984; Lipsey and Kravis 1985). The inference, quite at variance with the argument advanced here, is drawn from data on the export performance of American multinational corporations (MNCs). Between 1966 and 77 American MNCs increased their share of world exports, maintaining it through 1983 while the American national share dropped. There are major problems with the inferences the authors chose to draw from the data. First, much of the data represent automotives and aeronautics. But despite the high exports automotives generate from various countries, the competitive positions of Ford and GM have substantially weakened since 1966. Sales of military aircraft are not the best indicators of economic efficiency. Boeing, the dominant company in commercial aircraft, operates less as an American MNC than as an American domestic producer that exports substantially. This correction aside, America's competitive position in commercial aircraft is weaker now than it was in 1966. Airbus has become a major competitor; Japan is building an aircraft industry, in part as a subcontractor to Boeing, while established European companies and upstart Brazilians produce short-range and specialty craft. But most important, in these and other sectors, what does it mean that American multinationals export so much from diverse locations? Those export numbers could be as much a sign of weakness as of strength. They could indicate decisions to manufacture components, subsystems, and even final products in various cheap-labor locations abroad and export them back to the mother company in the U.S. - perhaps the company has failed to innovate in manufacturing and no longer has the skills to produce competitively in high-wage locations. The U.S. consumer electronics industry exhibited that kind of busy export performance as it was being sliced down by Japanese competitors who operated from a base that included rapidly rising wages, rapidly rising productivity, and a trajectory of innovation in production that proved decisive.

In sum, inferences drawn from the export performance of American MNCs do not undermine our hypothesis that there is an important link between America's competitiveness problem and our difficulties in manufacturing innovation.

1. The Success of Mass-Production and its Technological Basis

At the core, we propose, the difficulty lies not in our machines and technology, but in organizations and the use of people in production, in the strategies for automation and the goals we attempt to achieve with production innovation. The problem is not with our robots or our local area networks, but with our understanding of how to exploit their productive promise. In the first part of the century, American firms built the model of advanced production. What went wrong? How did we fall from our position of leadership?

Here we must simplify a very complicated story (Cohen and Zysman 1987). In the late 19th and early 20th centuries, the United States developed an industrial structure that projected this country into global economic preeminence. That structure rested on two fundamental innovations: mass-production and the hierarchical multi-divisional corporation.

Mass-production began in the early 19th century with producing interchangeable parts for guns; with Henry Ford's production of automobiles it became the model of how to produce in an advanced economy. It meant volume production of standardized products for a relatively homogeneous market. Volume allowed the specialization of tasks, both for machines and people. Moderately skilled workers, moreover, could produce sophisticated products.

The organization of people and machines turned on an underlying concept of how to produce. The concept was variously labeled Taylorism, for the management of people, or Fordism, for its market and production strategy. The hierarchical but divisionalized corporation, likewise, emerged in the United States to permit administrative control of complex activities on a continental scale (Chandler 1962; 1977).

During World War II and in the years that followed, this American system of management and production conquered the world. At home, the system defined the lines along which technological advance would proceed, and technological advance steadily improved the system's performance. Despite new technologies and new industries developing during the past forty years, the basics remained entrenched until challenged by foreign competitors using different approaches.

Why, then, did the system freeze? First, many sectors such as autos and steel became stable oligopolies with only marginally increasing demand, and high barriers to entry. These structures tended to divert competition from production costs or basic technological development to marginal product, process, and style changes. Also, complex social structures have resilience and inertia. Because the production structure developed elaborate systems of labor relations and comparably complex systems of management training, recruitment, organization, and reward, massive forces had structured themselves around the basic design of that production system. Changing it would mean changing them. Finally, there was the inescapable fact that the system worked. It won the war; it won the peace. It was successful beyond any precedent or any contemporary comparison, and it could be steadily improved. The mass-production paradigm was not going to change without outside pressure. Suddenly we were vulnerable to innovation from abroad.

2. Production Innovation and the Importance of Advanced Manufacturing

The innovations that emerged abroad took two forms. One involved nationally distinct government policies for managing advanced industrial economies, policies that favored investment over consumption and allowed government's direct participation in the protection and promotion of industrial development. The second, the central part of our story, came in manufacturing and more broadly in the organization of production. During the postwar period, the gap between America and its allies closed. Yet while attempting to imitate American practice, firms and governments abroad established distinct manufacturing systems that suited their economic circumstances and social settings. Later, as world markets changed, and as technology gaps among advanced nations narrowed, the newly established models of production proved to have significant advantages.

The emblematics of these production innovations are code words such as "just-in-time production" and "quality circles", which at once suggest and obscure concrete changes in the way goods are designed and produced. The innovations in the best firms extend beyond the shop floor to the nature of the product, beginning with a design concern for manufacturability and extending to a corporate strategy in which anticipated economies of scope can justify investments in new technologies that are difficult to justify through more traditional criteria, and that figure in the firm's strategic positioning against its competitors. Unfortunately, at present only limited systematic evidence exists to demonstrate that production organization differs sharply between countries, let alone that those differences are crucial to the success of firms. For now we find only clues drawn from narrower research projects. First we look at two images of production, one from Japan and the other from Italy. We use the word "image" intentionally, because images are more suggestive than models are robust and complete. From Japan emerges the picture of the high-volume, automated factory operating through the night with no lights and no workers. The Japanese are not simply copying American production with less expensive capital or even pushing the American model of mass-production to its logical conclusion. Something quite different is happening. For example, as part of a general reorganization of production, Japanese producers have reduced inventories and improved materials flows as well as altering quality control processes and substantially reducing labor content.

The important outcome is that the relationship between production and corporate strategy is altered. Manufacturing becomes a competitive weapon. The evidence is overwhelming that low cost has not been the only or the most important advantage of Japanese production innovations. The Japanese did not invent the color television, the video tape recorder, or the semiconductor. But they developed designs and manufacturing systems that created decisive competitive advantage. It was not Japanese advances in the design of microchips, but in the yields of the production systems, that have made them the largest microchip producers and exporters in the past five years. Equally important have been their innovations in the organization of production, which permit them to introduce new products rapidly and constantly to improve and adapt the workings of that system. Honda defended its market position in motorcycles in Japan by abruptly introducing an entire new product line. The product cycle from design to production for Honda automobiles is faster than any foreign rival's (Abbeglen and Stalk 1985). American producers, in contrast, typically do not innovate production incrementally. They tend to jump from one production plateau to another; change is slower and riskier (Wheelright and Hayes 1984). Japan's flexibility has developed from continuous production innovation, often with internal design of equipment and a skilled workforce able to understand and implement the continuous changes. Advanced production technologies are not an alternative to skilled workers. It is the capacity to manage the continuous evolution of the production system, and not merely the ability to operate an automated factory, that is the competitive meaning of post-industrial manufacturing.

Japan is not the only source of production innovation. In Italy networks of small firms have developed a different approach to innovative production organization, that of flexible specialization. Using modified traditional technologies, communities of small firms have established themselves as world-class producers in sectors such as textiles, apparel, and machine-tools. These horizontal networks involve shifting combinations of cooperation and competition, with today's collaborators being tomorrow's competitors. Similar networks of world-class machine-tool firms are found in Germany as well, suggesting that the model is not purely Italian.

The horizontal model of Italy and the vertical or Japanese model differ greatly from one another; furthermore, circumscribed within each general model are major differences in practice. Yet they share some common features, one of which is to limit inventories. The need for inventories is radically reduced, whereby some inventories are pushed back to suppliers who themselves learn to modify production to limit their own inventory needs. A second common element is a network of small suppliers tied to common tasks by market relations and direct hands-on contact rather than by administration and bureaucracy. Those fluid networks give flexibility to small and large companies alike. Some of the networks are vertical, with tiers of suppliers linked to large firms such as Fiat and Beneton in Italy or Toyota in Japan. Others are horizontal networks. These networks, these steps toward vertical disintegration of production, were not created deliberately. Rather, in Japan and

Italy hordes of small producers survived, in part through political protection, into the late 20th century. As a result, small firms account for more manufacturing in Japan and Italy than in other advanced countries. The networked system was created as producers, large and small, sought ways of competing in national and global markets in the 20th century. The pattern differed from that established under American conditions. The networks proved more flexible, and resolved problems that traditional administrative integration could not.

Rapid expansion in Japan, and in a less steady way in Italy, permitted capital investment and the introduction of new machines, and in the effort to catch up to more established technologies forced iterative production innovation. Introducing new machines opens the possibility of production reorganization, but does not assure it.[3] Nor do new production systems assure increased productivity. Indeed, new production systems rarely function perfectly when first introduced and initially may lower productivity. Yet rapid growth generated not only investment in new machines, but also new approaches to manufacturing, new organizations to implement them, and new strategies to gain advantage from them (Murakami and Yamamura 1982). The innovations that initially were ways of competing in a world in which our allies were laggards became unexpectedly the basis of advantage.

3. The Flexibility Question and the Rethinking of Manufacturing

Basic approaches to manufacturing are changing. An effort is being made to create the concepts and language to examine and discuss these changes, and flexibility is the code word (Sayer 1985; Piore and Sabel 1986; Coriat 1986, 1987; Coriat and Boyer 1986). Traditional mass-production is inherently rigid. It rests on volume production of standard products or components with

---

[3] This is emphasized by Wheelright and Hayes (1984). Often the introduction of new technology leads to a drop in productivity levels. Only when the reorganization is effective are the potentials of new equipment captured. Our view is that when equipment is crafted in-house to fit the needs of organization developed on the shop floor, the disruption is limited or non-existent.

specialized machines dedicated to specific tasks. Now the notion is to apply a set of more general-purpose tools to produce a greater range of products. Importantly, the bulk of manufacturing has involved batch production that was difficult to automate. Now new approaches and programmable equipment open batch production to increased automation, and reduce some of the cost difference between batch and series production.

Flexibility, a firm's ability to vary what it produces, rests on organization. As a matter of fact, flexible organization precedes flexible machinery and the flexible use of programmable equipment. The same machines can be used in rigid or flexible automation. Technology itself is channeled and formed by the conceptions of those who would use it. However, flexibility is an imprecise objective as much as a description, and has come to mean not one, but a variety, of ways to adjust company operations to shifting market conditions. Static flexibility suggests that a firm's ability to adjust operations at any moment to changes in the mix of products in the market is demanding. If one product is not selling, can production be oriented quickly to another? It implies adjustment within the confines of established products and a fixed production structure. This notion is captured in the distinction between economies of scale and economies of scope. Economies of scale are the notion that the cost of producing a single unit declines as volume increases. Economies of scope are gained not in the volume production of a single good, but in the volume production of a set of goods (Goldhar and Jelinek 1983). Scope and scale often move together: large-scale plants may be required to realize flexibility. The advantages of scale do not disappear. Very expensive production lines make possible the volume production of a variety of products. In some industries, such as semiconductors, the cost of a basic production line - economies of scale - has risen steadily even while application- and user-specific products have become possible. Economies of scope are created by standardizing processes to manufacture a variety of products.

Dynamic flexibility, in contrast to static flexibility, means the ability to increase productivity through improvements in production processes and product innovation. The capability to change quickly in response to product or production technology - to put ideas into action quickly - is the central notion. In a period when automation technologies permit new production strategies, dynamic flexibility is crucial (Klein 1986). Yet as Jaikumar points out, making flexibility and responsiveness the mission of manufacturing "flies in the face of Taylor's view of the world which for 75 years has shaped thinking about manufacturing" (Jaikumar 1986).

4. The Problem in the Evolution of American Manufacturing

Is American industry capturing the possibilities of new technologies, or is it caught in an increasingly obsolete production paradigm? The evidence, which by its nature is fragmentary, comes in two forms. The first is a large set of industry and firm case studies of international competition and production organization. These cases are more than anecdotes, for taken together they represent a substantial share of the economy and tell a consistent story, a story of slow and partial adjustment. In steel American firms import from Japan production know-how that was based on an earlier Austrian innovation. In automobiles American firms struggle to match the cost and quality performance that has enabled Japanese firms to capture a large, permanent share of the American market. In both sectors the recent drop in the dollar's value has closed the gap in final costs, but has not placed American firms on a competitive trajectory of technology development. The semiconductor industry recently was shocked to discover that its seeming technological advantage was vulnerable to production developments in Japan.

The production tools that embody know-how and innovation - machine-tools in metal bending industries, automatic looms and jet spinners in textiles, photolithographic and ion implantation in semiconductors - increasingly are imported. One offshore producer of apparel argues that on paper the economies permit him to bring production back to the United States, but the required skills and infrastructure no longer exist. They can be found in cheap-labor locations. It is not simply that a set of firms or sectors are in difficulty, but that the infrastructure of production know-how has weakened. A change in relative prices achieved through changes in exchange rates will not quickly reverse this erosion.

In the late 1960s and early 1970s, American firms faced with foreign competition often concluded that their rivals used low-cost labor to achieve competitive advantage. Few firms realized that innovations in production, usually achieved with limited technological advance and considerable organizational imagination, were occurring. The flight of American firms offshore to low-cost production sites represented, finally, a means to defend existing production structures. It sheltered firms from the need to rethink their own production strategies.

If our argument is correct that American industry is not effectively implementing the potentials of production innovation, what additional forms of evidence should we expect to find? First, the ways America uses advanced technologies would differ from the ways our best competitors use them. American firms would not capture the full potential of new technologies: rather than creating flexible systems, they would implement new technologies in traditional ways. Second, advanced technologies for innovative production would not diffuse as widely in the United States. Standard data sets for measuring economic activity do not address the question of production organization. Large-scale comparative studies that would directly test our notion do not exist. Yet there are narrower, more limited studies that support the argument. Let us consider two such studies.

The first question is how new technologies are used. One recent study compares the use of flexible manufacturing systems (FMS) for the production of comparable products in Japan and the United States. The average number of machines in the Japanese FMS was six, and in the American system seven (Jaikumar 1986). However, "the number of parts made by an FMS in the United States was 10; in Japan, the average was 93, almost ten times greater.... The annual volume per part in the United States was 1,727; in Japan only 258" (Jaikumar 1986). The Americans used the tools as instruments of an old-style approach to manufacturing. They also failed to exploit them for introducing new products. The rate of new product introduction was 22 times greater in Japan than in the United States. Jaikumar concluded that, with few exceptions, the flexible manufacturing systems installed in the United States show an astonishing lack of flexibility in use. In many cases, they perform worse than the conventional technology they replace. "The technology itself is not to blame. It is the management that makes the difference" (Jaikumar 1986). The risk is that the social inertia of existing arrangements lock American producers into reinforcing rather than replacing existing production systems. A few examples give a sense of the situation. General Motors invested $50 billion in production during several years only to discover that its margins were the lowest in the industry, its break-even volume point was the highest, and that no clear production strategy had emerged (Forbes 1987; Quinn 1986). The purposes of automation and the organization suited to capture the advantages of new technologies have not been worked out in many American firms; thus new technologies are not introduced or have limited impact when they are.

The second dimension is the diffusion of advanced technology. Arcangeli et al. examined the introduction of advanced automation technology into factories in advanced countries (Arcangeli et al. 1987). Their techniques and data sought to separate advanced from traditional manufacturing investment. Two conclusions are suggested. First, the United States leads the way in office automation, but trails in factory automation. Second, America invests more in traditional automation and less in flexible manufacturing than comparable countries do. The pace at which advanced technologies are introduced is slow: that is, only a small percentage of firms use such things as flexible manufacturing systems. Yet those American firms that use them tend to be leaders in their sectors. These data are consistent with studies of specific technologies, such as robots.

Numerically controlled machine-tools and the advanced languages to implement them emerged early in the United States, as did the technology and use of robots. However, as is widely known, they are used much more extensively in Japan than in the United States; diffusion is several times broader, with some 40% of the machines in smaller firms (Klein 1986).

The evidence is powerful. Aggregate trends reinforce factory and sector studies. The argument that there is a problem in the evolution of American manufacturing is now strong enough to require refutation rather than demonstration.

Despite the disturbing past, there is no reason that those trends must continue. The picture is complex and changing. Many American firms have begun to innovate in production organization. Allen Bradley, Black and Decker, Cypress Semi-conductor, Texas Instruments, and IBM all provide examples. It is not yet possible to judge whether there is new life in American industry or whether the successes are "valiant but isolated". It is not, in our view, because of a lack of evidence. The future is being created, and the outcomes are inherently not knowable (Electronic Business, September 15, 1986). The difficulty is that the more systematic data, of a variety of sorts, suggest that the troubles outbalance the advances. Jay Jaikumar of the Harvard Business School summarized the problem well: "The battle is on and the United States is losing badly. It may even lose the war if it does not soon figure out how better to use the new technology of automation for competitive advantage. This does not mean investing in more equipment; in today's environment, it is how the equipment is used that is important". A "manufacturing gap", the counterpart of the technology gap of earlier years, has emerged, and this time it is the United States that lags behind.

5. Conclusions: Important Linkages between Innovation and Manufacturing

We have tried to show here that weakness in production innovation is central to America's competitiveness problem. For a firm, production capability is a decisive competitive tool. It is not just a question of marginal cost advantages; a firm cannot control what it cannot produce competitively. There is little chance of compensating for production weakness by seeking enduring technological advantage (Cohen and Zysman 1987). A production disadvantage will quickly erode a firm's technological advantage. Only by capturing the "rent" on an innovation through volume sales of a product can a company amortize its R&D costs and invest in R&D for the next-generation product. The feeble American presence in next-generation consumer electronics indicates the cost of failure to produce competitively in the previous generation. Finally, if a firm simply tries to sell a laboratory product to someone else to produce, the value of the design is lower than that of a prototype, and prototypes are valued lower than products having established markets, as each step toward the market decreases uncertainty. A producer with a strong market position often can buy a portfolio of technologies at a low price and capture the technology rents through volume sales. For the firm, manufacturing matters.

Mastery and control of manufacturing is equally critical to the nation. This fact, so central to policy-making, has been obscured by a popular myth that sees economic development as a process of sectoral succession. Economies develop as they shift out of sunset industries into sunrise sectors. Agriculture is followed by industry, which in turn is sloughed off to less developed places as the economy moves on to services and high technology. Simply put, this is incorrect. It is incorrect as history and it is incorrect as policy prescription. America did not shift out of agriculture or move it off-shore. We automated it; we shifted labor out and substituted massive amounts of capital, technology, and education to increase output. Critically, many of the high value added service jobs we are told will substitute for industrial activity are not substitutes, they are complements. Lose industry and you will lose, not develop, those service activities. These service activities are tightly linked to production just as the crop duster (in usual statistics a service worker) is tightly linked to agriculture. If the farm moves off-shore, the crop duster does too, as does the large-animal vet. Similar sets of tight linkages - but at vastly greater scale - tie "service" jobs to mastery and control of production. Many high value added service activities are functional extensions of an ever more elaborate division of labor in production. The shift we are experiencing is not from an industrial economy to a post-industrial economy, but rather to a new kind of industrial economy.

The choices we make now will shape our future. We cannot simply imitate our most successful competitors, although we must learn from them. Just as new and innovative industrial solutions emerged abroad in response to American industrial success, so we must create our own innovations in response to new pressures. The innovations, moreover, will emerge incrementally. There will be no simple formulas, no one magic trick. Our choices, moreover, are sharply limited by a set of constraints and opportunities. In our view there are three principal constraints. First, as a nation we cannot compete in world markets by cutting wages. Not only will it not work because there are many willing to work at wages forever lower than those we can pay, but also it would mean a total and catastrophic change in our society. Happily there is substantial evidence that a highly skilled workforce can sustain the productivity and value added to be a highly paid one. Second, a retreat to defensive protection will not serve as a long-term policy to sustain high wages and productivity. Third, policies that are radically inequitable are unlikely to generate the broad political support required for a national commitment to long-term growth and innovation.

The opportunities are equally constricting. Ours is a world in which science and technology, capital and management know-how, are widely available. Consequently, our international competitiveness is based on how effectively we develop and diffuse technology and product and production know-how to our firms and how effectively we use those technologies. Effectively using those technical possibilities depends on management visions and worker skills. Simply put, in the long run investment in science, in technological development and diffusion, and in education are all that will sustain us.

Bibliography

ABBEGLEN, James C., and STALK, George (1985), *Kaisha: The Japanese Corporation*. New York: Basic Books.

ARCANGELI, Fabio, DOSI, Giovanni, and MOGGI, Massimo (1987), *Patterns of Diffusion of Electronics Technologies*. Prepared for conference on Programmable Automation and New Work Modes, GERTTD Paris VII, Paris 2-4 April.

CHANDLER, Albert (1962), *Strategy and Structure: Chapters in the History of the Industrial Enterprise*. Cambridge, Mass.: M.I.T. Press.

CHANDLER, Albert (1977), *The Visible Hand: the Managerial Revolution in American Business*. Cambridge, Mass.: Belknap Press.

COHEN, Stephen, and ZYSMAN, John (1987), *Manufacturing Matters: The Myth of the Post-Industrial Economy*. New York: Basic Books.

COHEN, Steve, TEECE, David, TYSON, Laura, and ZYSMAN, John (1984), *Competitiveness*, Vol.3 President's Commission on Industrial Competitiveness, November, available as BRIE Working Paper No.8. BRIE, University of California, Berkeley.

CORIAT, Benjamin (1986), *Automatisation Programmable et Produits Differencies*, GERTTD Conference.

CORIAT, Benjamin (1987), *Information, Technologies, Productivity, and New Job Content*. Paper presented at BRIE conference Production Reorganization in a Changing World, September.

CORIAT, Benjamin, and BOYER, Robert (1986), *Technical Flexibility and Macro-Stabilization*. Paper presented to the Venice Conference on Innovation, Diffusion, April 2-4.

DOSI, Giovanni (1984), Institutions and Markets in a Dynamic World, in: *The Manchester School* (forthcoming).

ELECTRONIC BUSINESS (1986), *The Manufacturing Zeal of Tracy O'Rourk*, September 15.

FORBES (1987), *Fiddling with Figures While Sales Drop*, August 24.

GOLDHAR, Joel D., and JELINEK, Marianne (1983), Plan for Economies of Scope, in: *Harvard Business Review*, November/December.

JAIKUMAR (1986), Postindustrial Manufacturing, in: *Harvard Business Rev*iew, Vol.64, 69.

THE JAPAN ECONOMIC JOURNAL (1986), *Honda Prepares to Survive Yen Rise up to 120 to U.S. Dollar*. 27 December.

KLEIN, Burton (1986), Dynamic Competition and Productivity Advances, in: LANDAU, R., and ROSENBERG N. (eds.), *Positive Sum Strategy: Harnessing Technology for Economic Growth*. Washington, D.C.: National Academy Press.

KRAVIS, Irving B., and LIPSEY, Robert E. (1984), *Productivity and Trade Shares*. Washington, D.C.: NBER Conference on Research and Recent and Prospective U.S. Trade Policy, March.

KREMP, Elizabeth, and MISTRAL, Jacques (1985), Commerce Exterieur Americain: d'ou vient, ou va le deficit?, in: *Economie Prospective Internationale 22*. Paris: Centre d'Etudes Prospectives et d'Information Internationales CEPII.

KRUGMAN, Paul, and HATSOPOULOS, George (1987), The Problem of U.S. Competitiveness in Manufacturing, in: *New England and Economic Review*, (Federal Reserve Bank of Boston, Jan-Feb).

LIPSEY, Robert E., and KRAVIS, Irving B. (1985), The Competitive Position of American Manufacturing Firms, in: *Banca Nazionale del Lavoro Quarterly Review*. June.

MURAKAMI, Yasusuke, and YAMAMURA, Kozo (1982), A Technical Note on Japanese Firm Behavior and Economic Policy, in: *Policy and Trade Issues*, 115-116.

PAVITT, Keith (1984), Sectoral Patterns of Innovation; Toward a Taxomony and Theory, in: *Research Policy*.

PIORE, Michael, and SABEL, Charles F. (1986), *The Second Industrial Divide*.

QUINN, Dennis (1986), *Dynamic Markets and Mutating Firms*, BRIE Working Paper No.26.

ROSENBERG, Nathan (1982), *Inside the Black Box*. New York and Cambridge: Cambridge University Press.

SAYER, Andrew (1985), *New Developments in Manufacturing and their Spatial Implications*. Working Paper No.49 (University of Sussex, Urban and Regional Studies), October.

SCOTT, Bruce R., and LODGE, George (eds.) (1985), *U.S. Competitiveness in the World Economy*. Boston: Harvard Business School Press.

WHEELRIGHT, Steven, and HAYES, Robert M. (1984), *Restoring our Competitive Edge: Competing through Manufactures*. New York: Wiley.

Part IV

Small Countries in an Innovating World Economy: Can State Policy Introduce Participation?

12

Small Industrialized Countries and the Global Innovation Race

The Role of the State in the Netherlands, Belgium and Switzerland

Rob van Tulder[1]

This chapter will consider the adjustment problems and the innovation policies of three small European countries: the Netherlands, Belgium and Switzerland. These countries are chosen because they can provide interesting additional information to the mainly "large" country analysis in this book. Both Switzerland and the Netherlands are countries with large "home-based" high tech multinationals. In previous periods this has facilitated a flexible accommodation to new technological developments and even put these smaller countries high in the league table of technological achievements (measured for instance by the number of patents).

Switzerland is an example of a Federal state with a rather weak central government. The Netherlands is a more unified

[1] University of Amsterdam, Department of International Relations and International Public Law; with thanks to Gerd Junne who provided extremely useful comments on the first draft.

small state with a centralised government. Belgium is an interesting example because its governmental organisation lies somewhere in between the Swiss and the Dutch "models". The Belgian national R&D infrastructure is dominated largely by foreign-owned multinationals and by small and medium-sized firms. Both the Netherlands and Belgium are EC member states, whereas Switzerland is not. These different national positions provide comparative material for assessing the conditions under which the state functions in addition to the analysis of two countries representing the "Scandinavian model" in the next chapter.

This chapter starts with an analysis of the particular problems the smaller countries face in the 1980s and the decades to come. The concept of the "small country squeeze" will be introduced. The national industrial and firm structure is analysed in order to find out what the starting position of these countries is. Then, the consequences of this background for the national research and development structure will be dealt with. Technology policy cannot merely be the outcome of an independent policy-making process of the central government, but involves a continuous conflict of interests between different groups in society, and between government agencies. The struggle over the formulation of technology policies in these three countries will be analysed. The effectiveness of the policies chosen is indicated on a number of issues.

1. Market Niches, the Technology Squeeze and Industrial Structure

In the post-war period particularly the smaller European countries have been successful in adopting industrial adjustment strat-egies. More often than not this implied establishing specific comparative advantages in selected market niches and linking international liberalisation with domestic compensation. Domestic compensation in the form of investment, employment and income policies was needed in order to counter the harmful effects of international liberalisation for large groups of the population. Peter Katzenstein comes to the following general observation:

The strategy of the small European states is flexible, reactive, and incremental. It does not counter adverse change by shifting its costs to others abroad; it does not attempt to preempt change by ambitiously reordering the economy at home. Instead, the small European states continually improvise in living with change. (1985)

Katzenstein concedes that "economic flexibility and political stability are mutually contingent" (1985) in the case of the small European states.

1.1 The "Squeeze"

The question remains whether this flexibility still holds for a period in which an acceleration in technological changes puts increasing pressure on the smaller countries, something which Katzenstein refers to but does not seem to alter his faith in the ultimate adaptability of the small countries' adjustment strategies. The process of increased pressure on the position of smaller countries has become better known as the "small country squeeze" (Kristensen and Levinsen 1983). Stankiewicz has elaborated this with regard to the place of basic technologies in the R&T policies of the small industrialized countries (1981). He comes to the conclusion that there are two threats to the traditionally strong position of the smaller countries in specialised niches of "medium tech" products in which their flexibility could be developed to a high degree of efficiency (Walsh 1987). On the one hand, the growing complexity of new core technologies such as microelectronics, biotechnology and new materials necessitates growing capital and human resources to be exploited in an optimal way. This growing complexity also implies that more fundamental research has to be performed, and thus a more active role of the government is needed since fundamental or basic research is often financed by governments. Due to more limited resources, the governments of the smaller countries face a particular dilemma of priority-setting in this context. Where do the particular comparative advantages of the smaller countries' research infrastructure lie and who is going to decide upon the destination of the public funds? The buyer *and* supplier markets for these highly complex technologies become more and more dominated by a small group of industrial superpowers, both politically and economically. On the other hand, the area of

Rob van Tulder

relatively simple products is increasingly dominated by Newly Industrialising Countries. Countries like South Korea in semiconductors (and many other products), or Brazil in computers, enter medium and high tech areas. Some of them seem to become increasingly able to produce complex technologies.

OECD statistics with regard to the composition of the sectoral output of industry in the smaller countries largely conform to this tendency for the early 1980s. Table 1 gives figures on the late 1970s and early 1980s.

Table 1: International Comparison of Sectoral Output Shares by R&D Content

		high tech (1)	medium tech (2)	low tech (3)	(1)+(2)
smaller countries					
Belgium	76–78	0.069	0.344	0.589	0,413
	81–83	0.069	0.354	0.577	0.423
Netherlands	76–78	0.117	0.229	0.654	0.346
	81–83	0.104	0.258	0.639	0.362
Sweden	76–78	0.101	0.282	0.617	0.383
	81–83	0.099	0.287	0.616	0.386
larger countries					
France	76–78	0.113	0.307	0.579	0.420
	81–83	0.122	0.325	0.554	0.447
Germany	76–78	0.124	0.376	0.500	0.500
	81–83	0.124	0.391	0.484	0.515
Japan	76–78	0.139	0.312	0.551	0.451
	81–83	0.158	0.331	0.512	0.489
UK	76–78	0.110	0.302	0.586	0.412
	81–83	0.197	0.238	0.565	0.437
USA	76–78	0.127	0.331	0.541	0.458
	81–83	0.157	0.298	0.544	0.455

Source: OECD 1986 (data relate to sales of value of output).

The smaller countries already have had a comparatively lower percentage of their sectoral output in "high tech" sectors, with the exception of the Netherlands and Sweden. In particular Belgium has the lowest value of the index for the high tech category, compared to other small European countries with considerable openness like Austria, the Netherlands, Sweden, Denmark and Switzerland (OECD 1986). In all instances, however, the part of high tech in the national product mix for the smaller countries has *diminished* (or stayed at the same low level in the case of Belgium), whereas it has increased in the larger countries (with Germany staying the same). Interestingly enough, according to these figures, the strength of the German economy has also been developed on the basis of a "medium tech" specialisation. The position at the lower technology end has declined for both the larger and smaller countries with the notable exception of the United States. The weakening position of the smaller countries in the high tech area can also be witnessed in their general trade performance. The collective share of Switzerland, Belgium and the Netherlands in world trade in "high R&D intensive products" declined from 11.2% of total world trade in 1980 to 9.9% in 1983 (Walsh 1987) as a consequence of the growing shares of industries from the United States and Japan. In Switzerland, for instance, the performance of the scientific instruments and machinery sectors deteriorated throughout the whole of the 1970s and 1980s, but the chemical (and pharmaceutical) industries, defined in the official statistics as a "medium tech" industry, remained strong.

The social, political and economic systems of small countries, therefore, are particularly geared towards the medium tech areas mainly as a result of their position in the international division of labour between the larger countries and the developing countries. In this area, the output shares of all small countries increased, largely off-setting the relative decline in high technology output. In general this could lead to the conclusion that a "technology squeeze" or a technology gap with the larger countries does not exist for the smaller countries. Such a conclusion seems premature, though, for a number of reasons. The most important reason is that it becomes more and more clear that, in particular, the *combination* of both high and medium tech is important in establishing a dynamic and flexible national economic structure which is able to adjust to changing technological paradigms. In the combination of high tech and medium tech (the last column of the table) the smaller countries not only score lower than the larger countries, but they also experience a slower growth than large countries such as Japan, France or the UK. In other words: there is evidence that the *technology gap* between the smaller and most of the larger countries is growing.

Since the smaller economies are more internationally orientated than the medium-sized and larger economies, these developments leave the "natural domain" of the smaller countries

Rob van Tulder

open to an international squeeze. Major developments in techno-industrial innovation increasingly take place beyond the reach of the smaller countries, which might leave them hardly any option but to concentrate on diffusion and application, rather than to produce the basic technologies themselves. This might seem an obvious focus for national state policies. Particularly in periods of rapid structural change, in which painful restructuring processes are needed, the smaller countries might have to deal with certain political and institutional "rigidities" which can hamper the success of previous flexible adjustment strategies.

With regard to Switzerland, for instance, the OECD in its 1984 country report suggested that there is evidence that the country is not renewing its technological base quickly enough and is endangering its comparative advantageous basis in the manufacturing sector. Technology policy does not come about in a societal vacuum, and it is not at all certain that the "best" strategy will be adopted. The second section will provide some examples from which it will become clear that the adaptability of the smaller countries has its limits.

1.2 Industrial and Economic Structure

The R&D performance of the smaller countries is very much affected by the presence of so-called "home based" multinationals. The three smaller European countries with some of the largest multinationals (Switzerland, Sweden and the Netherlands) also have the highest expenditures on R&D (measured as % of GNP) and the largest numbers of R&D personnel. All are comparable with the larger European countries in these latter two respects. If we compare the number of employees of the five largest firms in these three smaller countries with the size of the five largest firms in the larger countries, however, it becomes clear that these firms are still of a relatively smaller size. See table 2.

The five largest firms, though of relatively smaller size, dominate the national R&D structure far more than in the medium-sized and larger countries. In all these countries the five largest firms spend more than 50% of all the industrial R&D expenditures (GERD). In Sweden the five large manufacturing corporations (Ericsson, ASEA, Volvo, Saab-Scania, SKF, see next chapter) do around half of R&D spending, whereas this proportion is even higher in the case of the Netherlands (Philips, Shell, Unilever, AKZO, Dutch State Mines (DSM)) and Switzerland. The production and research interests for these firms, however, do not run parallel. The big Swiss corporations,

Table 2: Average Size of the Five Largest Firms in 1984

		number of employees of corporate group (thousands)					
	LARGER COUNTRIES				SMALLER COUNTRIES		
	US	UK*	BRD	Japan	Sweden	Switzerl.	Neth.
1972	451	219	195	–	51	70	121
83/84	444	167	223	134	67	85	100

ESTIMATED R&D CONCENTRATION IN 1983/84
(% of Gross Expenditures on Research and Development (GERD)

US	UK	BRD	Japan	Sweden	Switzerl.	Neth.
12	20	22	13	>50	>70	70

* Excluding Unilever and Shell

Sources: Eliasson 1986; Arnold 1986; van Tulder and Junne 1988.

Nestlé in food processing, Brown Boverie & Cie in machine-tools (now merged with ASEA of Sweden), Alusuisse in metal-working, Ciba-Geigy in the pharmaceutical and chemical industry and Hoffmann-LaRoche in pharmaceuticals, for instance, have most of their production abroad. In the case of Ciba-Geigy, the Swiss market only makes up 2% of the total turnover. For Nestlé and Brown Boverie this is 4% and 6% respectively. In the 1970s, 83% of the employees of the five largest Swiss companies worked outside Switzerland (Niehans 1977). Most of the Swiss companies, however, are very centrally organised and perform the bulk of their R&D in Switzerland, which gives Switzerland a high R&D figure as a percentage of GDP. Only one-third of research is done abroad. The national R&D structure is not only rather specialised, but also in the hands of a few major firms, which have big international interests and thus are very difficult for the national government to control. *Grosso modo*, the same pattern can be witnessed in the Netherlands.

In a context in which large multinationals are also in the process of internationalising their R&D efforts (van Tulder and Junne 1988), the link between international liberalisation and domestic compensation might become increasingly difficult to sustain. This is especially true if Sweden, Switzerland and the Netherlands do not find ways to broaden their R&D base in the direction of smaller and medium-sized firms which might become the strong and large firms of the future. Some other smaller countries (like Denmark, see the next chapter), with considerably lower R&D spending, might be in a better position than the highest scoring nations since their R&D infrastructure is more widely spread over smaller firms and research institutes.

In Belgium the R&D landscape is dominated to a lesser extent than in the other countries by a few firms, but in the Belgian case these firms are foreign. The four largest industrial R&D spenders undertake 25% of all R&D, whereas twenty firms account for 50% of all industrial research. The eight largest R&D firms employ more than 30% of all R&D personnel in Belgium (Arnold 1986). In 1983, it was estimated that half of all employees in the private sector served multinationals, of which 55% came from other European countries and 36% from the USA (European Industrial Relations Review, July 1983). Research indicates that the Belgian subsidiaries of foreign-owned multinationals have higher levels of productivity than local firms (Plasschaert and van den Bulcke 1983).

Next to some dominant multinationals, most smaller countries have also a larger than average proportion of smaller and medium-sized firms (Prakke and Zegveld 1982). The effectiveness of national policies thus very much depends on the way in which the SMEs can be reached. These policies have to be formulated very often in direct opposition to the policy proposals of the MNCs or their lobby organisations.

The last "structural" characteristic of the smaller countries to be mentioned in this context is their close links to the economy of one larger country in Europe with which they do a considerable part of their trade. This means also that this influences their position, by way of some indirect effects: for instance the networking (and thus the user-producer relations which enhance innovation on a broader scale) established by the links between Dutch companies and companies in NorthRhine-Westphalia is jeopardised because the centre of high tech gravity in Germany is shifting to the southern states of Bavaria and Baden-Württemberg. This process has been the topic of a study by the scientific council on government policy in the Netherlands. In this study concern is expressed for the deteriorating position of the Dutch economy *vis-à-vis* the German economy (WRR 1982). At the same time the opportunities for Swiss and Austrian subcontracting industries are changing favourably due to these processes. Many of the international alliances in which the firms of the smaller countries are engaged can only be understood in terms of the relationship with the large neighbouring country. The merger of ASEA of Sweden with Brown Boverie & Cie of Switzerland for instance had nothing to do with the objective of penetrating the Swedish or the Swiss markets. The large presence of BBC on the German market has been one of the major reasons for the Swedish willingness to merge and form the largest European engineering company.

2. The Role of the State

Is there reason to have great faith in the ultimate adaptability of the small European countries with regard to the global innovation race? This is to a large extent a matter of *effectiveness* of government policies formulated as the outcome of interest battles between different societal groups. In this context, a more independent role of the government with regard to conflicting societal interests is supposed to be necessary for any effective and broad policy. To substantiate the latter argument, the first part of this section gives a short assessment of the background of the post-war political flexibility of the smaller countries' governments. Then, a number of possible yardsticks, for "measuring" the effectiveness of government policies under the present circumstances of rapid technological change, will be considered. First, the strategies towards the development of "core technologies" (i.e. on the "high tech" end of the spectre) will be looked at. The strategies chosen in this context give an indication of the inclination of governments to support high risky investments in core technologies (often under the influence of lobby activities by large firms) and the price they have to pay for it. Second, the impact of government policies on industrial research is briefly analysed in order to obtain a view of the room to manoeuvre of governments. Third, the matter of the industrial infrastructure will be tackled. It will be considered to what extent smaller and medium-sized firms can be reached under the circumstances analysed in the previous sections.

2.1. Macro-Fordism and Neo-Corporatism

Governments of the smaller countries have been particularly "innovative" in pursuing flexible responses to changing international circumstances in the post-war period. A number of scholars have categorised the dominant post-war capitalist accumulation model as "Fordism" (e.g. Coriat 1979; Hirsch and Roth 1986). This concept can be analysed at different levels in society, and very often it has only been considered at the micro level. In the latter sense an industry-sociological approach has been adopted linking the introduction of the conveyor belt with higher wages at plant level. The analysis can also be applied to the macro or national level. This has been of particular importance to the success of a number of European economies and especially of the smaller European countries. Their political flexibility has been embedded in a "macro-Fordist" system in which negotiations between employers and labour unions, linking productivity increases (due to process innovations) with increases of purchasing power at the plant level ("micro-Fordism"), was broadened to national and tripartite negotiating practices. Thus, especially in the smaller European countries "macro-Fordism" dominated "micro-Fordism". As a result, the public sector grew rapidly. In the first ten to fifteen years after the Second World War the share of public spending (as a percentage of GDP) did not differ very much among the larger and smaller countries. During the 1950s, some of the large industrialised countries even had a larger share of public spending in GDP. In the two decades thereafter, the smaller countries rapidly overtook the position of the larger countries. Even Switzerland experienced a more rapid growth of the public sector than most large countries. "The growth of public spending in 'conservative' Switzerland exceeded the growth of public spending in 'socialist' Britain" (Katzenstein 1983). Central bargaining structures, the important role of big companies, and strong labour unions lie at the basis of this remarkable growth (Cameron 1978). At the central level of most small countries an important fusion of interest has led to what can be called neo-corporatism or macro-Fordism. The redistributive role of the government and the strong centralised power of the labour unions has been identified as an important reason why the European small industrialised countries have managed to resist an inherent "peripherisation" tendency that has been experienced by most present-day developing countries (Senghaas 1982). In most of the larger countries a decentralised form of interest articulation (very often without government interference) led to a far more pluralistic structure. What has been part of the comparative advantage of the smaller countries in the previous decades, however, seems to become more of a liability in a period of rapid technological change. The macro-Fordist or neo-corporatist system of policy formulation has increasingly become jeopardised, certainly in the area of technology policy, which is now more and more considered to be an area of "metapolitics", and it remains an open question whether this can lead to new and flexible responses to changing circumstances. This raises dilemmas for an effective state policy. Several considerations of effectiveness will be dealt with in the next part of this chapter.

2.2 The Increasing Need for R&D Funds and International Markets

The technology squeeze approach, already referred to, implies that a growing number of technologies are of increasing complexity and thus R&D expenditures have to rise rapidly. This is especially the case with specific applications of microelectronics, such as large digital public switching equipment, fourth and fifth generation computers, megabyte semiconductors, and 32-bit microprocessors. The development costs for these items run in the hundreds of millions of dollars or even surpass the 1 billion dollar mark. In some areas of *application*, like highly automated factories for large-scale production (for instance in the automotive sector), the design and manufacture of aircraft, the aerospace sector, costs are also increasing rapidly. For instance, the design and production of a single aircraft is estimated to run over $2 billion. Increasing development costs necessitate economies of scale or large markets. The smaller countries have been traditionally weak in these areas with only a few exceptions. Industries in these areas needed vast markets and thus international liberalisation. Most smaller countries, however, managed to specialise in niches. The present problem for the policy of many governments, however, is that the core technologies not only represent significant market share, but that these technologies are *strategic inputs* for almost all the products in which the smaller countries have specialised in. Traditionally, national economies could substitute the loss of market share in the areas where these specific economies of scale were necessary with other products. This limited their dependence. With regard to core technologies, much more so than in the past, there are no substitutes and the decision to "make" or "buy" becomes a national issue of utmost importance.

Under these circumstances governments can basically adopt three strategies:

1. Invest large sums in the design, the development and even the commercialisation of core technologies in order to create their own independent high technology base.
2. Follow the policy of the large firms and subsidise their choices for certain core technologies and products.
3. Leave the development of core technologies to other countries or to major domestic firms, concentrating on the quick diffusion of know-how and subsidising investment in technology niches by smaller and medium-sized firms.

The choice of any strategy (or a combination of the three) is influenced by the national economic and R&D infrastructure which determines the medium-term national capabilities, and by the lobby power ofHmajor actors, particularly the large multinationals. The first two strategies involve an immense pressure on (scarce) public resources. For the small countries concerned, investing in expensive core technologies means also that they become more dependent than previously on a large international market to amortize the original expenditure. As I will illustrate below, this can result in particularly difficult situations. The third strategy indicates an acceptance of certain limitations of the small countries' capabilities.

Looking at the whole group of small European countries, only the Swedish, the Swiss and the Dutch governments followed one of the first two strategies. In this sense, contrary to what Katzenstein notes, they have tried to do some "reordering" of the economy. The Swedes and the Swiss tried to develop their own, more or less national, capability in computers and large digital switching equipment. The experience of both countries shows that the choice of the first strategy has been rather unsuccessful.

The Swedish government chose an offensive policy in the second half of the 1970s. It influenced the computer industry to withdraw from the production of mainframe computers and supported the merger of the two largest Swedish computer firms (Datasaab division of Saab-Scania and Stansaab) in order to create cooperation in R&D and in marketing peripheral equipment and special purpose computers. The government took a majority share in the newly created firm. In this way the government linked the fate of its computer policy with that of one company. The new company, Datasaab AB, however, proved very weak and losses of hundreds of millions of krona had to be covered by the government. This put a heavy claim on the total Swedish budget for supporting electronics. More than 90% of the total SEK 425 million in support of electronics in the 1970-79 period went to Datasaab (Hingel 1982). In 1980-81 Ericsson took the company over. This ended an expensive state experiment. A positive outcome might have been that it kept the computer capability under Swedish control. This proved to be the case for a only short timespan, however, because in 1988 Ericsson sold the computer division to the Finnish company Nokia.

Without possessing a major home-based multinational, the Swiss government tried to develop a national digital public switching system in the 1970s and early 1980s. In cooperation with Siemens and the Swiss subsidiary of ITT, the Swiss telecommunications firm Hasler received SFr. 300 million over a period of fourteen years. Problems with the development of advanced computer software, other delays and insufficient financing (for instance to create sufficient training and retraining facilities) turned the project into a failure. The Swiss are now procuring switching equipment from abroad and produce under licence, although still with the aim of becoming 100% self-sufficient in producing the licenced technology themselves by the end of the 1980s. One of the consequences of the failure was that Hasler merged with Autophon, a large Swiss producer of telephones forming a SFr. 2 billion firm (Ascom) with a world market share in telecommunications of 2% (Bulletin SKA, 1 February 1987). The failed experiments in Sweden and Switzerland seem to have had the useful consequence that the governments in these countries do not seem to be very much inclined to invest in such projects any more.

The Dutch government has been far more susceptible to the lobbying power of multinationals and predominantly chose the second strategy, thereby largely linking the effectiveness of national policies to the commercial fortune of individual products or technologies. This is *de facto* a "national champion" strategy and proves no less risky than the previous strategy.

The inherent risks can be illustrated by the case of AKZO. The Dutch government subsidised around half of the Dfl. 600 million development and production cost of a new superfibre (Aramide). A patent struggle with DuPont (and the US government) came about in which the AKZO product has been barred from other big markets. The Dutch government now finds itself in the uncomfortable situation of lobbying for support other governments in the European Community to get at least some of its investments back. The same can be said about the aid for the development of a new generation of aeroplanes by Fokker, which has cost the government more than Dfl. 1 billion. Due to a number of mistakes, technological problems, the fall of the US dollar, and of course a highly competitive market to operate in, the company faces big problems in surviving bankrupcy. The Dutch government also supported the investment of Philips in submicron-technology with at least Dfl. 200 million, the so-called Megachip project in conjunction with Siemens. According to a number of observers, the firm only used the government subsidy to finance existing plans. Without government support the project would have been executed anyway.

As can also be observed in the case of the Netherlands and Switzerland, the innovation programmes in Belgium very often did not really involve a strategic analysis of the technology area (in this case: microelectronics), but rather a regrouping and a re-labelling of existing programmes. The reaction of the Belgian government, however, was not based on the request of specific companies. The Belgian government turned more or less to the third strategy, since there was no great pressure from "national champions" in any area. Where strong firms exist, they tend to be in the company of a number of other firms, very often small and medium-sized firms. The lack of large, strong firms in the high tech area, therefore, forced the government to adopt a niche strategy from the start. A good example is the action programme for information technologies (the Maystadt programme). According to Arnold this programme involved the

> judgement that there was no opportunity for Belgium to enter the high-volume standard IC market, but that it was important to have a national capability in custom circuit design and manufacture. (Arnold 1986)

2.3 Direct Financing of Industrial Research

The influence of governments over national research can rise through the greater financial control over research done in *industry*. The control over the direct impact on commercialisation of certain technologies can be enhanced if governments finance the R&D in firms. Investing in basic research and in the general university framework gives governments only an indirect influence on developments.

Public financing of industrial R&D in Belgium, the Netherlands and Switzerland is rather low compared to the larger countries. Whereas the UK government funded almost 30% and the French and German governments funded around 20% of industrial R&D, these figures were around 9% in Belgium, 6% in the Netherlands at the end of the 1970s (Arnold 1986),[2] and 1.4% in Switzerland (CPE 1983). This is partly because of the low expenditures for military purposes in these smaller countries. The effect is that the direction of industrial R&D in the smaller countries is dominated by the larger companies whereas in the larger countries government procurement and

---

[2] In the Netherlands, the percentage of industrial research financed by the state increased in the 1980s to 9% in 1988 (measured as primary distribution, Government White Paper on Science Policy, September 1987). It does not seem likely that this has been accompanied by an increase in government influence over company R&D policies.

research policy (if wished) can have an important impact on the *direction* of private research strategies.

The bargaining process on the political priorities of innovation policy is the least open in Switzerland, where the firms exert their lobbying power in closed committee "militia" of industrialists, university representatives and civil servants from the ministry of economic affairs.[3]

In the Netherlands, the growing influence of industrialists over industrial policy in general has been more open and can be observed by the number of official advisory committees chaired by representatives of the multinationals.[4]

In Belgium, the situation is less clear because of the lack of firms with really big R&D laboratories in the country. A major integrating role is played by the "Société Generale", a holding company controlling around one-third of Belgian industry. The Generale plays a role for the Belgian economy comparable to the "Wallenberg consortium" in Sweden. Unlike its Swedish counterpart, the Belgian holding company was oriented predominantly towards the strong points of the Wallonian economy, i.e. the large steel and other "old" industries. Only in the second half of the 1980s did the holding company start to change its course somewhat towards more "high tech" industries and towards Flanders. The Generale for instance took part in the ITT-CGE (Alcatel) merger in telecommunications. It is not surprising under Belgian circumstances that the shift in policy of this holding more or less runs parallel with some of the shifts in the central government's decisions to pursue a more explicit innovation policy. The 1984 proposals of the Minister of Science Policy, Maystadt, tended to adopt a more selective strategy towards support of research on strategic areas and the valorisation of research for the Belgian economy as a whole, without

---

[3] In the early 1980s, the Swiss did not want to participate in the "small country" debate within the OECD.

[4] Major examples are the Commission on reindustrialisation called after the chairman of Shell (Wagner), the technology policy commission chaired by the chairman of Philips (Dekker) and several other committees chaired by managers of the large multinationals (Steenbergen on telecommunications policy, Pannenborg on procurement policy, Rathenau on microelectronics policy).

taking regional specificities into consideration. As a result, the share of industrial research expenditure funded by the government stayed at the low level of 9% during the first half of the 1980s (OECD 1986). The general research scene, however, as in the Netherlands, became gradually more geared towards the needs of industrial competitiveness. In the national budget for scientific research and teaching, the share of aid to industrially oriented research rose to 18% in 1985.

The moderate influence of the budgetary policy of the state on the companies' policies limits the margins of policy formulation and of the effectiveness of any policy pursuing other goals than those of the dominant firms.

2.4 Small and Medium-Sized Firms

The "old boys' research network" particularly in Switzerland and the Netherlands created a framework in which quick formulation of priorities in innovation policy can be achieved. In Belgium, on the other hand, an innovation policy was practically absent before 1984. Margaret Sharp notes with regard to the effective formulation of a biotechnology policy:

> One of the most successful government programmes in Europe has been that of the Dutch government which has succeeded in combining the efforts of industry and academe within the overall planning framework of their Biotechnology Action Programme. But the Dutch benefit from being a small country which means that thereHare really only five firms of importance in this field - Shell, Unilever, Dutch State Mines, AKZO and Gist Brocades - and it is relatively easy to get them all around a table with the relevant academics to forge a unified programme. A somewhat similar situation arises in Denmark and Sweden, which likewise show a consistency of effort which seems lacking in some other countries, most notably the UK. (Sharp 1987)

For biotechnology, the same can be said of Switzerland with three major firms in this area: Ciba-Geigy, Hoffman-LaRoche and Sandoz. The fact that large firms help to *formulate* policy priorities could, however, also often result in a squeeze on smaller firms.

Why should one dwell on the issue of smaller firms, in particular for the smaller countries? Small and medium-sized firms have been considered especially valuable as sources of new ideas and innovations. In addition there are other arguments concerning technology policy such as that a more equal distribution of economic power and less market concentration leads to more economic efficiency, and especially that smaller firms act as a good buffer to sharp fluctuations in employment (Rothwell and Zegveld 1982). In short, the smaller firms have been very important for the smaller countries because they provided a "flexibility buffer" and thus facilitated a niche market oriented strategy. At the same time the labour unions, organised in the larger firms, managed to develop strong central bargaining structures which stimulated corporatism and the redistributive role of governments. With rapid technological developments, however, it becomes clearer that at present most large firms "create" unemployment in the home country due to their higher capacity for rationalisation *and* internationalisation, whereas smaller firms have difficulties in following the pace of technological developments. Thus at both ends of the economy flexibility of the economy tends to decline and the squeeze results in high levels of unemployment. This mechanism could explain much of the extremely high unemployment in the Netherlands as well as Belgium in the 1980s. Since the early 1980s the unemployment of French-speaking Wallonia in Belgium, for instance, ranks very high in Europe. Only Ireland has higher figures. This region is traditionally dominated by heavy industry, and thus by large firms which used to be the bearers of the whole of the countries' industrialisation. The Dutch economy as a whole has also experienced very high unemployment rates, whereas the Swiss managed to keep official unemployment very low, basically due to their ability to pass on this burden to their migrant workers.

While the large firms limit their employment, it becomes especially important for the broader effectiveness of government policy to reach small and medium-sized companies either directly or indirectly. While the "rigidities" of political and economic institutions make it relatively easy to get "consensus" superficially among the major actors, as has been noted by Sharp, the same structure makes it more difficult to change policies in the direction of smaller sized firms. Due to the limited resources of the smaller countries, there is a more direct trade off between the interests of smaller and larger firms. For example, in Switzerland a 1984 government proposal to provide innovation assistance to small and medium-sized enterprises was defeated, apparently because it was felt that this involved the Confederation in taking an "anti-big-business' stance" (Arnold 1986). In the Netherlands, a large innovation stimulation scheme (INSTIR) for R&D support explicitly aimed at smaller and medium-sized firms was changed in 1987 since it was, paradoxically, too successful in reaching SMEs. Around 50% reached SMEs which prompted the larger firms to complain that they did not receive a share in proportion to their contribution to national R&D expenditures.

The approach taken by Belgium for instance in supporting its three main universities (Leuven, Ghent and Brussels) to form an independent company seems to have had, perhaps, more interesting and direct results. The Inter-University Microelectronics Centre (IMEC), in less than a year after its opening, is carrying out research on so-called application specific integrated circuits (ASICs) for more than 70 companies worldwide (New Scientist, 4 June 1987). The facility is far more reachable for smaller and medium-sized firms and a transfer of technology to national firms in the regions seems more likely. If we consider the Megachip project of Philips within this context, there have been no arrangements to create "spin-off" effects to universities or local industries (van der Eijk 1988). This also seems unlikely because of the highly strategic nature of the project for the firm. Thus the increase in R&D spending of Philips in the Dutch economy has no immediate positive effect on the knowledge base in semiconductors of the Dutch economy.

3. Participation for whom in the Technology Race?

In the 1980s none of the smaller countries have been able to abstain from efforts to develop a more coordinated innovation policy. Even the Swiss with their long tradition of "laissez faire" policy agreed upon a Federal Law on Research in 1984 in which some national coordination on research priorities was pursued (CPE 1983).

In this concluding section I will consider a number of issues which can give an indication of the effectiveness of the policies chosen by the three smaller countries in order to withstand the technology squeeze, and participate in the innovation race in such a way that the society as a whole is able to withstand the peripherisation pressure as defined by Senghaas.

First, in all three small countries considered, the result of the battle between interests over innovation policies has been that the share of government R&D funding as a percentage of GDP has not increased.[5] Thus the priorities' battle in these countries implied substituting one purpose for another. There are indications that this has largely been to the benefit of the larger firms (either directly or indirectly, through more industry oriented university research) in Switzerland and the Netherlands, whereas in Belgium this process has been more balanced and resulted also in support for smaller and medium-sized firms, especially in Flanders. The *ineffectiveness* of these policies in raising the overall national R&D effort, however, is also clear since total R&D funding as a percentage of national GDP hardly increased in the first half of the 1980s. In the case of the Netherlands, for instance, the five largest R&D spenders as a group increased their R&D spending (measured as % of sales), but they did not spend this in their home country. A recent correction of the official statistics on R&D expenditures in the Netherlands notes an increase in private R&D expenditures after 1984 (government expenditures remaining the same), which must be attributed largely to the change in the policy of one company, i.e. Philips. It is hardly secret, given Dutch experience, that this rise is at least partly financed by the public budget in the form of tax measures, indirect subsidies and the like, which make it very difficult to issue any statement on the effectiveness at large of state innovation policies in triggering larger R&D spending from firms themselves. In some of the larger countries like Germany, Japan or the United Kingdom the governments did not raise their R&D spending either, but private funding did increase in the early 1980s. In Denmark and Sweden the governments chose to raise public R&D expenditures, which also triggered additional private R&D. It does seem, therefore, that an active government policy in the smaller countries is needed, since large firms do not seem to be inclined to raise their R&D

---

[5]   In the Netherlands this stayed around 0.98%, in Belgium around 0.60% and in Switzerland around an estimated 0.30% according to the OECD/STIID Data Bank in the 1981-87 period.

spending in these countries without "domestic compensation". The international innovation race does put an upward pressure on the R&D funding of most firms, with the larger ones being clearly inclined to invest in the larger countries.

Second, participating in a race in which every actor invests in the same technologies is not very wise for the smaller countries, since they have, by definition, only limited resources and less international political and economic clout. This indicates that it does not suffice any more to follow the strategies of the large and dominant firms. A separate political strategy has to be developed in which a clear concept of the place of the country in the international context should be developed. This has not happened in any of the countries, which means that the policies which are not aimed at education or other basic infrastructural facilities will only be effective *by accident*.

At the same time and partly as a consequence of the above mentioned lack of understanding of the small country position, the emphasis on industrial "competitiveness" is interpreted only in a very limited sense. The attention to social, political, cultural and other factors which represent a broad assessment of the small country's challenges and opportunities has been considered to be of minor interest. A better assessment of the social and economic consequences, and the strategic nature of high technology fields, however, could give governments an instrument of political choice for deciding which research to fund. The increase in state funding for industrial R&D in the Netherlands, for instance, on the one hand has been accompanied by a tremendous shift in the priorities of nationally funded research towards "industrial productivity and technology": in 1980 this category made up 11% of all government funding (from all ministries); in 1988 it has grown to almost one-third of the whole budget. On the other hand, the percentage of research for "societal structures and relations" declined rapidly from 11% to 4% of all funding in the same period. In 1987, this development prompted the National Advisory Body for Science Policy (RAWB) to express its concern over the lack of funding for research in the humanities, implying, in my interpretation of their statement, that it is not enough just to follow the research and development trajectories set by the larger firms. This should be complemented and checked by research into national priorities, social assessments, and the like, in order to be able to make a better and more conscious use of scarce resources. In a period of rapid technological transition, the political influence of the companies, which in large part dominate the direction of the national industrial research effort, has increased.

Third, a perhaps surprising result of the previous comparative analysis is that with regard to reaching small and medium-sized firms the Belgian (i.e. Flanders) "strategy" seems to be more effective than that of the other two countries.

Fourth, in pursuing international linkages within the framework of European cooperation programmes, there is the danger that "islands of innovation" will be developed in the smaller countries which have no links with the domestic infra-structure. This might be the case with the participation of the larger companies in the case of Switzerland and the Netherlands, and for the participation of research institutes especially in the case of Belgium. A link between research priorities aimed at international projects and national (or regional) research goals is difficult to establish under such circumstances. This can perhaps be summarised as the problem of *spin-out*, a development which has always been of particular relevance for the smaller countries (Walsh 1987) and which becomes of increasing importance with the internationalisation and growing cooperation within the research community.

In short, the "comparative advantages" of the smaller countries run the risk of becoming eroded, partly due to the very success of previous strategies. The effectiveness of policies is hampered by the structural power and conservatism of a few actors. The government policies of the three countries chosen seem to have been affected very much by the interests of only a limited number of actors. In the Netherlands and Switzerland these were mainly large firms and some research institutes. In Belgium these are Flanders and also some research institutes. It remains to be seen whether these strategies, along with such obvious strategies as raising the level of education, which are adopted by all countries (see Ergas (1986) for an assessment of the Swiss system), will provide the desired domestic compensation which restores the unique position and the specificities of the small industrial countries of Europe. There are some indications that this might be successful in the area of telecommunications, as for example with the growing popularity of the Dutch "model" of deregulation in other European countries (large as well as small), but, in general, faith in the ultimate adaptability of the small European countries dealt with in this chapter appears to be somewhat misplaced on the basis of recent experiences.

Bibliography

ARNOLD, Erik (1986), *Policies for Electronics, Computing and the Information Technologies in four smaller OECD Economies: Belgium, Canada, the Netherlands and Switzerland*; A report to the National Swedish Board for Technical Development, Sussex, January, 229p.

CAMERON, David (1978), The Expansion of the Public Economy: A comparative analysis, in: *American Political Science Review*, LXXII, 4 (December), 1243-1261.

CORIAT, Benjamin (1979), *L'atelier et le chronométre*, Christian Bourgois Editeur, Paris, 142p.

CPE (1983), *European Policy Studies Papers, no.29*, Brussels, 68p.

VAN DER EIJK, Eelco (1988), *Het Mega-Project; een analyse van de betrokkenheid van Philips en het Ministerie van Economische Zakenbij de gemeenschappelijke ontwikkeling van sub-microntechnologie door Philips en Siemens*, Amsterdam, MA thesis, 67p.

ELIASSON, Gunnar (1986), International Competition, Productivity Change and the Organization of Production; in: H. de JONG and W. SHEPERD (eds.), *Mainstreams in Industrial Organization*, Martinus Nijhoff, Dordrecht, 127-158.

ERGAS, Henry (1986), *Does Technology Policy Matter?*, Centre For European Policy Studies Papers, no.29, Brussels, 68p.

HINGEL, Anders J. (1982), *Social Change and Technology in Europe, Current Events in Scandinavia; European Pool of Studies*, report no.9, Brussels, 80p.

HIRSCH, Joachim and ROTH, Roland (1986), *Das neue Gesicht des Kapitalismus, vom Fordismus zum Post-Fordismus*, VSA-Verlag, Hamburg, 258p.

VAN KASTEREN, Joost (1987), Laveren tussen strijdige belangen; onderzoeksbeleid in Belgie: partijstrijd is een gewoon verschijnsel geworden; in : *Wetenschapsbeleid*, The Hague, 9e jaargang, no.10, 7-10.

KATZENSTEIN, Peter (1985), *Small States in World Markets, Industrial Policy in Europe*; Cornell University Press, Ithaca and London, 268p.

KRISTENSEN, Peer Hull, and LEVINSEN, Jorg (1983), *The Small Country Squeeze*, Forlaget for Samfundsokonomi og Planlaegning, Roskilde, 336p.

NIEHANS, Jürg (1977), Benefits of Multinational Firms for a Small Parent Economy: the Case of Switzerland; in: T. AGMON, and Ch. KINDLEBERGER (eds.), *Multinationals from Small Countries*, MIT Press, Cambridge, Mass. 1-39.

OECD (Organisation for Economic Cooperation and Development) (1986), *Economic Survey: Belgium-Luxembourg*, 92p.

OECD (Organisation for Economic Cooperation and Development) (1987), *Economic Survey: Switzerland*, 83p.

Rob van Tulder

PLASSCHAERT, S., and VAN DEN BULCKE, D. (1983), *De Impact van multinationale ondernemingen in gastlanden: een overzicht*. Tijdschrift voor Economie en Management, Vol. XXVIII, nr.1, 41-62.

PRAKKE, Frits, and ZEGVELD, Walter (OECD rapporteurs) (1982), *Innovation in Small and Medium Firms*, Paris, 274p.

ROTHWELL, Roy, and ZEGVELD, Walter (1982), *Innovation and the Small and Medium Sized Firm, Their Role in Employment and in Economic Change*, Frances Pinter Publishers, London, 268p.

SENGHAAS, Dieter (1982), *Von Europa Lernen, Entwicklungsgeschichtliche Betrachtungen*, Edition Suhrkamp, 356p.

SHARP, Margaret (1987), Biotechnology, in: W. KRUMBEIN, and U. HILPERT, (eds.), *Staatliche Modernisierungspolitik gegenüber dem industriellen Wirtschaftssektor*, FAST paper no. 182, Brussels, 87-93.

STANCKIEWICZ, Rikard (1981), The Place of Basic Technologies in the R&D Policies of the Small Industrialized Countries; in: P.H. KRISTENSEN, and R. STANKIEWICZ, (eds.), *Technology Policy and Industrial Development in Scandinavia*, 88-101.

VAN TULDER, Rob (1984), *Je zult maar klein zijn*, mimeo, Amsterdam, 101p.

VAN TULDER, Rob (1987), *The Factory of the Future, Productivity and Income*; International Metalworkers' Federation, Geneva, 61p.

VAN TULDER, Rob, and JUNNE, Gerd (1988), *European Multinationals in Core Technologies*, John Wiley and Sons, Chichester, 300p.

WALSH, Vivian (1987), *Technology, Competitiveness and the Special Problems of Small Countries. A Survey of the Literature*; IKE Workshop on Technological Change and the Competitiveness of Small Countries, Denmark, August 18-21, 53p.

WETENSCHAPPELIJKE RAAD VOOR HET REGERINGSBELEID (WRR) (1982), *Onder invloed van Duitsland*, Den Haag, Staatsuitgeverij, 227p.

13

National Styles in Technology Policy

Comparing the Swedish and Danish State Programmes in Microelectronics/ Information Technology

Andrew Jamison[1]

This chapter compares the ways in which the state has responded to the "microelectronics revolution" in Sweden and Denmark. In both countries, the responses can be termed neo-corporatist, in that they were based on alliances and agreements between the state and the interest organizations of the private sector. In both countries, the so-called national programmes in microelectronics/information technology have been conceptualized not simply as government plans, but as joint undertakings by state institutions and private firms to contribute to the formation of a new kind of technological capacity.

---

[1]   This chapter is part of the project, 'Industrial renewal through national programmes for microelectronics'. I am grateful to my colleagues in the project, Hans Glimell and Ulrik Jorgensen, for their comments. Special thanks to Jan Annerstedt, who contributed to the text and helped me edit the final version.

For all their similarity, however, the state responses in Sweden and Denmark have differed in orientation, direction and approach. As I intend to show in the pages that follow, these differences can be said to reflect different "national styles" of technology policy. But first, let me briefly describe the two programmes.

As one of its last decisions in 1983, the Swedish *Riksdag* passed legislation for a comprehensive programme for information technology. As the first of what was planned to be four steps, the National Programme for Microelectronics (NMP) was started in close cooperation with some of Sweden's largest private enterprises. Six months later, just before midsummer, the financial committee of the Danish *Folketing* gave its blessing to Denmark's biggest technological undertaking in this century: 2,140 million Kroner (some US$200 million at 1984 prices) for a joint state-industry technological programme. Formally, this Technology Development Programme (TUP) was placed under the direction of the National Agency of Technology in the Ministry. Its main objective was to "promote the necessary transformation of the Danish industry to use high technology".[2] It should give Danish industry as a whole, not just specific sectors of industry, better possibilities to attain the same technical level as that in countries with competing industrial firms. Especially by exploiting information technology, the national programme was intended to strengthen Danish industry, which until then had been threatened by the international technological development.

The Danish national programme emphasized diffusion of new technology through a number of joint state-industry activities, from demonstration projects of model factories to the provision of technical and financial support to small firms and cooperative research institutes. "Correctly used", the programme contended, "technology may now become a positive development factor precisely in an industrial structure like the Danish. Information technology makes it possible for both small and medium-sized companies to obtain advantages at a moderate cost which

[2]

A Tec nological Development Programme, English-language version of *Et teknologisk udviklingsprogram*. Teknologistyrelsen (National Agency of Technology), December 1983. (I have slightly modified the English translation, following the original Danish text.)

306

used to be reserved for large enterprises, in such fields as information gathering, administration, product development and production - while at the same time strengthening the flexibility and good working climate which have traditionally characterized these undertakings" (Teknologistyrelsen 1983).

A broadly framed national information technology programme in Sweden was laboriously constructed by a large number of public agencies in cooperation with industrial and research interests in the early 1980s, but only the NMP became government funded. The *Riksdag* could only agree "to encourage the development of microelectronics"; the remaining three parts of the information technology programme, to further microelectronics application and stimulate potential innovations in relations with the new technology in other sectors of the society, were simply left out.

The National Microelectronics Programme (NMP) would stand alone for the foreseeable future as the only source of "fresh" government money to the area. From the Swedish government, some 550 million Krona (or US$70 million), less than a third of the Danish expenditure, would be devoted over a five-year period to research and experimental development (R&D) in microelectronics. The main effort would be a small number of advanced projects run by government-backed industrial consortia, dominated by a few big corporations.

The overall programme objectives were derived from an economic interest in protecting a continuous supply to Swedish industries of microelectronics and to secure, in the medium term, Sweden's competitive strength in the area of semiconductor technology. Particularly emphasized in the legislation of 1983 was the "generational shift" in electronic component technology, from standard components to custom-made specialized semiconductors. Swedish industry, the government argued, was in an advantageous position to develop custom-made components and thus "reduce the lead" of the United States and Japan.[3]

---

[3] *Nationellt mikroelektronikprogram.* Stockholm: Regeringens proposition 1983/84:8. An official English version of the planning document, on which the government proposition was founded, is published as *National Microelectronic Programme*, Stockholm: Swedish National Board for Technical Development (STU Information No 424, 1984). The ideas for a national

Sweden and Denmark thus responded to the microelectronics challenge in two strikingly different ways. The Swedes supported activities primarily on industrially relevant research and development, while the Danes focused on the diffusion and application end of the innovation process. The two programmes had different ambitions, different institutional orientations, as well as different levels of expenditure. As such, the two programmes can also be expected to have different kinds of effects on their respective socio-economic environments.

These differences, I would suggest, are not merely accidental. It is not simply by chance, or political whim, that Denmark and Sweden have responded differently to the microelectronics revolution. For better or worse, the technology policy-makers have been affected by their national cultural traditions. They have been influenced, in their choice of policy measures and their assumptions about what policy can achieve, by what we might call national styles of technology policy.

In all countries, I would contend, there are national styles of technology policy, even if they are seldom examined or compared very systematically. For even though there is an international technological development process, to which all countries must accommodate themselves, or a kind of *technological imperative*, there are significant differences as to how that accommodation takes place. There is also, we might say, a *cultural imperative* in the process of technological development. Comparing national styles in technology policy-making is one way of showing the cultural imperative at work and indicating that even industrial development must be coupled with cultural patterns and traditions.

1. National Styles in Science and Technology Policy: Devising a Comparative Model

Most of the attempts that have been made to compare national, or more broadly cultural, differences in relation to science and technology can be grouped into three main categories:

---

information technology programme were collected in a 265 page volume called *Svensk informationsteknologi* ('Swedish Information Technology'), Stockholm: ASF/STU/UHA, 1984.

(a) philosophical,
(b) ethnological, and
(c) institutional or organizational.

Within each category, "culture" means something different.

For the philosophically-oriented analysts, culture is primarily a cosmological characteristic; it is the values and motivations and the ideals that lie behind the material representations of science and technology. Since Lewis Mumford's classic work on the subject, *Technics and Civilization* (first published in 1934), this is the way in which the cultural conditioning of technology is perhaps most commonly viewed. Culture is seen to influence technology by providing it with its metaphysic, with a set of background assumptions and fundamental attitudes to nature and knowledge, as well as to the artifacts themselves.[4]

In relation to national comparisons of science and technology, this philosophical approach has primarily sought to identify some distinctive style of thought or of conceptualization that can be associated with a particular national character or "spirit". In an earlier work, I have characterized these distinctive national patterns of thinking as a national *metaphysical bias* that can be found among scientists and technologists in a particular country (Jamison 1982).

In the history of technology, there is similarly a long tradition of associating national patterns of industrial development with particular cultural traditions; at the beginning of the first world war, Thorstein Veblen produced an ambitious comparison of British and German industrialization in this vein, linking the one to the "habituation of the workshop" and the other to the habituation of a strong, central, state bureaucracy (Veblen 1915). In our day, attempts have been made to relate American indus-

---

[4] After Mumford, some of the more significant contributions to this genre have been made by the American medieval historian, Lynn White (1978), e.g. *Medieval Religion and Technology*, University of California Press. In recent years, there has developed a growing literature in the 'philosophy of technology'; for a sample of recent articles, which are highly relevant to the concerns of this chapter, see Carl Mitcham and Alois Huning (eds.) (1986), *Philosophy and Technology II. Information Technology and Computers in Theory and Practice.*

trialization to a "pastoral ideal" or, more specifically, to "republican values" ; and, of course, Japanese industrialization has come to be seen, by many authors, as associated with a particular kind of mentality, the strong cohesive group mentality with roots going back to the samurai warriors of the traditional past (Marx 1964; Kasson 1976).[5]

One need not accept all or, for that matter, any of the specific arguments to admit that this approach does raise an important question, which any comparison of national styles must attempt to answer in some way, namely, how is technological development influenced by the "mentality" or dominant belief-system of the country in which it takes place? More operationally, we can ask how dominant groups in different countries have expressed their particular ideologies of industrialization and technological development.

This general, philosophical approach to the cultural influence on technology has not, of course, been the only way to get at these matters. In recent years, several historians of science and technology have come to consider culture in much more specific terms as the "way of life" of particular groups of scientists and engineers. They have pointed to conflicts in engineering work between a university, or professionalizing, culture on the one hand and a workshop, or artisan culture, on the other.[6]

In this sense, culture is the characteristic of a group, rather than an entire society; it is the shared experience and background of a particular grouping of people, rather than the cosmological characteristic of an entire social formation. In this perspective, conflicts between cultures are formative influences on science and technology. National comparisons would thus be between the different combinations of sub-cultural influences, the

---

5   For some particularly insightful articles on the influence of Japanese culture on technology, see the special issue of the *Canadian Journal of Political and Social Theory*, 8.3 (fall 1984). See also Erik Baark and Andrew Jamison (eds.) (1986), *Technological Development in China, India and Japan. Cross-cultural Perspectives*. Macmillan.

6   Some of the best examples of this new historiography are Merritt Roe Smith (1977), *Harper's Ferry Armory and the New Technology*. Cornell University Press; David Noble (1978), *America By Design*. Knopf; and David Noble (1984), *Forces of Production*. Knopf.

relative strength in Germany, for instance, of a professional poly-technical engineering culture and its relative weakness in Britain.[7]

Finally, we can think of a third category of cultural analysis, which has become especially important in our innovation policy era. Culture, in this perspective, is the particular institutional framework of the technology policy-makers themselves, the organizational forms in which decisions about technological development have been made in a particular national or local context. Thus, analyses of MITI, Japan's Ministry of International Trade and Industry, seek to elucidate the particular policy culture that has been developed, the consensus shaping, the intimate contacts between state and industry, the forms of state support, etc. Whether it be the possibilities for inter-organizational communication or the breaking down of the barriers between management and employees, some cultural factor is pointed to as the key factor in explaining technological success.[8]

Obviously, each of these three approaches captures something important, and yet, as is so often the case in these types of analysis, each often tends to mistake the whole for one of its parts. I suggest that we think of the three approaches as corresponding to three distinct, but inter-connected, structural levels through which a social formation influences the development of science and technology policy. We can follow the philosophically-oriented analysts in seeking to identify cultural influences on a national *macro level*, where the national ideological discourse is conducted, national priorities are set, or not set, and where the dominant perceptions of technology and industrial development are formulated.

It is important, however, not to reduce this macro level to a matter of cosmology or ideology; on the contrary, the ideologies of particular national elites shoud be seen in relation to particu-

---

[7] See, for example, the comparison of 'regional styles' of electrification in Berlin, London and Chicago, in: Thomas P. Hughes (1983), *Networks of Power*. Johns Hopkins University Press.

[8] See Chalmers Johnson (1982), *MITI and the Japanese Miracle*. Stanford University Press. For a recent examination of the Japanese model, see Christopher Freeman (1987), *Technology Policy and Economic Performance. Lessons from Japan*. Frances Pinter.

lar developmental strategies and experiences. Culture here can be thought of as the conceptions of science, technology, and industrial development that are identifiable with particular dominant classes or interest groups in the society.

What seems especially significant are the ways in which these groups or classes perceive threats or challenges to national sovereignty or identity. By identifying challenges and threats, ideological leaders mobilize cultural resources for technological policy-making; they legitimate particular policy measures or programmes by appealing to a usually latent national identity. As such, cultural expression, as I see it, is based on a socio-economic basis; but it is neither determined by that basis, as some self-styled "historical materialists" would have it, nor does it determine the socio-economic developments. At this macro level, cultural discourse can be thought of both as the product of particular developmental experiences, as well as the contextualizer of new developments. Culture both reflects and reshapes economic "conditions", and at the macro level this cultural influence is primarily exercised through particular cultural figures: ideologists, publicists, politicians, political leaders, and the like.

The ethnologically-oriented analyses direct our attention to cultural influences on a micro level, or the level of the scientific/technical practitioners policy. Here culture is a shared value-system, derived from a common institutional or occupational experience.

We can then think of the policy culture as a level in between the other two, mediating between them, and, in various ways, connecting the macro and micro levels with one another. Comparisons of national styles in technology policy need to include comparisons on all three levels. For it is my contention that the success of technology policy can in large measure be explained in terms of the effectiveness by which the policy-makers at the intermediate *meso level* manage to link together the perceptions and ideologies at the macro level with the particular competences and orientations of the scientific/engineering base at the micro level.

2. The Macro Level: National Ideologies of Industrialization

Let us then begin our comparison of Swedish and Danish technology policy at the macro level. As was the case in most of the other countries of 19th century Europe, in both Denmark and Sweden there developed what we might term particular national perceptions of industrialization. In both countries, political and cultural leaders incorporated the British and, somewhat later, the continental experiences of "industrial revolution" into a particular kind of macro level discourse. Industrialization, as a "universal" phenomenon, was assimilated to Danish and Swedish cultural traditions and, interestingly enough, it was assimilated in two rather different ways.

For one thing, the ideological starting-points were different. Denmark had been one of the leading mercantile nations, "a model of enlightened despotism since 1660" (Olwig 1984). It ruled over an extensive trading empire, and its grain exports provided a significant amount of revenue for the royal coffers. It was a country dominated by its capital city, and by the German financiers and experts who had been brought in to manage the Danish commercial interests. At the beginning of the 19th century, however, Denmark was thrown in upon itself; Norway was lost to Sweden as a result of the Napoleonic wars, in which Denmark suffered defeat at the hands of Britain. The merchant fleet was cut in half, the overseas markets were diminished considerably, and the price of grain fell drastically - all of which led to the so-called national bankruptcy of 1813 and the rather rapid institution of "bourgeois democracy" and parliamentary rule.

At the same time, and no doubt partly as a result of the economic and political downturn, Copenhagen experienced something of a cultural renaissance in the first third of the 19th century. Hans Christian Andersen, Sören Kierkegaard, the sculptor Bertel Thorvaldsen, the scientist Hans Christian Örsted, and a number of other significant artists and writers all actively took part in the creation of what might be called a national cultural identity. German romanticism merged with Nordic mythology and a rediscovery of the Danish countryside to produce a peculiarly popular culture in which peasant values and the skills of the craftsman took on almost heroic proportions. It was the Danish farmer and artisan, in the fields of Sealand or the heaths of Jutland, who became the epitome of Danish values.

Already in the 18th century, Ludwig Holberg had given voice to this cultural identity, and in the 19th century it became, particularly through the multifarious activities of N.F.S. Grundtvig, the dominant conception of Danishness (Jamison 1982). Grundtvig wrote histories of Denmark and collected Nordic myths, he wrote hundreds of hymns for the Danish Church, and, perhaps most importantly, he inspired a network of people's high schools throughout the Danish countryside, where "education for life" was opposed to the dead, bookish learning of the universities and the hated Latin-dominated school system.

Like his contemporaries, Grundtvig travelled to England and reflected critically on the experience of English industrialization. While he praised English "free enterprise" for being a constructive life force, he hoped that England would "admit that she was on the wrong path in sacrificing hundreds of thousands of human beings to her machines ... The same will to fight that created these machines will also understand either how to destroy them again or how to place them in a serviceable and servant-like relationship to human activity and human happiness" (Thaning 1972). It is not clear whether or not he met Robert Owen, but Grundtvig was certainly inspired by Owen's critique of mechanization and by the cooperative movement that was developed by Owen and his followers.

The struggle of Grundtvig and his contemporaries for the Danish language and the Danish soul provided a range of cultural resources that would, in the second half of the 19th century, enter into the "class-consciousness" of the peasantry, whose class struggle was perhaps the main factor in the transformation of Denmark into a modern industrial nation. The ideology of industrialization in Denmark was oriented, first and foremost, to the industrialization of agriculture. That ideology contained, we might say, an "assessment" or critical evaluation of the experiences of England and a conscious attempt to assimilate industrial development to Danish conditions. The ideology that emerged in the powerful farmer's movement oriented Danish industrial development into cooperative, relatively small-scale, and artisan-based directions - and it certainly owed something to the cultural influence of Grundtvig, Andersen, and the other re-creators of a Danish national identity in the first decades of the 19th century.

In Sweden, the situation was quite different. Swedish culture had flourished in the 18th century, in the mercantile age, after the great power ambitions of the 17th century had been abandoned. Sweden experimented with parliamentarism, as well as with chemistry and mechanics, and there was an intensive exploration of the country's natural resources in an effort to improve the financial situation after the imperial adventures of the previous century. But little of economic significance came from all the experimentation - political or scientific - and the early 19th century brought on something of a backlash against the utilitarianism and enlightenment values that had been so prominent. Romanticism and the revival of Nordic mythology tended to nourish a more provincial and backward-looking "national character" in Sweden; indeed, it has been written that "in the middle of the nineteenth century, Sweden was a little country of civil servants, without political influence, a country which seemed to have atrophied in old forms, an out-of-the-way corner of the world well protected from life-giving impulses from the outside" (Lindroth 1952).

In the mid 19th century, Sweden was perhaps among the most economically underdeveloped countries of Europe, but interestingly also one of the most literate. Traditional ways of doing things could thus be perceived as a hindrance to development by significant segments of the population. Therefore, the Swedish ideology of industrialization that emerged in the latter half of the 19th century represented a more explicit break with the past and with some of the more visible forms of a national cultural tradition than was the case in other countries.

Sweden had already experimented with industrial production - through its decentralized and paternalistic mill system, based on the extraction of mineral resources and the exploitation of the enormous forests - but was now assisted by foreigners. Literally, the new ideas of economic growth were brought in by British mercantile capital that was used to speed up and restructure the mills, lay the ground for a machine tool industry and, at least modestly, link this northern country with what was still a British world economy. As the commercial houses of Gothenburg and Stockholm expanded, the ideology of industrialization became unabashedly internationalist, so much so that many observers have identified a kind of national inferiority complex and *lack* of national identity as being central ingredients of the Swedish national character.[9]

The ideology of industrialization in the late 19th century was not so much Swedish as a home-grown concoction of foreign ideologies, sometimes practised in Sweden while they were still being preached in their homeland. The creative borrowing of cultural resources from abroad seems to have been particularly important in Sweden. Even today, the dominant conceptions of industrialization and technological development continually emphasize the need for internationalizing the Swedish ecnomy and the Swedish culture, as well. Mixing American pragmatism, British empiricism and later Keynesianism, French positivism and German social-democracy, Sweden's ideological leaders have created a justly famous middle way between capitalism and communism, an ideology of rationalization and organization and systematic investigation of social and economic problems.

What seems to be peculiarly Swedish is the emphasis given to planning, coordination, and efficient management, a legacy perhaps from the mercantile age when mineral wealth gave the Swedish state a head-start in establishing agencies of state administration. The strong interest in system and order that one finds in Swedish culture certainly predates industrialization - and they very likely have something to do with the fact that mining, that most artificial of medieval activities and most conducive to capitalist modes of operation, was a disproportionly influential activity in pre-modern Swedish society.[10]

---

[9] One of the earliest analysts of the Swedish national character, Gustav Sundbärg, devoted an entire chapter of his aphorisms on *Det Svenska Folklynnet* to 'bristen pa nationell instinkt' (or lack of a national instinct). His little book, which was written at the turn of the century as an appendix to the state investigative commission's report on emigration, also contains a good many comparative comments about Danish and Swedish national character.

[10] As a cultural influence in Sweden, the copper mines of Bergslagen were extremely important in medieval times; indeed, it has been suggested that St. Bridget, Sweden's only medieval cultural personality of international renown, was the first to describe a blast-furnace, in her 14th century revelations (cf Hermann Kellebenz (1974), Technology in the Age of the Scien-

Obviously, these national ideologies of industrialization have only an indirect effect on contemporary technology policy: they form, we might say, the ideological frame of reference within which technology policy is constituted. We can see their influence primarily as a source for the perceptions of challenge and threat that inform technology policy: they help us better understand what a particular policy is responding to - as well as why the response takes the particular conceptual form that it does.

In our case, the different national ideologies lead to different perceptions of the challenge that is seen in structural terms as a threat to, but also a possibility for, the entire national industrial structure. The situation is reminiscent of the 19th century, when a recreation of national identity accompanied, and to some extent effectuated, the process of industrialization. In our time, an appeal to national identity - to the small and medium-sized Danish industrial firms - is part of a response to a new kind of technological situation. The form the response has taken now, as in the 19th century, is to encourage a conscious and comprehensive diffusion of new technology to meet the external, structural challenge.

To respond to the challenge of the industrial revolution, Denmark assimilated, among other things, the British cooperative movement to its own cultural climate. England provided a paradigm or model for the Danish farmers to follow and adapt to their own needs. Their cooperative dairies and slaughterhouses supplied them with an organizational form for modernizing and industrializing agricultural production. Not merely by chance has the Technology Development Programme taken as a reference point the British Alvey programme, which also includes a comprehensive diffusion of information technology into the national economy.

In Sweden, the microelectronics revolution has primarily been perceived as a threat to national security and economic independence. It is seen not so much as a structural, but rather as a *strategic* challenge. It is a threat to key industrial firms that supply the Swedish military with its electronic components, and for whom the new generation of semiconductors represents a

---

tific Revolution 1500-1700, in: Carlo Cipolla (ed.), *The Fontana Economic History of Europe*, vol.2. Collins and Fontana).

menace to their competitive position. The new technology is thus seen through a different kind of ideological framework, one in which the role of the state is primarily to ensure the competitive strength of Swedish companies.

As in the 19th century, the macro level discourse in contemporary Sweden is concerned with finding a pragmatic response to a changing international environment. The state plans, systematizes, forecasts, and, most crucially perhaps, attempts to coordinate a research and development effort that the industrial firms cannot manage entirely on their own. But the international orientation of the Swedish macro level discourse has made it difficult for any particularly effective Swedish model of technology policy to emerge. The official Swedish response has been to borrow from Japan, the United States, France and Britain various paradigms and models and put them together in a coherent programme. By leading policy-makers Sweden is perceived as a fully-fledged industrial nation, certainly small, but big enough to sustain a coherent national system of industrial innovation. The problem, however, is that a big country perception of the microelectronics challenge has been difficult to correlate to the industrial needs and the science and technology capabilities in this small country.

3. The Micro Level: The Scientific/Engineering Culture

The different orientations of science and technology in different countries are not merely the result of different perceptions of industrialization and technological development. They are even more a reflection of the fact that industrialization proceeded differently in different countries, making use of different natural resource allotments, scientific and technological institutions, and developed in turn different industrial structure alignments. So while both Sweden and Denmark can be characterized as having followed a Scandinavian "path" of development, their paths have nevertheless led to quite different scientific/engineering cultures on the micro level.[11]

---

[11] On the Scandinavian 'path' of development, see Dieter Senghaas (1985), *The European Experience. A Historical Critique of Development Theory* (translated by KH.-Kimmig), Berg Publishers. For an introduction to

In both Sweden and Denmark industrialization was in large measure based on the development of export-oriented branches which refined or processed products that had previously been exported in a non-refined form. In Denmark, the largely agrarian economy was transformed into an agricultural processing industry, and it was the export niches carved out by these new industries that made it possible to develop a diversified national economy with a large number of small firms producing primarily for the domestic market. It was refined agricultural products - butter, bacon, cheese, and beer - that gave Danish industrialization its particular character, and which led to an extremely decentralized industrial structure in the Danish economy even in the 20th century.

The Swedish industrial structure, on the other hand, rather rapidly came to be dominated by a relatively few export-oriented firms that specialized in products derived from the mines and the forests - iron and steel, ball bearings, chemicals, pulp, paper, and somewhat later machinery and automobiles. At its core, Swedish industry has always been a heavy industry, and it has been highly concentrated on those firms that have been able to make small but important improvements in already invented products. Some of the larger corporations were in fact founded by an inventor becoming an entrepreneur. Thus, at an early stage, research and especially development work played a significant role in Swedish industrial strategy.

These historical experiences are not without their contemporary relevance. The scientific/engineering cultures in the two countries are very much a reflection of the different industrial traditions. In Denmark, already in the 19th century, an elaborate system of technical services was set up for the agricultural processing industries, with consultants, cooperative research institutes, and adult education at the people's high schools. In the 20th century, this system was extended to other branches, through the Technological institutes established in Sealand (1906) and Jutland (1943) to serve local industry with management expertise and ideas for product and process development,

Scandinavian industrialization, see Lennart Jörberg (1970), The Industrial Revolution in Scandinavia 1850-1914, in: Carlo Cipolla (ed.), *The Fontana Economic History of Europe*, vol.4 (published as a separate book), Fontana.

319

and the network of twenty branch-oriented cooperative research institutes established under the Academy for Technical Sciences.

On the other hand, there is a long tradition of university-based technology in Denmark; already in 1829, Hans Christian Örsted, as one of his many efforts to infuse natural science into Danish culture, established his own version of the Ecole Polytechnique, and for the better part of the 19th century, its graduates were far too academic for the needs of Danish industry.

At the micro level, the scientific/engineering culture in Denmark has thus had two rather distinct component parts: on the one hand, a relatively autonomous academically-oriented culture focused around the university and on the other a service-oriented culture primarily consulting for the needs of the relatively small and diversified industrial structure. In our case, the first culture has provided much of the basis for a "critical" research about the social implications of information technology, while the other culture has provided much of the infrastructure and expertise for the comprehensive programme of diffusion. There has, however, been a rather wide gap between the two sub-cultures, and this has been one of the tensions in the Danish programme.

In Sweden, the scientific/engineering base has come to be concentrated within the large export-oriented firms. Some 70% of all R&D takes place in the private sector. The industrial laboratories at Ericsson, ASEA, Volvo, Saab-Scania, and SKF perform more than half of Swedish industrial R&D. The engineering way of life in Sweden has thus tended to be predominantly corporate, concentrated on the large Swedish-based transnational corporations, with the state contributing resources and some direction primarily through its aerospace projects.

Compared with Denmark, the Swedish state has exercised considerably more influence over the academic culture, where the so-called sectorial R&D policy has led to university scientists and engineers identifying more with a particular government sector than with any more autonomous academic culture.

In recent years, the academic system has expanded considerably in the name of regional development. Thus the newest technical university has been located in the far north, in Lulea, to contribute to the economic development of the region. And, throughout the country, regional colleges and "high schools" are expected to become knowledge resources for the revitalization of the national economy. Nowhere is the proliferation of science parks and the like more rapid or extensive than in Sweden, where, in 1985, there were some 79 different centres, parks, foundations, etc., all encouraging university-industry cooperation.

Another important component of the R&D system in Sweden is the military, which has the largest research institute in the country - now also regionalized to four different locations - and which has also been the largest single source of state R&D funding. It is also from the military that the sectorial R&D policy, applying customer-contractor principles, has spread to other sections of the Swedish R&D system. It is no surprise then, that it has been largely through the military that the Swedish response to the microelectronics challenge has come.

As opposed to the Danish micro level cultural split, between an academic culture on the one hand and a technology service culture on the other, the Swedish micro level has been characterized by a segmentation of R&D work or fragmentation of innovative activities into various branches and sectors. There is thus little of a unified scientific/technical culture at the micro level in Sweden; instead, allegiances have been to the respective firm or sector in which the scientist or engineer has worked. And this has meant that international contacts have also been made through the sector or the firm. This has no doubt been one of the contributing factors to the difficulty that the Swedish technology policy-makers have had in developing a more comprehensive policy response to the microelectronics challenge.

4. The Meso Level: The Technology Policy Culture

By now, it should be somewhat clearer why Sweden and Denmark have developed different policies in the area of microelectronics/information technology.[12] At the macro level, where

---

[12] The remaining text of this chapter is built upon reports by Jan Annerstedt on Danish technology policy in the 1970s and 1980s and by Hans Glimell on Swedish technology policy in the same period. Both reports are included in Hans Glimell (ed.) (1988), *Industriförnyelse i Norden* (Industrial Renewal in the Nordic Countries), Roskilde: Forlaget Samfundsökonomi og Planlægning. An English edition is in preparation.

fundamental national priorities are debated and decided upon the ideological perceptions have been different: the challenge of microelectronics has been seen through different ideological frameworks. And at the micro level, the infrastructural preconditions have also been very different - a decentralized Danish system of technical service institutes stands opposed to a concentrated Swedish system of industrial R&D, dominated by the large corporations and the military.

The two programmes, however, are not merely the result of two different macro and micro levels. For the technology policy culture itself has exercised a strong influence on the way in which the programmes have been conceived. This meso level is populated by the planners, organizers, administrators and managers who actually implement technology policy, and they have their own cultural traditions and "ways of life". What sort of influence has this meso level culture had on our particular case?

In Sweden, there have been several responsible state agencies, but two have been particularly important - namely the National Board for Technical Development (Styrelsen för teknisk utveckling, STU) and the military procurement agency (Försvarets materiel verk, FMV). STU was founded in 1968 as a new central agency for technology policy to be part of the Ministry of Industry, established in 1969. It was created both to take over what had previously been carried out by the Technological Research Council, as well as to support technical development work in industry. It was thus a component of the "active" industrial policy that characterized the late 1960s and early 1970s - and yet it became difficult for STU, in practice, to play a particularly active role in industrial policy-making. For as the 1970s progressed, industry policy in Sweden came primarily to consist of attempts to "save" traditional branches of industry, like shipbuilding, iron and steel, that were being hard pressed from international competition. STU primarily supported cooperative research in these branches, or it developed more general support programmes for new technological fields, related to these industries. Support for electronics, however, was fairly limited.

State support to electronics firms was primarily a result of military procurement programmes, in particular telecommunication systems and computer-based systems for military aircraft and missiles. There was thus little coordinated effort within the technology policy culture to follow international developments within electronics at large. The most active policy concerns came from another arm of the Ministry of Industry, which, in the 1970s, carried out a voluminous and detailed investigation of the electronics industry. However, no concrete planning efforts were based on this ambitious analysis.

Worth mentioning though is the activity at the planning division at STU, which grew increasingly interested in the late 1970s and early 1980s in the new high-technology fields, and developed a certain activity in technological forecasting and long-term planning. But that activity, oriented towards so-called three-year plans of technological development, never became a foundation for a national programme for information technology. Instead, some sectorial and military interests in microelectronics were fused.

It was thus from within a fairly limited segment of the technology policy culture that the national microelectronics programme was formulated. In meetings between FMV's electronics expert and STU's electronics expert - who previously worked at FMV - the microelectronics programme was conceptualized. Both men recognized, at the end of the 1970s, that something new and extraordinary had to be done in Sweden to respond to the global microelectronics challenge. For the military procurement agency, the key factor was the American VHSIC programme, as well as the American technology export restrictions. For the STU administrator, the key factor was the generational shift in components which represented a challenge to the competitive position of Swedish industry. At a later stage, a microelectronics expert with industrial experience both in the United States and in Sweden was brought in as a consultant, and it became his task to combine the two orientations of the FMV and STU policy cultures and apply them in a realistic way to the actual situation of the industrial "micro level".

Unsuccessful attempts to broaden the focus of the programme, to create a "national programme for information technology", were made in 1983-86, but all those various efforts had trouble winning political approval. Too many sectors and agencies were involved in information technology in one way or another to make it possible for any more comprehensive programmes to be accepted. The fairly developed, but fragmented policy culture in Sweden thus led to one fraction of interest defining the microelectronics policy rather than a "national" interest grouping.

The social democratic party, returning to government power in October of 1982 after six years in opposition, found it necessary to take some kind of policy initiative in the area of information technology. Its perception of the challenge of microelectronics, however, was limited to the strategic challenge; and its conceptual tools were similarly limited to pragmatic, systematizing responses. During his first meeting at STU's headquarters in Stockholm the new minister of industry was confronted with ideas of new government support to information technology, and he immediately asked for a more detailed proposal in the field of microelectronics.

The result, as presented by STU, was later to become the NMP - the National Programme for Microelectronics. The focus was put on only one segment of the R&D system, the major corporations already involved in the development of microelectronics. These companies were considered to be of strategic national importance and should, therefore, receive public support. There was no more general response forthcoming from the government.

Only at a later stage of the policy process were the many regional initiatives developed into an arm of national technology policy, eligible for government support. The same is true for the state encouragements to science parks and the like, that could only marginally be connected to the microelectronics programme. As such, the Swedish policy in the area of information technology was both limited and fragmented.

In Denmark, the Technology Development Programme also came into being in large measure because a new government wanted to show that it could take a new initiative in a new area. But the preparation within the technology policy culture - well before it attained official government support - had taken a very different course. Having a much smaller budget than its Swedish counterpart, the National Agency of Technology was, for one thing, a much more broadly-based organization with a number of very different support schemes under its authority. In the late 1970s, it had devised a system of initiative areas, where it was charged with focusing on new areas of technology - and it would be the chairman of the initiative area in information technology who would be the main catalysing force in the making of the Danish Technology Development Programme. At a small-scale, high-level planning meeting in August 1983, financed but not arranged by the National Agency of Technology, individuals from government and industry drew up a "national programme" for information technology of 700 million Danish Kroner. This information technology programme became the central ingredient of what was soon to become the Technology Development Programme, a joint 2.1 billion undertaking by government and industry.

The "industrial modernists" that stood behind this new programme were a different kind of technology policy actors than their Swedish counterparts. They were engineering consultants, leaders of high-technology firms, heads of government labs or other specialists working in government. All of them had good connections throughout Danish industry, but they did not officially represent Danish industry or have a government function. They were alarmed by such signals as the comparatively old production technology of the typical Danish firm and they were stimulated by the growing activity that other European countries were taking in the area of information technology. The ESPRIT programme in the Common Market was especially significant as policy incentive in Denmark. The contacts with British consultants in information technology and with the persons behind the UK Alvey Programme were particularly well developed, and British responses and eventually policies were known in Denmark at an early stage.

The size of the Danish Technology Development Programme, however, was largely a result of an early government backing and the extremely broad basis of support that was able to be solicited for an ambitious programme. That support was won over the criticisms of the powerful shipping industry. And it was won in large measure because it was formulated in a way that corresponded to the dominant conception of the microelectronics challenge in Denmark - namely that what was at issue was the modernization of the entire national industrial structure. But the technology policy culture of Denmark could produce a more comprehensive and ambitious programme also because it was less fragmented; indeed, the trend had been more toward integration than fragmentation, as the National Agency of Technology had, in the course of the 1980s, become an ever more central, and professional arm of the Ministry of Industry.

Another factor of policy importance was the fact that industry policy in Denmark was not branch oriented to the same extent as in Sweden; it rather was oriented toward general kinds of support, where the old and multifaceted technical service organization had been a key ingredient. The Technology Development Programme could thus be seen as continuing in a well-trodden policy tradition, and because of that, it received the early support and encouragement, as well as political acumen, of senior staff members in the Ministry of Industry, especially the conservative top industrial policy-maker of the ministry.

Interestingly enough, the organization and policy ideas of the Technology Development Programme have come to serve as models for initiatives in other areas of science and technology policy. At present, two new programmes are being implemeted in Denmark. The first one is a ten-year national programme in the area of biotechnology to include both research and development work in some of the larger industries and government laboratories. The second new national programme is directed toward new materials technology. It includes measures for both R&D and the diffusion of technology; so, in a way, it combines ideas from the first Technology Development Programme with those of the Biotechnology Development Programme.

Indeed as opposed to Sweden, where the microelectronics programme is likely to be a brief parenthesis in the development of technology policy, the Technology Development Programme in Denmark can very well come to seem at the beginning of a new policy era. In late 1986, the Danish government announced plans for a new, more interventionist ("active") industrial policy, where state support for the effective diffusion of new technology in industry is given pride of place. The organization implication of the new policy was a more professionally staffed Ministry of Industry and, in 1987, a far-reaching reform and restructuring of key administration agencies in ministries responsible for science policy, industrial policy, regional policy as well as trade policy.

While in one country the microelectronics challenge thus seems to have led to a general transformation of the range and ambition of several policy areas, in the other, the challenge has been met in a much more pragmatic and non-dramatic way. In Denmark, the Technology Development Programme has been the subject of media attention from the outset, while in Sweden, the National Programme for Microelectronics has received almost no media coverage.

It is, of course, too early to draw any far-reaching conclusions about the relative success or failure of the two national programmes. But I do hope that I have indicated something of the role that national cultural traditions - both of the long and short term - have played in the conception of the underlying cultural factors; policy initiatives can be expected to be less successful. Indeed, the above analysis indicates the importance of infusing technology policy with some sort of cultural understanding. Most policy-makers would, I suggest, improve their performance if they adopted a more culturally-reflective approach to their activity.

Bibliography

JAMISON, Andrew (1982), *National Components of Scientific Knowledge. A Contribution to the Social Theory of Science*. Lund: Research Policy Institute.

KASSON, John (1976), *Civilizing the Machine. Technology and Republican Values in America*. Grossman.

LINDROTH, Sten (ed.) (1952), *Swedish Men of Science*. Stockholm: Almqvist & Wiksell.

MARX, Leo (1964), *The Machine in the Garden. Technology and the Pastoral Ideal in America*. Oxford University Press.

OLWIG, Kenneth (1984), *Nature's Ideological Landscape*. London: George Allen & Unwin.

TEKNOLOGISTYRELSEN (1983), *A Technological Development Programme* (English-language version of Et teknologisk udviklingsprogram), Copenhagen: Teknologistyrelsen (National Agency of Technology), December.

THANING, Kaj (1972), *N.F.S. Grundtvig*, translated by David Hohnen. Copenhagen: Det Danske Selskab.

VEBLEN, Thorstein (1915), *Imperial Germany and the Industrial Revolution*. Macmillan.

Part V

Conclusions

14

State-Induced Participation in New World Markets

Some Comparative Conclusions on Trends in Internationalization through Techno-Industrial Innovation

Ulrich Hilpert

Ongoing change in international markets creates a continual need for techno-industrial innovation in the Western industrialized countries. But the more the future of their socio-economic development relies on science-based industries, the more those countries must foster innovation and participation in new world markets. It is not simply a question of how to promote and support the activities that may already exist in each country. It is also a question of the organization of the innovation process itself within the limitations presented by national settings and the variations between technologies. This *brings the state back in*. The techno-scientific progress that is basic to techno-industrial innovation is related to, and is a product of, state activities. Access to appropriate markets is facilitated by state activities. And the orientation of the enterprises that make up the neces sary industrial structure for these research intensive products is contingent upon incentives that are set by state policies.

These changes in the international division of labour relate national socio-economic development to products and markets that will neither be developed nor supplied unless the state is able to create the necessary conditions. Techno-scientific progress and the existence of appropriate markets are basic to the process that aims at economic development but it is not clear where this path of techno-industrial innovation finally leads. The socio-economic impacts, yet to unfold, are not fully known, and technology assessment has to face a twofold dilemma. Being aware both of the increasing competition from Newly Industrialized Countries (NICs) in old and mature industries and of the potential of science-based industries governments in Western industrialized countries are designing policies aimed at a growing participation in new world markets.

But national conceptions of state innovation policy differ fundamentally and their outcomes diverge markedly. Participation in the international race for techno-industrial innovation calls for stronger state engagement. The efficacy of these state policies is basic to successful economic development. The innovation process leads to a more differentiated international division of labour and only a small number of countries can participate successfully in the new world markets. State policies reinforce advantageous initial conditions. Disadvantageous initial conditions hinder the state's concentration on the introduction of successful techno-industrial innovation, but state policies may still allow the opportunity to manage competition from the NICs. Although these initial conditions determine the effects of the state's engagement to a great extent, there is hardly any opportunity to participate in the innovation process without the state's playing a pro-active organizing role.

Given this importance of initial conditions, it is very much to be doubted whether particular governmental ideologies can claim to be the source of successful techno-industrial innovation. The American example of the microelectronics revolution has shown an affinity between neo-conservative and neo-liberal concepts and high tech development. The message was spread that engagement in high tech and a decrease of governmental funding (in social policy in particular) would lead to economic growth. Little attention was paid to the enormous funds spent by the Pentagon and on particular programmes (such as on biotechnology). So neo-conservative governments in European countries generally followed the idea of rolling back the state. But, to be economically successful, they had simultaneously to develop the state's new role in techno-industrial innovation. Comparative research leads us to draw conclusions that indicate an increasing segregation in national socio-economic development, an increasing role for the state in innovation-led socio-economic development, and a trend towards depoliticization in that particular area. Trends towards the internationalization of development therefore have to be understood as national attempts to introduce what is perceived to be an exclusively economic process. Existing trends are supported, problems of industrial change and restructuring are expected to disappear in an age of innovation-induced growth. But policies that are not designed with sufficient regard to the concrete initial conditions have to face developments that reduce national sovereignty and perpetuate existing problems. They are the consequences partly of the internationalization trap and partly of unintended consequences.

1. The Internationalization of Innovation and National Socio-Economic Development

The strong interest that is paid to techno-industrial innovation in all Western industrialized countries represents a response to changing competitive relations in the world market. This is, of course, not the end of mass-production, but it does indicate some basic changes in the field of old and mature industries. The modernization of these industrial sectors, increasing complexity, the growing interrelation between economies and industrial sectors, and the opportunities to apply scientific breakthroughs create a situation that has consequences for the internationalization of innovation. These occur in two ways: (i) on the one hand, industrial sectors that are unable to stand international competition decline, while on the other hand those sectors that can be modernized, or that are already innovative, balance industrial decline by their growing participation in world markets; and (ii) scientific research and the development of new key technologies call for enormous funds that require large markets for amortization. These markets transcend the size of the internal markets of most Western industrialized countries. Although the specific situation may vary in different countries, the general tendency is one of convergence.

Techno-industrial innovation can take place only insofar as there is an industrial structure that is prepared to make use of techno-scientific progress and which has access to appropriate markets. This introduces a fundamental difference to earlier phases of innovation, because successful innovation is so closely related to market size. It creates a process of selection, according to the size of available (or creatable) market, and it calls for different policies in different national situations. The United States and Japan, with large internal markets, will not really be aware of this question, because they are able to amortize their investments. Smaller markets cause severe problems in some technologies in some European countries which attempt to participate in these markets. Their decisions and the success of their policies are vitally dependent upon developments that take place outside their national influence. Small European countries have become wholly dependent upon international developments and upon the market niches that appear. National sovereignty is surrendered regarding economic development and the trends in world markets determine even the national policies that *can* be designed.

Even though this may indicate that large internal markets provide the opportunity to determine national policies, the changes in old industries' competitive positions in world markets affect sovereignty as well. Large internal markets may provide better initial conditions for successful techno-industrial innovation, but the linkages with the international economy constrain both innovation policies and responses to international market conditions. European attempts to set up Airbus Industrie indicate that large internal markets do not create sovereignty from the international competition. In addition, European countries show quite clearly that large internal markets may form an advantageous initial condition for some industrial sectors, but they will not affect the problems of decline in old industrialized regions. Regional grading replicates the internationalization of techno-industrial innovation.

The relation between the internationalization of techno-industrial innovation and regional growth or decline also indicates that successful national innovation depends upon particular socio-economic conditions. The need to compete in world markets has an immediate influence not only upon regional policy but also upon the structure of science. The organization of research and its functionalization to produce advances appropriate to industrial needs and to particular economic opportunities determines the future development of science. So, via the internationalization of innovation a situation is created that interrelates science and industry in such a way that development can hardly take place outside the relationship with the world markets.

Because of the inevitable decline in some sectors (such as steel and shipbuilding) and the limited recovery in mature industries due to new technologies (such as textiles and watchmaking) future social developments are closely related to sunrise industries. But there economic growth creates relatively small numbers of jobs and requires highly qualified specialist labour. So, what takes place in the field of economic development indicates a tendency towards the internationalization of social development as well. The concrete way in which societies develop depends upon economic tendencies that are introduced by participation in the international division of labour. Industrial structures, again, are the key for a clear understanding of social development. With regard to the national importance of old and declining industries, this relationship is clearly evident. But, by contrast, the innovative industries introduce a contradictory development. They are less labour intensive and given their mix of old and new technologies they require highly qualified labour employed in highly flexible small and medium-sized firms.

To the extent that the internationalization of socio-economic development fits with particularly favourable local conditions, their advantageous developments may be introduced, as we identify in some small countries and in the well-known growth regions. Large countries that do have old industries as well as sun-rise ones have to face the social problems of internationalization in addition to the industrial ones. Small countries, though incapable of competing in frontier technologies, may find their opportunity in attractive market niches dependent upon utilization of high tech. It is not surprising therefore that, due to convergences in industrial structures and engagement in world markets, similar fields of scientific research are selected. Nor is it surprising that similar difficulties emerge in these countries. The extent of engagement in particular fields of techno-industrial innovation forms an important initial condition for the concrete form of national socio-economic development that takes place.

But, depending upon the size of internal markets, policies can provide incentives for innovation and development that correspond with the opportunities provided by the internationalization process. Transport and energy systems as well as various environmental technologies provide opportunities for state-led development instead of development based upon international markets. Hence there can be opportunities to reintroduce national sovereignty instead of depending upon world markets. Given a sufficient size of internal market, the state, playing its new role, can drive national socio-economic development away from dependency on international markets and can introduce a development that serves mainly national needs.

2. The Role of the State and the Generation of Techno-Scientific Progress

Internationalization introduces new conditions for the realization of techno-industrial innovation and changes the role of the state fundamentally. The importance of scientific research and the long lead times between the first engagement in research and the final technology are making more difficult the selection of fields that turn out to be successful. This makes the state's decision to foster a new technology, or not, vitally important. The fact that accurate technology assessment is impossible at the early stages of decision-making, and that social groups are not yet sufficiently prepared to formulate their particular interests, leads to a situation where state policies are designed according to the government's general conception of the capitalist economy and its understanding of the international division of labour. But techno-industrial innovation can take place only in those fields that are made ready by the supply of appropriate techno-scientific progress. Hence the state can play its important role only insofar as the generation of techno-scientific progress takes place.

So, a new role of the state is indicated by its being based not upon existing interests and industrial sectors but upon the promotion of innovations. But the national situations vary greatly. There is no single pattern that can be identified as forming the basis of state action. It is the way the process takes place in the particular national situation and the way the state contributes towards it that enables one to determine its impact. Techno-scientific progress forms the germ cell of techno-industrial innovation. It is the state's engagement to generate such progress that makes particular industrial developments possible. Variations between the countries indicate the close niches between state and national settings. The extent to which new technological advances are applied outside dominant industrial sectors indicates the extent of the state's autonomy.

It is interesting to note that the state, in all of the countries and cases discussed here, plays an important role in inducing innovation. The attention given to deregulation in the field of telecommunications shows a strong similarity to the creation of larger and more appropriate markets in energy technologies, aircraft or in the media. Although in this field organized interests aim to change existing structures, the state's engagement in creating markets for technology-based or technology-related developments is fundamentally important. This creates the situation in which techno-scientific progress can be turned into attractive technologies. Countries with large internal markets can limit their policy mainly to organizing the circumstances in which techno-scientific progress is generated. The development of a highly effective research structure and its engagement in frontier technologies calls for intensive state intervention (e.g. comparing the U.S. with Japan). A lack of sufficient state action in inducing techno-scientific progress and poor technology transfer to industrial applications (e.g. in Italy and Britain) creates severe problems for participating in the global race for innovation.

Given the great importance of states playing their new role, and of the generation of techno-scientific progress, it is unsurprising that the technologically stronger European countries (France and West Germany), as well as the successful efforts of advanced small industrialized countries, show a strong concentration of state activity upon the generation of appropriate techno-scientific progress. In different ways states play their roles by assuring the supply of scientific knowledge. In France it is by direct intervention. In Germany it is the functionalization of science by supporting research projects and, in the small countries, it is the attempt to introduce small research institutes that supply the particular technology mix necessary to underpin their opportunities for innovation. Thus the role of the state, in generating techno-scientific progress, is clear.

Comparative analysis shows that the more science-based economic developments are, the more important is state activity. It also shows that beyond the need to introduce innovation or to catch up with competitors, there is also the opportunity and the need for the state to determine possible future fields of innovation. But it is also clear that the opportunities and need to play an active role are related to a country's initial conditions. The fewer the initial conditions present for a successful national path of techno-industrial innovation, the more an active role by the state is necessary for participatation in attractive new world markets or market niches.

3. The Depoliticization of Innovation Policies

The management of the problems of industrial decline under the condition of participation in the international division of labour prompts the question of how to induce innovation and economic development to counterbalance this tendency. The state's innovation policy is aimed at the adaptions of the national industrial structure to enable it to meet the opportunities presented in new world markets. Hence the dynamism of these new world markets can be used to generate a corresponding dynamism within the domestic economy. Though the specificities of particular national innovation policies may vary from state to state, the roots of such variations lie not in the ideological differences between governments, but in the different initial conditions which have prevailed in different states. These differences imply the need for different policy measures in order to overcome different problems and to address the requirements of different new world markets. Because these various policies are all aimed at overcoming the problem of deficient initial conditions to participate in new world markets, which is seen as the key issue in the prevailing paradigm of economic development, they tend to be the focus of little dissent.

Discussion of innovation policies is frequently reduced to a technical question "how to be successful?". It does not address the issue of different political paths and ideas that may be available to a state. It concentrates on the appropriate engagement of frontier technologies and may also include the economic effects of different technologies. It always makes particular reference to the timely engagement of techno-scientific research, the availability of required scientific knowledge, the inducement of technology transfer and science industry linkages, and to the position that can be achieved in the new world markets and in the changing international division of labour. The more future economic development relates to development in science-based industries, the more policies must take account of the generation of techno-scientific progress. The promotion of academic research does not cause political controversy because science itself and the progress it produces is regarded as part of a purely scientific and technical logic of development.

Dealing with technology policies and the new role of the state, governments claim beneficial economic development to be the outcome of their policies and to indicate that they can harness the innovation process successfully. It is not surprising, therefore, that the orientation towards techno-industrial innovation is not politically questioned in Western countries. Criticisms in industrial policies of the innovation process are made regarding social participation in the benefits of economic development. Criticisms are made of governments that are not prepared to support the scientific research to underpin the innovation process. But the generally close correspondence between the new role of the state and the supply of new technical knowledge required by capitalist economies for their growing participation in world markets is not called into question.

Innovation policies demonstrate a very specific mode of depoliticization. Political discussion is very much concerned with initial conditions and policy instruments. Hence innovation policy is seen as a purely technocratic matter. This view is derived from prevailing liberal and conservative ideologies which see economic growth as the primary purpose of innovation policy. Policies based upon this presupposition are portrayed as being both radical and creative, and address themselves simply to the task of managing and facilitating the innovation process. Thus, at a very early stage in policy formation, innovation policy can be created as depoliticized and attention can be allowed to focus purely on technical and managerial issues. The paradox of this position is that it ignores the reality of innovation policy-making, which is highly politicized, especially in its very early forms when particular fields of scientific activity are selected for public support. Thus it is not surprising that conservative and liberal ideologies call for a clearer orientation of scientific research towards economic needs and for closer science-industry linkages. Having identified the particular logic of the innovation process under capitalism and, apparently determined that it is based upon value-free scientific progress, the conservatives can proclaim themselves as the natural allies of progress and declare that future social welfare necessitates societal adjustments to the needs of innovation. Social-democratic ideas of applying techno-scientific progress and innovation to broader social problems appear to be inappropriate in this depoliticized situation. Doubts about the efficacy of such an approach are raised and scepticism of social-democratic innovation policies appears to be justified. Conservatives, thus, are able to present themselves as being "progressive", whilst damning their social-democratic opponents as "reactionary". The depoliticization of innovation policy and its gearing to the international division of labour provides little opportunity to break away from the dependence of socio-economic change upon the logic of the industrial innovation process. Once the state adopts its new role in generating techno-scientific progress by functionalizing scientific research, there are few opportunities to introduce a different logic of economic development utilizing the particular scientific knowledge in the branch of science concerned.

4. State-Induced Innovation through the Internationalization of Policy - Between the Internationalization Trap and Unintended Consequences

The process of techno-industrial innovation calls for an early engagement of the state in promoting the necessary techno-scientific progress. It is this relationship, between the role of the state and the importance of science and research, that introduces the basic changes in the policy-making process and a *new* role of the state. A move away from policies and policy instruments based on the medium of money brings change to the very centre of the economic system. Key technologies are characterized by this new form of state activity. It is most important to be clear that techno-scientific progress forms the germ cell of the innovation process and gives it its initial impetus, but successful economic development requires, as it were, a *magic triangle* of available markets, an appropriate industrial structure and a lively and capable research structure. Here the state acts and induces innovations using mechanisms fitted to particular national settings.

The depoliticization of innovation policies and the loss of share in world markets for the products of old industries, leads to a little questioned orientation towards the *new* world markets for science-based products. This strategy that is regarded as forming the basis for successful economic recovery is demonstrated by the Japanese and German successes and by the Italian, French and British problems in managing their declining industries. But this internationalization simultaneously raises problems that reach beyond the erosion of national sovereignty discussed earlier. The increasing orientation towards world markets gives rise to industrial structures that are congruent with the national advantage in the international division of labour and to a research structure that provides this particular national industrial structure with the techno-scientific progress it requires. Economic development, therefore, depends crucially upon international markets, and innovation can be generated only to the extent that the relevant techno-scientific progress, that is its primary source, has already been generated. Saturation of some international markets or sudden changes in the demand for particular science-based products cannot easily or quickly be offset, leading to economic and political crisis and to social disruption. The normal development of markets thus transforms the advantage of a strong position in new world markets into an internationalization trap as the market matures. Attempts at managing these economic problems, by making the process of techno-industrial innovation permanent, may disguise the problem by increasing internationalization but the trap is rarely avoidable.

Although the tendencies to internationalization are widespread the results and the extent of the trap differ widely between nations. Countries with large internal markets (such as the

United States and Japan) form a significant part of the world market for the products concerned. Similar tendencies in techno-industrial innovation lead to different forms of internationalization, and the risk of the trap varies according to differences in their internal markets. The availability of internal markets presents the domestic manufacturer with an advantage that does not necessarily demand the most advanced and most expensive technology in order to be successful. Thus there is a risk of falling behind frontier developments. Small countries (such as the Netherlands, Belgium, Switzerland and the Scandinavian countries) on the other hand are nearly completely dependent upon international markets and on the international orientation of their processes of techno-industrial innovation. But their strong orientation towards small market niches and the importance that is given to smaller and highly flexible production units limits the risk of their falling into an internationalization trap. The most uncomfortable situation is that of larger European countries that neither form a significant part of world markets individually nor follow the paths of smaller countries. They have to engage in world markets that are very important to their national processes of techno-industrial innovation. They are obliged to fall into the internationalization trap as they try to manage their internal process of industrial change. No matter what their differences may be, it is the case that new technologies generate new markets, but these markets are, by their nature, international and it is by no means certain that all the nations who endeavour to supply them will be economically successful.

Beyond the problems of the appropriateness of specific forms of techno-industrial innovation and of the internationalization trap lie even more important issues: the relationship of state technology policies to the initial conditions present (e.g. research and industrial structures) and the impact of technologically induced industrial change on regional and social development. The importance of the initial conditions demonstrates that there are very few opportunities for processes of techno-industrial innovation to be completed outside the established industrial structure. The innovation processes in question, therefore, follow older paths of industrialization, industrial specialization and the international division of labour, so favouring those that meet the conditions for participation. At the same time industrial development becomes intensively science-based but scientific research is a limited resource. Increased funds and stronger support for research in general are not sufficient to meet the specific needs of techno-scientific progress. Thus techno-scientific progress is generated in those scientific fields that are thought generally to be most appropriate for providing innovatory opportunities within the prevailing national industrial structure, and hence are those expected to be most likely to deliver economic growth.

There is a close relationship between industrial and scientific development and the meeting of market opportunities. The shortage of scientifically qualified manpower and the need for techno-scientific progress create a situation in which the national capacity to generate an appropriate economic setting to meet the needs of new world markets is vital and techno-scientific progress is an integral part of that setting. The smaller a country is or the less capable its research structure, the greater is the need for selecting appropriate fields of research and for discriminating between alternative opportunities for scientific investigation and developments of science. In other words, the increasing orientation on science-based development in Western industrialized countries introduces an organisation of scientific research which turns out to be strongly characterized by the national competitive position in the system of the international division of labour rather than following the intrinsic logic of scientific research.

So because of the internationalization of national development and the need to take cognizance of existing national systems for techno-industrial innovation, the limits within which states can induce the generation of techno-scientific progress are so narrow that only minor deviations from a particular path are practicable. But the incapacities of the research structure and the existing path of innovation, based as it is on the needs of the existing industrial structure, each lead to unintended consequences. In making use of such opportunities the existing industrial orientation is continued and reinforced, so that the pursuit of some comparative advantages leads to the unintended consequence of damaging the pursuit of other potentially fruitful paths. The importance and problems in this science-industry interrelation and the need for optimization introduce a tendency for the processes of techno-industrial innovation to be located at places that supply the initial conditions of research and industry structures. In each country, even in the smaller ones or those that are most highly industrialized and densely populated, these initial conditions are unevenly distributed and concentrate on a small number of regions. So policies that may introduce the required techno-industrial innovation at the national level have unintended consequences at the regional level.[1]

Severe international competition in science-based industries induces developments that systematically generate unintended consequences in regional development. This, in turn, overlaps with the social tendencies induced by techno-industrial innovation. Industrial decline in Western countries puts people out of work who find it very difficult to obtain in the new growth industries. These new or innovative industries are characterized by (i) their jobless growth; (ii) their demand for highly skilled labour; (iii) the devaluation of skills that are related to earlier forms of production; and (iv) by the significant decrease in the need for unskilled or semi-skilled workers. While on the one hand the appropriate highly skilled labour is extremely scarce, on the other hand there is a significant part of the workforce that is inappropriately skilled. Re-education programmes cannot solve the problem because many of those workers out of a job are not prepared to acquire the necessary new skills. Even if they are willing to do so, the high value added in the new industries necessitates a relatively small number of employees.

This change due to techno-industrial innovation systematically generates the unintended consequence of social marginalization that strengthens the ethno-cultural problems in Western countries. It is significant that the processes of techno-industrial innovation and industrial decline are strongly regionalized so that, in addition to economic change, there are major regional changes in social structure. The notion of a depoliticized techno-

---

1   This strong inter-regional grading is the consequence of the fact that some regions are well endowed with the necessary initial conditions to attract and retain high technology-based growth industries, whilst old industrialized and peripheral regions are generally much less well endowed so that they get more and more cut off from the process of techno-industrial innovation.

industrial innovation that is oriented towards world markets and that will achieve beneficial economic effects faces not only the problem of internationalization but also the generation of unintended consequences in other areas of the socio-economic system that are more intensive, the more successful the state-induced innovation process is.

Even though the state appears to be able to induce national processes of techno-industrial innovation according to the national settings the analysis of the role of the state takes one far beyond straightforward technology policy. It indicates clearly that the state's earliest decision on research policy forms the platform for future development and the choice of how the dynamics of national techno-industrial innovation are related to world markets. There is, of course, the opportunity to relate some innovation processes much more to certain internal markets (for example in environmental technologies) but it is characteristic of the state in Western countries that it looks to an increasing internationalization of national development and to new world markets for the generation of beneficial economic effects. Here, it is most important to be aware of the universal consequences of this new role of the state: it is not only that state policies serve as a basis for economic development, but that they determine the development in other policy fields and in society at large. The outstanding importance of techno-industrial innovation for the development of the socio-economic system and the new role of the state lend major importance to the analysis of unintended consequences, because they indicate the interrelationship and interdependency between different policy fields. The analysis of governmental ideologies is also highlighted because the developments and unintended consequences induced by state policies vary significantly according to government ideologies. The analysis of state policies on techno-industrial innovation and the way the state plays its new role thus become highly important for the understanding of socio-economic development in modern capitalist societies.

Index

manufacturing 262; solar technology 89; telecommunications 217, 228
Niehans, J. 287
Nixdorf 118
NMP *see* National Microelectronics Programme
Noble, D. 310n
Nokia 293
Noll, A. 229, 230
Nonet, P. 52
Nora, S. and Minc, A.: Nora–Minc report 54, 113, 115, 124, 170
Nord Aviation 196
Nordenstreng, C. 45
Northern Telecom 220, 228
Norway 313
NRDC 136-7
NTIA (National Telecommunications and Information Administration) 164
NTT 215–16, 219–32

OEC 227
OECD (Organization for Economic Cooperation and Development) 111, 112n; chemicals 99, 102; R&D 296n, 297, 300n; small industrialized countries 284, 286; telecommunications 110, 111, 112n
off-air broadcasting 46, 50, 57–8
off-shore broadcasting 44
Office of Technology Assessment 67, 68
Ohmae, K. 46
Oki 227
Olwig, K. 313
ONERA 192, 205
Opta, L. 175
organization: of Airbus Industrie 200–10; of techno-scientific progress 31–6
Organization for Economic Cooperation and Development *see* OECD
Orsenigo, L. 13, 20; on biotechnology 133–57
Örsted, Hans Christian 313, 320
OTA *see* Office of Technology Assessment
OTS satellite 125
Owen, R. 314

PABX 114
Pannenborg 296n

Papon, P. 93
Parkhill, D. 164
parliament *see* politics
Parsons, D.J. 143
Paschen, H. 70
Pavitt, K. 263
Pearce, A. 192
Pearson, R. 143
Pechiney-Ugine-Kuhlmann 102
Pelissolo, J. 104
Pentagon 7, 8, 34, 332
Petzman, S. 51
pharmaceutical industries *see* chemical
Philips 116, 217, 287, 294, 296n, 299, 300
Pierson, J. 203
Piore, M. 6, 269
PIRDES (Programme Industrielle de la Recherche et du Développement) 91
Plan Câble 120, 126, 128
Plasschaert, S. 288
Plessey 112, 122
policies/policy-making: biotechnology 133–57; broadcasting and new media 48–62 *passim*; depoliticization of 338–40, 341; nature 52–9; new model for designing 36–8; options analysis and technology assessment 70–1; relevance 59–62; science and techno-industrial innovation 28–38; small industrialized countries 13–14, 18–19, 24–7, 289–92; solar technology 94–5, 98; and state's changing role *see* science; telecommunications 112–17, 118–19, 222–4 (*see also* liberalisation); videotex 160, 161–76; *see also* Japan, R&D; national styles; science and techno-industrial innovation
politics/political 41–2, 333; and Airbus Industrie 190, 192–4; and biotechnology 136; and broadcasting and new media 53–4; decisions about future socio-economic development 70–3; depoliticization of innovation policies 338–40, 341; generation of innovation *see* policies; small industrialized countries 285, 290–1, 296, 324; and technology assessment 68–9, 70–3, 77–80; and telecommunications 113,

SOCIAL SCIENCE LIBRARY

Manor Road Building
Manor Road
Oxford OX1 3UQ
Tel: (2)71093 (enquiries and renewals)
http://www.ssl.ox.ac.uk

This is a NORMAL LOAN item.

We will email you a reminder before this item is due.

Please see http://www.ssl.ox.ac.uk/lending.html
for details on:

- loan policies; these are also displayed on the
  notice boards and in our library guide.

- how to check when your books are due back.

- how to renew your books, including information
  on the maximum number of renewals.
  Items may be renewed if not reserved by
  another reader. Items must be renewed before
  the library closes on the due date.

- level of fines; fines are charged on overdue books.

Please note that this item may be recalled during Term.